NAVAL STRATEGIES
OF THE
CIVIL WAR

CONFEDERATE INNOVATIONS AND FEDERAL OPPORTUNISM

JAY W. SIMSON

CUMBERLAND HOUSE

NASHVILLE, TENNESSEE

Copyright © 2001 by Jay W. Simson.

Published by
CUMBERLAND HOUSE PUBLISHING, INC.
431 Harding Industrial Drive
Nashville, Tennessee 37211
www.CumberlandHouse.com

Cover design by Bateman Design, Nashville, Tennessee.

Library of Congress Cataloging-in-Publication Data

Simson, Jay W., 1953–
    Naval strategies of the Civil War : Confederate innovations and federal opportunism / Jay W. Simson.
        p.   cm.
    Includes bibliographical references and index.
    ISBN 1-58182-195-6 (pbk. : alk. paper)
    1. United States—History—Civil War, 1861–1865—Naval operations.
2. United States. Navy—History—Civil War, 1861–1865. 3. Confederate States of America. Navy—History. 4. Strategy—History—19th century.
5. Mallory, Stephen R. (Stephen Russell), 1813–1873. 6. Welles, Gideon, 1802–1878. I. Title.
E591.S56 2001
973.7'57—dc21

                                                                2001032541

Printed in the United States of America

1 2 3 4 5 6 7 8—05 04 03 02 01

To the Western Ohio Civil War Roundtable in great
appreciation for your support and encouragement

and

To Lynn, Stephanie, Crystal, Terry, and Nathaniel
just because you are all so special to me

CONTENTS

INTRODUCTION

ONE OF THE MOST little known aspects of the American Civil War has been the naval strategies followed by the Union navy and the infant Confederate navy.

This may be the first book that attempts to show how the strategic concepts of Stephen R. Mallory, the Confederate secretary of the navy, and Gideon Welles, the Union secretary of the navy, were formulated and put into action.

Mallory managed to create a multifaceted strategy for the Confederate navy. His strategic vision was one of the most powerful weapons in the Southern navy's scant arsenal. He emphasized technological innovation and individual merit and competence as he sought to match quality against the Union navy's numerical superiority.

Welles, on the other hand, never had the luxury of formulating an independent strategy for the Union navy. He followed Abraham Lincoln's national strategy as laid down in the Anaconda Plan—consisting of a naval blockade of the Southern seacoast and a combined army-navy thrust down the Mississippi River that was originally intended to end at New Orleans. Although Welles followed the national strategy, he was not wedded to it when opportunities presented themselves.

This is the story of two very different approaches to naval strategy in the American Civil War. Until now, it has been mostly an untold story, a story hidden in the more general histories of the war and of the confrontations on inland rivers, coastal areas, and on the high seas as two American navies clashed.

The Civil War's naval conflict can provide lessons for naval strategists and theorists. Ironically many of these lessons were lost on one of the most influential of these theorists, Alfred Thayer

Mahan, who himself was a veteran of the war and who even wrote a history of that conflict's naval war. He failed to use his own experience to provide an insight into the limitations of seapower, a term that Mahan himself coined.

PREFACE

An Opening Union Failure

I t was the spring of 1861. Abraham Lincoln had just been inaugurated as the sixteenth president of the United States. The country itself, however, was in the middle of the greatest crisis of its eighty-five-year history.

Since the previous December a total of seven states—South Carolina, Mississippi, Florida, Alabama, Georgia, Louisiana, and Texas—had taken the momentous step of leaving the Federal Union. No one on either side was prepared for what followed, least of all the U.S. Navy. The previous administration of James Buchanan had adopted a policy of doing nothing, ostensibly so that the situation would not get any worse. Simply speaking, they dropped the whole situation in President-elect Lincoln's lap.

According to Princeton historian James M. McPherson, Lincoln's election in November of 1860 marked a political revolution. On the issue of slavery, Lincoln was a moderate. He had no intention of outlawing the South's "peculiar institution," only restricting it from the territories. The acrimonious debates of the 1850s had split Lincoln's opposition among three candidates: Stephen Douglas of Illinois, John Bell of Tennessee, and John C. Breckinridge of Kentucky. Although Lincoln only won 40 percent of the national popular vote (54 percent in the North), he won 180 electoral votes (a minimum of 152 was required). Even if the opposition had combined against Lincoln in every free state, he still would have won the White House with 169 electoral votes.

The election represented an end of an era when the South, through the Democratic Party, held the balance of power in the federal government and could therefore ensure the continuation of slavery. The result of the political revolution represented by the 1860 presidential election, according to McPherson, was a conservative counterrevolution aimed at nullifying the disaffection of the Southern states. South Carolina seceded on December 20, 1860; Mississippi on January 9, 1861; Florida on January 10, 1861; Alabama on January 11, 1861; Georgia on January 19, 1861; Louisiana on January 26, 1861, and Texas on February 1, 1861.

Many of the Secessionists, however, also saw their struggle as a political revolution that was designed to circumvent or even prevent a social revolution. They wished to prevent the freeing of the slaves from the planter aristocracy and oligarchy that ran the South. Moreover, they opposed any efforts granting civil rights equal to those held by the Southern slave owners. As a result the United States tottered on the edge of an abyss leading directly to civil war.

Lincoln, prior to his inauguration, had apparently opted for the strategy of continuing business as usual. He would take no overt step toward war, but at the same time he was obliged to hold and occupy whatever Federal property existed within the seceded states. In practical terms these were Forts Pickens, Jefferson, and Taylor in Florida and Fort Sumter in South Carolina. The most important of these was Fort Sumter, which stood on a man-made island four miles from downtown Charleston and directly at the entrance to the harbor.

Fort Sumter was of masonry construction with walls forty feet high and eight to twelve feet thick. The facility had only just been completed. It was designed to mount 146 heavy cannon and to garrison 650 troops. Many believed this fort could stop anything from entering—or leaving—the harbor.

At the time South Carolina seceded from the Union, the only Federal troops in the area were eighty soldiers under the command of Kentucky-born Maj. Robert Anderson. They garrisoned Fort Moultrie, an obsolete defensive work dating back to the Revolutionary War. Moultrie was a mile across the bay from Fort Sumter and stood at the tip of an island easily accessible from the mainland and exposed to capture from the rear. While Anderson himself sympathized with the South, he remained loyal to the Union.

Therefore, while President Buchanan dithered, Major Anderson acted. He interpreted his ambiguous orders from the War Department as giving him the option to move his command from Fort Moultrie to Fort Sumter if necessary to deter an attack. He did so on the evening of December 26, 1860. His purpose was not one of defiance but simply to preserve the existing and very fragile status quo, knowing that if he were to be fired upon, it would mark the beginning of civil war.

For political and symbolic reasons Fort Sumter was of supreme importance. South Carolina had been the first of the Southern states to leave the Union. As long as the U.S. flag flew over the fort, the Palmetto Republic's independence from the Federal government was in doubt. To validate its claims to being a legitimate independent government, the republic of South Carolina and the new Confederate States of America—which soon succeeded it—had to control this fort. Although Florida's Fort Pickens dominated the Pensacola Navy Yard, the Florida forts were of limited strategic or political importance as compared to Fort Sumter.

Lincoln was in a quandary over what to do about Fort Sumter. He would just as soon avoid war, if he could. But he refused to countenance any role for himself in overseeing the dismemberment of the Union. Yet he had also pledged not to start a war. In his inaugural address, he had said: "In your hands, my dissatisfied countrymen, and not in mine, is the momentous issue of civil war. The government will not assail you. You can have no conflict without being yourselves the aggressors."

Nevertheless, he was determined to hold the forts. The apparent unimportance of the Florida forts made their retention relatively easy.

Fort Sumter was another story, for it was short of provisions. If something were not done soon, that fact alone would force its surrender without requiring the Confederate and/or South Carolina authorities to fire a single shot.

Lincoln's cabinet was divided on the issue. General in Chief Winfield Scott declared that Sumter could only be relieved by a force of at least twenty-five thousand men supported by a large fleet. Neither existed. The strength of the U.S. Army at this time consisted of just sixteen thousand men—most of whom were scattered in tiny outposts across the western frontier that were intended to defend settlers against the tribes of the West. The U.S. Navy had only three ships in North American waters since most of its vessels were spread out across the oceans, protecting American maritime commerce. Therefore, in Scott's opinion, due to the government's temporary military impotence, the only other option was to evacuate the garrison.

That may have been the militarily sensible thing to do, but Lincoln knew that it would not be the politically sensible thing to do.

Secretary of War Simon P. Cameron and Secretary of the Navy Gideon Welles reluctantly concurred with Scott's opinion. Secretary of State William Seward also wanted to evacuate Fort Sumter, but for his own political as well as military reasons. He advised Lincoln that such a gesture of peace and goodwill would reassure the states of the Upper South, which had not yet seceded, and strengthen the Unionists in those states that had seceded. Seward went so far as to establish unofficial contact with Confederate peace commissioners and leaked information to them and to the newspapers that Sumter would be evacuated.

Until Lincoln reined him in, Seward was angling to make himself the Union premier while reducing the president to the status of a figurehead.

Although Lincoln himself had not yet made a decision, he came close to letting Seward have his way. Of the seven members of his cabinet, only two—Secretary of the Treasury Salmon P. Chase and Postmaster General Montgomery Blair—favored relieving Fort Sumter. Chase felt the garrison should be resupplied, but only if that could be done without risking war. Blair demanded that the fort be held whatever the risk. Being from the Border State of Maryland (which was as divided as the rest of the country), he believed that surrendering the fort would discourage, not encourage, Southern Unionists. Blair was further convinced that meekly surrendering the fort without any resistance at all would mean the end of the United States as one nation. That was also Lincoln's opinion.

Blair went further than simply advocating that Fort Sumter be retained. His brother-in-law was a former naval officer, Gustavus

Vasa Fox, who had a plan for the relief of Fort Sumter. Fox was then a thirty-nine-year-old maritime businessman living in Massachusetts. Blair introduced him to the president, and Fox used the opportunity to present his plan for the relief of Sumter. He suggested that a troop transport, escorted by warships, be dispatched to the sandbar just outside of Charleston Harbor. Fox said that men and supplies could be transferred to tugs or small boats and, under cover of darkness, move across the bar and from there could easily reach Fort Sumter. The guns of the warships and the fort itself could then be used to suppress any attempt by Confederate shore batteries to interfere.

In addition, Lincoln, always the astute politician, was realizing that Northern opinion was hardening against the Southerners. Newspapers were demanding that Fort Sumter be relieved. Letters favoring the relief of the fort were pouring into the White House, many of them from prominent Democrats.

Meanwhile, Seward continued to tell the Confederate commissioners that the fort would be surrendered. Events came to a head at an emergency cabinet meeting held on March 29, 1861. In this meeting Lincoln read to the cabinet an explosive message from General Scott, who may well have been influenced by Seward, that advocated not only the evacuation of Fort Sumter but also the abandonment of Fort Pickens in Florida. Scott's message stated in part: "The evacuation of both the forts [Pickens and Sumter] would instantly soothe and give confidence to the eight remaining slave-holding States, and render their cordial adherence to this Union perpetual."

When it was realized that Scott, a native of Virginia, was advocating what amounted to unconditional surrender to the Southerners, his contention that the relief of Fort Sumter was a practical impossibility was immediately rendered suspect. Secretary of War Cameron was absent, and in the cabinet vote that followed, Seward was supported only by Caleb Smith, the secretary of the interior. The other four—Welles, Chase, Blair, and Attorney General Edward Bates—supported resupplying Sumter. Furthermore, all six favored securing Fort Pickens.

Thus determined to relieve Fort Sumter, Lincoln on April 4 authorized the Fox expedition. The ships selected for the task included the steam corvette *Powhatan,* armed with one 11-inch Dahlgren smoothbore and ten 9-inch Dahlgren smoothbores; the steam gunboat *Pawnee,* armed with eight 9-inch Dahlgren smoothbores and two 12-pounder cannon; the Revenue Service (the forerunner of the U.S. Coast Guard) cutter *Harriet Lane,* armed with three 9-inch Dahlgren smoothbores and one 30-pounder rifled cannon; and the *Baltic,* an unarmed troop transport and supply ship. Aboard the *Baltic* were two hundred soldiers scraped together from various harbor garrisons to reinforce the eighty-man garrison of Fort Sumter.

Instead of following Fox's original plan, the flotilla was now ordered to land supplies only. It was not to force its way into Charleston Harbor unless the Confederate shore batteries opened fire on the supply boats. Lincoln planned to notify the governor of South Carolina, Francis W. Pickens, that he was sending in provisions only. The political purpose behind the change in plans would be to place the Confederacy in the wrong by forcing the Southerners to fire on the delivery of food for hungry men, thus uniting the North and dividing the South. If the Southerners allowed the provisions to reach the fort, peace and the status quo would be preserved.

But Seward was not yet done playing political games. Fox's flotilla was greatly weakened when the *Powhatan,* its most powerful ship, was diverted through the machinations of the secretary of state, much to the disgust of Welles. He discovered that Seward, using his influence with the president, was interfering with his department. Welles believed that the *Powhatan* had been assigned to Fox's expedition; however, Seward persuaded Lincoln to issue orders turning the ship over to Lt. David D. Porter. Seward instructed Porter not to steam to Charleston but to head for Pensacola and Fort Pickens. Welles, when he learned of Seward's interference, had the orders rescinded. Porter, however, had already sailed. Welles then sent dispatch boats with new orders to Porter, which Porter refused to accept. Thus Fox's flotilla lost its single most powerful and important element.

The weather provided the next obstacle. While Fox's vessels were on their way south from New York City to Charleston, a storm scattered the little flotilla. This caused sufficient delay that, by the time they succeeded in reaching the scene, the Confederate batteries that ringed Fort Sumter were about to open fire. Upon being informed by the governor of South Carolina of Lincoln's proposal to bring supplies to the garrison, Confederate President Jefferson Davis decided that Fort Sumter must be reduced before Fox and his flotilla arrived. Davis made his final decision for war at a cabinet meeting held April 11. The Confederate batteries under the command of Brig. Gen. P. G. T. Beauregard opened fire at 4:30 A.M. on April 12.

Rough weather prevented Fox's flotilla from launching boats to attempt to resupply the fort. In addition, without the *Powhatan,* Fox was loath to risk his ships to enemy fire. After thirty-three hours of intense bombardment, the fort's commandant, Maj. Robert Anderson, surrendered on April 14.

The Federals were allowed to fire a final salute to their flag, during which a Union soldier—the only person to be killed in the entire affair—died after one of the guns burst. With its flag flying and band playing, the Fort Sumter garrison was marched aboard the *Baltic,* and Fox and his flotilla headed back to New York.

Thus for the Union navy the American Civil War had begun in an atmosphere of disorder and defeat. It remained to be seen if Gideon Welles could bring order out of chaos and victory out of defeat. His greatest asset was that he had an established navy and infrastructure in which to make the attempt. His Southern counterpart, Stephen R. Mallory, had neither.

NAVAL STRATEGIES
OF THE
CIVIL WAR

1

The Protagonists

A T ITS MOST BASIC element, the story of the Confederate and Union naval strategies in the Civil War is the story of the struggle between two opposing methods of operation utilized by two vastly different men. One of these men was the "One-Man Band" who created the Confederate navy out of nothing—Stephen R. Mallory of Florida. The other was a Connecticut Yankee who knew next to nothing about naval operations. He would stumble upon a team approach to leadership and as such would live up to the nickname given him by Abraham Lincoln in one of his more humorous moments—"Old Father Neptune." That man was Gideon Welles of Connecticut.

The two men held equivalent offices. Mallory served the Confederate States of America as Jefferson Davis's secretary of the navy. Welles served Lincoln as the U.S. secretary of the navy. As such they were the administrators who ranked between their presidents (as commanders in chief) and the various naval commands. But they soon became more than that.

The organizations they led were mirror images of one another. The foremost reason that underlay this sameness was that the Confederate Congress based its naval organization on what it was already familiar with—that of the U.S. Navy. The Confederate Department of the Navy's internal organization reflected that of the old U.S. Department of the Navy and consisted of the same or equivalent bureaus charged with the same or equivalent responsibilities.

In their bureaucratic organizations each department was similar, except where the U.S. Navy Department was organized into bureaus, the Confederate Navy Department was organized into offices. Eventually the U.S. Navy would have thirteen bureaus. The Bureau of Construction, Equipment, and Repairs was charged with doing exactly what its title implied until 1862 when it was broken up into the Bureau of Construction and Repair, the Bureau of Steam Engineering, and the Bureau of Equipment and Recruiting in the name of greater efficiency. There was a Bureau of Medicine and Surgery, which was responsible for the physical well-being of naval personnel. The Bureau of Navigation oversaw five sub-bureaus, which included the Naval Observatory, the Naval Almanac Office, the Chaplain Corps, and the Naval Academy. There was also the Office of Detail, which oversaw the assignments given to naval officers. All naval weaponry was overseen by the Bureau of Ordnance. The feeding and clothing of naval personnel was handled by the Bureau of Provisions and Clothing. Naval technology was handled by the Bureau of Steam Engineering. Developments during the war led to the creation of the Office of the General Superintendent of Ironclads, which oversaw the construction of all those warships. Other bureaus included the Bureau of Yards and Docks, the Bureau of Naval Boards and Commissions, and the U.S. Marine Corps.

In the beginning the Confederate Navy Department made do with four "offices." The Office of Provisions and Clothing had enormous responsibilities including manufacturing, acquiring, and distributing uniforms and equipment along with being the paymaster for all the officers, sailors, and other persons employed by the Confederate navy. The Office of Medicine and Surgery attempted to see to their general health and operated major naval hospitals. The Office of Orders and Detail served to oversee the navy's paperwork and personnel assignments and policies. Finally there was the Office of Ordnance and Hydrography. Charged with arming naval vessels, it became the most technological of the navy's bureaucratic offices as decisions were made to build ironclads and experiment with new weapons technologies.

As time went on there would also be the Submarine Battery Service, which sought to develop and expand submarine warfare using torpedoes as stationary naval mines and to find ways to provide them with mobility either through submarines or torpedo launches. There was also the Navy Department's Secret Service, which concerned itself, not with collecting naval intelligence, but with obtaining warships and naval war materiel abroad.

Naval personnel would be eventually divided between the regular navy, the volunteer navy, and the provisional navy. Enlisted personnel remained in the regular navy along with the overabundance of officers inherited from the old U.S. Navy. The volunteer navy would absorb the privateers and form a pool of talent from which the Submarine Battery Service drew personnel as needed. Concentrated in the provisional navy were the officers that Mallory eventually entrusted with the main Confederate naval effort.

This mirroring was also carried over into the naval ranks themselves. Before the Civil War the U.S. naval ranks included those of captain, commander, lieutenant, and master. There was also the designation of flag officer for the senior captain in command of a squadron of vessels. This had replaced the unofficial and honorary rank of commodore, although in practice the two terms were used interchangeably.

The need for a hierarchy of flag ranks was seen first by the Confederacy. The Confederate Congress approved legislation establishing the ranks of admiral, vice admiral, rear admiral, and commodore. Although a number of naval officers held the rank or designation of commodore, there were only two admirals. Franklin Buchanan was named to the rank of admiral as a reward for his command in the March 1862 battle of Hampton Roads. He became the highest-ranking Confederate naval officer. The second admiral was Raphael Semmes, who was promoted to the rank of rear admiral following his two-year cruise as commander of the commerce raider CSS *Alabama*. Semmes later commanded the James River Squadron that protected the water approaches to the Confederate capital at Richmond, Virginia.

During the war the U.S. Congress established the naval ranks of lieutenant commander and ensign (for graduates of the Naval Academy). The Confederacy did not follow suit, keeping the old designations of lieutenant commanding and passed midshipman. There were no admirals in the Union navy until the rank of rear admiral was created specifically for David G. Farragut after his April 1862 victory at New Orleans. As the war was ending, the rank of vice admiral was created, again specifically for Farragut, in part as a reward for his August 1864 victory at Mobile Bay.

Mallory had not solicited the job of secretary of the navy. He was, however, amply experienced in naval matters and quickly devised a strategy that he believed would bring victory to the infant Confederate States. His strategic vision became one of the few advantages that were to be enjoyed by the infant Confederate naval service. He was also blessed by the fact that his president knew next to nothing about naval affairs and seldom interfered with his conduct of the naval war. (Unfortunately, Davis considered himself to be as good or even better a general than his actual generals and insisted upon being his own secretary of war and his own general in chief, often to the detriment of Confederate military efforts.) In fact, Davis eventually became Mallory's chief defender. Mallory in turn became one of the two cabinet members to serve in the same post from the birth of the Confederate government, through the war, and on to the final collapse of that government.

Welles, unlike Mallory, did not attempt to set or implement a separate strategic plan for the Union navy. He merely followed the national strategy that had already been laid down by Lincoln and his first general in chief, Bvt. Lt. Gen. Winfield Scott, in the Anaconda Plan. Welles, however, was not adverse to adopting innovative strategic concepts and taking strategic shortcuts in following Lincoln's national strategy. Welles also knew what his own limitations were and eventually eased into an entirely different approach from Mallory's in leading the Union's naval war effort.

STEPHEN R. MALLORY was not a native Southerner. He was born in 1811 in the town of Port au Spain on the West Indies island of Trinidad, which was then a British possession. His father was a construction engineer from Connecticut and his mother was an Irish immigrant. When young Mallory was about a year old the family left Trinidad and moved to various places before finally putting down roots in Key West, Florida, in 1820.

Florida at the time was little more than a sparsely populated territory. The town of Key West, at the tip of the Florida Peninsula, amounted to little more than a tiny group of buildings perched precariously on a coral outcropping. The most profitable business was wrecking. Passing ships often ran aground on the coral reefs. If the ship's captain and crew stayed with the vessel, the locals might be asked to help salvage the ship and/or its cargo. If the ship were abandoned, it became fair game for the wreckers.

Mallory's formal education consisted of about twelve months in a country school near Blakely, Alabama, when he was nine and three years at a Moravian academy in Nazareth, Pennsylvania. After his father's death he helped his mother run a boarding house at Key West. When he decided to become a lawyer, the young man studied law between 1830 and 1834 under Judge William Marvin. He specialized in admiralty law and was admitted to the bar in 1834. While still preparing for his bar exam, he was named the inspector of customs at Key West in 1833. From 1836 to 1838 he obtained some practical experience in seagoing affairs when he commanded a small vessel in the campaigns against the Seminoles in the Everglades.

Like his mother, Mallory was a Roman Catholic, and in July 1838 he married Angela Moreno, a woman of Spanish descent from Pensacola, Florida. His being a Catholic placed him outside the planter aristocracy that controlled the antebellum South. His religion, however, did not hold him back as he began to climb the ladder in Florida Democratic Party politics. From 1837 to 1845 he was the county judge of Monroe County, and in 1845 he was named collector of the port at Key West.

Physically, Mallory was described by one observer in 1867 as a "stumpy, roly-poly fellow . . . his eyes were large and blue, with an attractive air of puzzlement about them; his nose had a little tilt which the ladies of Washington and Richmond thought quite charming."

In 1850 the Florida legislature elected Mallory to the U.S. Senate, as a Democrat, and he was reelected in 1856. Appointed chairman of the Senate's Naval Affairs Committee in 1853, he became a major civilian spokesman for U.S. naval policy and a major proponent of American naval power.

His primary concern as chairman of the Naval Affairs Committee was the abundance of superfluous personnel within the navy that caused him to champion the Naval Retiring Board. Mallory knew that the rate of promotion within the peacetime navy was glacial since it was based solely upon seniority. He was convinced that many officers were simply vegetating in the lower ranks and that they had lost any inclination to improve their professional expertise by the time they reached the middle to higher ranks. Others were either ill, too advanced in age, narrow minded, overly conservative, and lacking any impulse for improvement of either themselves or their service by the time they reached relative senior rank. While there were many gifted and superior naval officers, they tended to be overshadowed by those who were prone to routine or red tape or who were incompetent or infirm.

The Naval Retiring Board was given the responsibility of checking the records of all serving officers and proceeded to mercilessly prune the deadwood, although it did risk hitting some officers who did not deserve such scrutiny. These instances created for Mallory hatreds and controversies that would later dog his efforts as Confederate secretary of the navy.

The case of then Lt. Matthew Fontaine Maury was the most important of these incidents. Maury was the highly competent superintendent of the U.S. Naval Observatory. But in 1839 he was injured in a carriage accident and walked with a pronounced limp for the rest of his life. Because of his age, time in grade, and disability (which tended to make him ineligible for sea duty), he had been placed among the deadwood, that is the 201 officers who had been deemed by the board to be expendable. When the list was published in 1855, there was a political explosion. Maury's inclusion in the list of officers to be retired became a cause célèbre by those who opposed the Naval Retiring Board and the act of Congress that had created it. After considerable controversy the Navy Retiring Board Law was so amended by Congress as to be effectively nullified. After the controversy died down, however, an unofficial list was created by the secretary of the navy. Whenever possible, overage and unfit officers were placed upon this list with no publicity and were then simply left "awaiting orders."

This proved to be a workable, although imperfect, solution to the problem since many of the most senior officers within the navy proved themselves amply able to dodge this bullet, particularly if they had any political influence at all.

Maury himself was retained and evaded the unofficial retired list thanks to his admirers in and out of government. But from that moment, Maury and Mallory carried a deep rancor against each other.

This incident would have serious repercussions for the Confederate navy as many of the older, more senior, and more conservative naval officers followed their states out of the Union. (This should not be surprising since the counterrevolution of 1861 that led to the founding of the Confederate States of America was a conservative reaction to the election of Lincoln.) Therefore, Mallory tended to interfere with officers like Josiah Tattnall, George N. Hollins, and Duncan N. Ingraham—who were actually doing quite well—and using the problems created by overage incompetents like Victor Randolph as his justification. (Tattnall, Hollins, and Ingraham in the course of the war would be replaced by younger officers who in Mallory's opinion were considered to be more "energetic.") Senior officers, however, who tended to be fire-eaters, like Franklin Buchanan, Mallory had no trouble at all with. He also made mistakes in judgment in favoring daring and rash officers of the likes of a William Webb over the sober experience of a Josiah Tattnall.

As a proponent of American naval power, Mallory had worked hard to modernize the old navy. Mallory's efforts resulted in the construction of six modern steam-powered, screw-propeller-driven frigates, along with six first-class and six second-class steam sloops of war, also propeller driven. He got these ships through the Southern-controlled Congress by making sure that the drafts of these ships would be too deep for most Southern harbors, thus they would never pose a direct threat to these ports.

Mallory also favored the *Stevens Battery,* which represented the first attempt to create a seagoing ironclad warship. She was conceived and begun well before the French and British built their first seagoing ironclads following their introduction as mobile floating batteries during the Crimean War.

The *Stevens Battery* was the brainchild of naval architect and engineer Robert Livingston Stevens. The vessel had been first proposed as early as 1842 and had been originally intended to serve as a harbor defense ship. Her original mission would have been simply to help defend New York Harbor. But the vessel plans began changing as the technology changed. These changes caused delay after delay after delay, even after her keel had finally been laid down in 1854. Mallory soon became an enthusiastic booster of the project.

The changing technology had caused Stevens to make drastic changes in the ship's design. Her armor was increased and her guns were upgraded to two 10-inch pivot-mounted rifles fore and aft and four 15-inch smoothbores to be mounted within an armored casemate. Pivot guns were able to fire forward, aft, or on either broadside through more than one gun port. In addition, Stevens had also decided that his ship would be a true steamship without masts or sails. Her engines were designed to provide her with a top speed of sixteen knots. These changes forced the lengthening of her hull, drastically deepened her draft, and increased her projected displacement from fifteen hundred tons to forty-five hundred tons.

When Stevens died in 1856, Congress decided (over Mallory's strenuous objections) to deny the additional funding necessary to complete the ship. Many members of Congress who opposed the *Stevens Battery* cited her deep draft as a primary excuse for refusing to allocate the funds to finish her construction.

The *Stevens Battery* may well have influenced the design of most of the later Confederate-built ironclads. As the *Stevens Battery* evolved, her plans and specifications did call for the use of rifled guns and an armored casemate (both of which were carried over into Confederate ironclad designs).

In 1858 President James Buchanan recognized Mallory's abilities and offered to appoint the Floridian to be the American minister (ambassador) to Spain. Mallory, however, wished to remain in the U.S. Senate and declined the appointment.

Although a strong supporter of the South while in the Senate, he opposed secession. Nevertheless, Mallory resigned from the Senate on January 21, 1861, after his state left the Union. He was offered the post of chief justice of Florida's admiralty court, but he turned it down. He then turned his efforts to preventing war from breaking out between the North and the South. Mallory's political enemies accused him of obstructing Florida authorities from seizing Fort Pickens that January. What he had actually done was to confer with senators from other states—and had received support from them—in advising against violence at that time. Mallory also used his influence with President Buchanan to keep U.S. warships from entering Pensacola Harbor and to prevent reinforcements from being landed at Fort Pickens.

Confederate President Jefferson Davis nominated Mallory to be the Confederate secretary of the navy on February 25, 1861. Mallory had not sought the office and was at first unaware of his nomination. The primary reason for his nomination was political, in that he was from Florida, which had been allotted a prominent cabinet appointment because of the date of its secession. Davis also had known Mallory from the time they both were in the U.S. Senate. He chose Mallory primarily for his experience and demonstrated expertise in naval affairs and for his interest in innovations and improvements in both ship design and naval ordnance. The Florida delegation to the Confederate Congress, however, originally opposed the nomination because of their misunderstanding of his actions involving Fort Pickens. Mallory's nomination was the only one of the Davis cabinet appointments that was delayed in the legislature, although he was eventually confirmed on March 4, 1861.

Mallory also tended to be distrusted because he liked high living, a taste that may have possibly have derived from his humble beginnings at his mother's boarding house. Further complicating matters was his friendship with Judah P. Benjamin, who during the life of the Confederacy served in the Davis cabinet as attorney general, secretary of war, and secretary of state. Possibly the friendship grew out of the fact that both men were not of the planter aristocracy and they were of the wrong religions, Mallory a Roman Catholic and Benjamin a Jew.

Mallory controlled the activities of the Confederate Navy Department down to the minutest of details, becoming in effect the Confederate navy's primary one-man band. His collaborators—such men as Franklin Buchanan, Catesby ap Roger Jones,

Raphael Semmes, John Mercer Brooke, James D. Bulloch, and John L. Porter—were also one-man bands in their own areas of expertise. They achieved much, but they never reached the level or coordination of the Union navy under its secretary, Gideon Welles. Mallory would prove himself tireless in developing quickly made and ingenious fighting ships and naval ordnance. Mallory would also be imperturbable through the loss of New Orleans, Norfolk, the various Atlantic coastal enclaves, and control of the Mississippi River.

It was these losses that later led to a congressional investigation of Mallory's department. The investigating committee eventually reached the conclusion that the naval secretary and his department had done—and were doing—as well as could be expected given the overwhelming odds they faced in confronting the well-established Union navy.

Most naval historians also share this opinion.

GIDEON WELLES of Connecticut was fifty-eight years old at the beginning of the war. He was born in 1802 in Glastonbury, Connecticut. Unlike Mallory's family, the Welles family was fairly prosperous and was able to send Welles to the local Cheshire Academy. Upon graduation he traveled extensively and wrote about the places he visited and the people he met. Several of his articles were published by the *New York Mirror* in what was his first foray into journalism. Welles's family, however, believed that such activities were beneath his dignity, and he dabbled in various business ventures while at the same time flirting with small-town politics.

Welles in time became the most loyal member of Lincoln's cabinet. Like Mallory, Welles would serve his president from the beginning to the end of the great conflict. Shortly after his appointment as secretary of the navy, Lincoln had humorously dubbed Welles Old Father Neptune because of his full flowing white beard and the wig that he habitually wore somewhat askew. Welles would also earn the title for his overseeing the transformation of the U.S. Navy from a small but competent coastal and commerce defense force into a naval force capable of taking on any of the navies of the world. Aside from that, he also tended to look just a bit like cartoonist Thomas Nast's depiction of Santa

Claus, although he was just a little too tall and he lacked the round little belly.

Welles grew up surrounded by old-fashioned New England Federalists and Whigs, but in the election of 1824 he threw his political lot in with the newly revised Democratic Party of Andrew Jackson. Throughout the rest of his life he remained at heart a Jacksonian Democrat.

In the 1824 election Welles allied himself with John Niles, publisher of the *Hartford Times and Weekly Advertiser.* In addition, Niles was an adroit politician and soon recognized the talents of the young Welles. He put him to work as an editorial writer. Together Niles and Welles assembled a powerful Democratic Party organization in Connecticut. As a reward for his efforts, Niles was made postmaster of Hartford in 1829. When he was elected to the U.S. Senate, Welles succeeded him as postmaster in 1835. Welles lost the post when a Whig, William Henry Harrison, became president in 1840. Welles campaigned enthusiastically for James K. Polk in 1844 and was rewarded with the position of chief of the U.S. Navy Department's Office of Provisions and Clothing. In this post he demonstrated that he was an outstanding administrator, but the office gave him no actual experience or conception of naval operations themselves.

As a Jacksonian Democrat, Welles was also a supporter of states' rights, but he sincerely disapproved of what appeared to him to be the Southern desire to nationalize the institution of slavery. He went so far as to break ranks with the Democratic Party and to give his support to the Wilmot Provisio, a legislative proposal to keep slavery from any of the territories obtained from Mexico during the Mexican War.

In a speech before Congress on January 7, 1847, Welles said: "The time has come, when Northern Democracy should take a stand. Everything has taken a Southern shape and has been controlled by Southern caprice for years. We must satisfy the Northern people . . . that we are not expanding the institution of slavery as a result of this war."

In keeping with this position, as the years passed, he objected more and more to the direction being taken by the Democratic Party (whose national machinery was firmly controlled by the

Southern planter interests) concerning the issue of slavery. Finally in 1855 he broke completely with the Democrats and joined the antislavery Republican Party. He then decided to run in 1856 for the office of governor of Connecticut. He lost the one-sided race but gained national attention and recognition in the process. As a result he earned for himself a position on the Republican National Committee; this in turn ensured him a critical place at the Republican Party Convention of 1860 that was held in Chicago. There he originally opposed Lincoln's nomination in favor of a candidate more clearly opposed to slavery, Salmon P. Chase of Ohio.

When it came time to form his cabinet, Lincoln sought advice from several quarters, including that of his vice president, Hannibal Hamlin of Maine. Hamlin made it clear that it was important that a New Englander be named to the cabinet. For the post of secretary of the navy, Hamlin therefore suggested the names of three New Englanders. Welles was one. Also included for consideration for the post were two Massachusetts men, Charles Francis Adams (who eventually became the American minister, or ambassador, to Great Britain) and Nathaniel Banks (who became a spectacularly unsuccessful political general).

Welles himself believed that he was going to be named postmaster general, but that post went to a Border State Republican, Montgomery Blair. Knowing his own lack of experience and expertise in naval affairs, Welles was somewhat surprised when he learned of his being named secretary of the navy.

Unlike Mallory, Welles was thus distinguished by his lack of formal experience with naval affairs and operations. Lincoln himself joked originally that Welles did not know bow from stern or port from starboard. But Lincoln realized that Welles was an able administrator who had no real need to be a seagoing salt. Welles in his turn took what could have been a weakness and turned it into one of his greatest strengths as the Union's secretary of the navy.

For soon, unlike Mallory, Welles would not be facing the challenges of a civil war at sea alone, for fate had given Welles a partner. His name was Gustavus Vasa Fox—the same Fox who had come up with the scheme for the relief of Fort Sumter and who had been forced to watch helplessly while the fort was bombarded into submission. Fox, like Welles, was a New England man, being from

Massachusetts. He was also a former naval officer who had resigned his commission to become a maritime businessman. As such he knew ships and the sea. In addition, Fox also boasted impeccable social and political connections. This was in part due to his wife's sister who was married to the politically important and powerful Montgomery Blair of Maryland, Lincoln's postmaster general. This connection had enabled Fox to mount the Fort Sumter expedition in the first place.

When the post of chief clerk of the U.S. Navy Department became vacant, Fox sought the job. Although the title was insignificant, it was actually the second-ranking civilian position within the Navy Department. In effect, the chief clerk functioned as the secretary of the navy's primary assistant. Welles, however, already had a candidate of his own in mind for the position, William Faxon, who was a confidant of Welles. Faxon was already serving as a clerk within the department and was looking forward to the appointment.

To placate Fox, Welles suggested to Lincoln that Fox be reinstated in the navy at his former rank and then be given a command of his choice.

Once again Blair used his influence on Fox's behalf. Blair, who had easy access to the president, told Lincoln that posting Fox to a sea command would be a waste of his organizational talents. He argued that Fox's skills could be better used in Washington and not patrolling the coast of the Secessionists.

Lincoln, not wishing to offend Welles, proceeded cautiously. Rather than instructing Welles to appoint Fox to the position of chief clerk, Lincoln merely asked Welles to consider it. Welles appreciated the situation and looked for a solution that would please both his friend Faxon and his president. The solution was reached when Congress on July 24, 1861, as part of a general bill to expand the navy for the war, authorized the appointment of an assistant secretary of the navy. Fox was quickly appointed to the new position. In a short time the relationship between Welles and Fox became a truly formidable partnership.

Fox brought to this partnership his superb knowledge of naval affairs, his wide contacts in Washington political circles, and his strong personality. His appointment also brought the beginning of a team approach to the problem of controlling the far-flung operations of the Union navy at war. All policy decisions and all final decisions—whenever there was no consensus about a solution—were made by Welles. The day-to-day details, however, were handled by Fox. Eventually it seemed that Welles and Fox had merged and were like two sides of the same coin, since they never appeared—to outsiders—to be in disagreement.

Since the post of assistant secretary was brand new and thus did not have any rigidly defined responsibilities, Fox was able to invent his own areas of responsibility. He quietly took on the functions of what would eventually become the office of chief of naval operations nearly half a century before that position was actually created. This relieved Welles of a considerable burden and of direct control and responsibility for naval operations themselves. Since responsibility for the daily operations of the navy had been delegated to Fox, Welles was left free to set and define policy.

Thus Welles began to compensate for his lack of knowledge and experience in naval affairs. Welles also compensated in other ways, through such portions of his character that included raw determination and his total lack of pretension.

It became Welles's pattern, whenever he was confronted by something he did not understand or lacked firsthand knowledge about, to name a board of experts to study the problem or situation. Such boards included the Blockade Strategy Board and the Ironclad Board. The Blockade Strategy Board soon became an embryonic planning staff—laying the foundation for the Union blockade of the Southern seacoast—while the Ironclad Board did yeoman's work in determining the Union navy's answer to Confederate Secretary of the Navy Mallory's major technological innovation, construction, and operation of a steam-powered ironclad warship.

2

The Mallory Approach

ALTHOUGH STEPHEN MALLORY HAD not sought the post of secretary of the navy in the Davis cabinet, he did have some definite ideas about how the Confederate naval effort should be handled. Between his nomination by Davis on February 25, 1861, and his confirmation by the Confederate Congress on March 4, 1861, Mallory's ideas evolved into a well-thought-out and comprehensive strategy for the Confederate navy.

He knew that Confederate naval strategy would have to be based upon the environment and the conditions imposed upon it. The environment was the eastern coastline of the Confederate States, the Gulf Coast, and the Mississippi River. The primary adverse condition faced by the Southern navy lay in the overwhelming, indeed near total, naval preponderance of the Union—in that it had an organized naval force and infrastructure that the Confederacy did not—which appeared to give the Union the initiative at sea. The only ships that the Confederacy had seized were a few Revenue Service cutters and the obsolete and almost totally useless steam gunboat USS *Fulton*. Another condition, the naval strategy of the Union itself, would help determine the ways and directions of possible reply. Finally, there was the new technological framework that seemed to offer the Confederacy and its infant naval service the best hope of seizing the naval initiative from the Union.

The environment of the war (the naval war, that is) as represented by the Southern coastline measured thirty-six hundred nautical miles (starting from Virginia, down around the Florida Peninsula, and along the coast of the Gulf of Mexico to the mouth of the Rio Grande) with more than eighty-nine harbors or navigable river mouths to be defended. In addition to the maritime frontier, there were also the inland waterways to be defended because the entire territory of the Confederacy was crossed by navigable rivers to a great distance from the sea. Finally there was the Mississippi River itself, an internal sea eleven hundred nautical miles long. Then there were the Mississippi's tributaries, whose water level tended to be high at the end of the spring and low in the late summer and early autumn. This was an immense area, and the biggest question facing Mallory was determining how this huge expanse could be defended. Initially the Confederacy attempted to defend most of it with land-based fortifications that unfortunately soon proved to be inadequate, primarily due to steamships along the Atlantic seacoast and the use of ironclads as part of the Union thrust down the Mississippi.

At the beginning of the war, Mallory unfortunately did not fully consider the question of coastal defense, leaving it primarily to the Confederate army and local authorities. Experience soon caused him to rectify this error.

When Lincoln called for seventy-five thousand men to suppress the "rebellion," Confederate President Davis responded with a proclamation of his own, calling for one hundred thousand volunteers and for privateers to be unleashed against Union commerce. Lincoln thereupon upped the ante with a new proclamation calling for the establishment of a naval blockade. It was soon understood that this was to be followed by a Federal advance down the Mississippi River to New Orleans, which would thus cut the Confederate States in two.

The basic Union strategy soon became apparent. It was the North's intention to close off the Confederacy from the rest of the world and suffocate it while cutting it into two mutually insupportable portions. Therefore, it became the first objective of Mallory's new navy to break the blockade. Although circumstances (primarily the danger from Union amphibious operations) would later cause Mallory to emphasize other priorities, the effort to break the blockade would never be abandoned.

Mallory well knew that whatever naval forces the Confederacy was able to develop would be unable to meet the already well-established U.S. Navy toe to toe. He knew that his navy would always be inferior in numbers because the Union had too much of a head start and the South would never be able to match the industrial capacity of the North. Therefore, Mallory brought with him the convictions that soon became the basis of his strategic plan for the Confederate navy.

First, he was convinced that steam-powered ironclad warships had the potential to be the ultimate naval weapon of the day. Mallory was convinced that such ships would enable the Confederate navy to break the blockade and to even seize control of the seas off the East Coast of North America.

Second, he believed that Northern maritime mercantile commerce was susceptible to attacks by high-seas raiders. Therefore, Mallory reasoned, the North (specifically New England) could be driven to its knees and forced to sue for peace if its maritime commerce could be threatened with destruction. What was revolutionary about Mallory's concept was that his commerce destroyers would be commissioned naval vessels, not privateers. Privateering (the fitting out and arming of private or civilian vessels under government license or letters of marque to attack enemy merchant ships), despite the proclamation of President Davis, was dying out as a practical means of making naval war and had already been outlawed by most European nations.

Third, all Confederate naval vessels—if possible—should be armed with large-caliber rifled naval guns. Mallory was convinced that the rifled cannon invented by Lt. John Mercer Brooke was the best weapon of its type available to the South. Mallory realized that eventually all smoothbore naval cannon would be replaced by rifled guns.

Fourth, promotions and appointments should be governed by demonstrated courage and merit, not by the long-established tradition and principle of seniority as it then existed in the U.S. Navy.

Mallory took immediate steps to put his commerce-destroying plans into operation as quickly as possible. Knowing that the city of

New Orleans, besides being the largest city in the Confederate States, was also a considerable shipbuilding center, the largest in the South, he sent Cmdr. Raphael Semmes to New Orleans with orders to find and convert any suitable vessels into commerce raiders.

Although Mallory decided that Union maritime commerce would be a primary target in his strategy, he had absolutely no faith in the use of privateers to attack it. First, Mallory knew that the lucrative practice of privateers had never successfully affected the outcome of any war. In addition, it was next to impossible to subordinate privateers to the regular navy and thus provide some coordination or direction to their activities. Their attacks tended to be piecemeal, and since they were not part of the navy, but private individuals, they could not be subordinated or controlled in order to increase their effectiveness. Furthermore, since privateers were private individuals, they could be accused of piracy. (In fact, the Lincoln administration did press such charges against the first privateers captured during the war. It took threats to regular Union prisoners of war and European pressure to prevent Union authorities from executing the captured privateers.)

In addition, although the United States was not a signatory, recent European treaties had banned privateering, and Mallory believed that if the Confederate States were to attract European support they had best conform to European practices. Britain had been a major mover in the effort to ban privateering, primarily because as the leading maritime mercantile power it had the most to lose if the practice were to continue. When Britain took further unilateral action to ban privateers' prizes from their harbors and to prohibit British subjects from becoming privateers themselves (an action quickly copied by the rest of Europe), Confederate privateers were dealt a major blow since they had no place to take their prizes except for Confederate ports. As the blockade tightened, fewer and fewer prizes were able to get through and most of them were recaptured and returned to their owners. The lack of neutral ports in which to dispose of their prizes and the blockading of Confederate ports combined to make privateering unprofitable and eventually doomed the practice.

Mallory decided that the Confederacy should replace privateering by embarking upon a policy of commerce destroying conducted by regularly commissioned naval warships. Thus his ships would operate in accordance with current European international law.

Knowing that the South could never match the shipbuilding capacity of the North, he decided in May 1861 to dispatch two naval procurement agents to Europe. Mallory planned to buy what he needed in Europe, since the Confederate States did not have the manufacturing capability to compete with Northern industrial might. The first of these agents, James D. Bulloch, a former U.S. naval officer, was sent to Liverpool, England, as a civilian employee of the Confederate Navy Department. His original mission was to secure the construction of vessels that would be suitable to serve as high-seas cruisers to destroy Northern maritime commerce. The second was a serving naval officer, Lt. James H. North. His mission was to purchase or contract the construction of ironclad warships suitable for breaking the Northern blockade of the eastern and gulf coastlines.

Bulloch was to enjoy considerable success in his mission, but North would be an almost complete failure. These two appointments show that while, in general, Mallory was an excellent judge of the men he would need to carry out his strategy, he was still capable of making grievous errors in those judgments upon occasion.

Meanwhile, Semmes had succeeded in finding two ships, *Habana* and *Marques de la Habana*, that might do as commerce destroyers. *Habana* was a small passenger packet that normally plied the sea lanes between New Orleans and Havana, Cuba. *Marques de la Habana* was a steam-powered former Mexican warship and pirate ship that had been captured by the U.S. Navy in 1860. Semmes recommended the purchase, conversion, and armament of both ships.

Habana was armed with an 8-inch shell gun and four 32-pounders and renamed CSS *Sumter*. Under the personal command of Semmes, she also became the first Confederate raider cruiser. Eventually there would be ten of them (along with a few privateers and tenders) that would prey upon the North's maritime commerce. *Marques de la Habana* was armed with a 9-inch Dahlgren smoothbore and six 32-pounders and renamed the CSS *McRae*. This ship never ran the blockade to become a raider cruiser and was sunk while attempting to help defend New Orleans in 1862.

CSS *Nashville* was the second Confederate raider cruiser to put to sea. *Nashville* had originally been another small passenger vessel that plied the waters between New York City and Charleston, South Carolina. When South Carolina led the secession parade in 1860, the ship had been seized as enemy property. In the fall of 1861 she was armed with two 12-pounder howitzers and sent to sea. Her original mission was to take the Confederacy's first two diplomatic commissioners to Great Britain and France. At the last minute plans were changed, and *Nashville* slipped through the blockade at Savannah, Georgia, carrying mail, as was officially claimed by her captain and the Confederate government. Union officials, however, were convinced that she was being used as a decoy for the blockade-runner that was actually transporting the commissioners through the blockade.

Stopping briefly at Nassau—and destroying a Union merchant ship on her way—*Nashville* proceeded to Great Britain and arrived at Southampton on November 1, 1861. Her arrival caused considerable consternation and sensation since she was the first Confederate warship to arrive in a European port. Charles Francis Adams, the American minister to the Court of St. James, demanded that the ship and her crew be seized by British authorities as pirates.

British foreign secretary Lord John Russell, however, refused. He found that the *Nashville* was a warship of a belligerent power with a regularly enlisted crew. While she remained in a British port, the British would prohibit anything that would substantially increase her fighting power, but she would be permitted to conduct any necessary repairs to permit her to put to sea again. In addition, since the Union and the Confederacy were both belligerent powers (in the eyes of British authorities), if ships of both powers were moored within the same British port and a ship of one power were to leave the port, the vessel of the other belligerent power would not be permitted to leave for at least forty-eight hours. For example, if the *Nashville* were to leave Southampton, any Union ships also at Southampton would not be permitted to leave the harbor until forty-eight hours later. Following Britain's example, such belligerent rights were soon granted the Confederacy by the other European powers and were thus soon extended throughout the world.

Nashville left Southampton for her return voyage to the Confederate States on February 5, 1862, with a cargo of Enfield riflemuskets. After managing to avoid Union cruisers searching for her (while meanwhile destroying a second Union merchant ship), she returned to Savannah.

All in all it had been a successful cruise. The *Nashville* had destroyed two merchant ships, each with a value greater than her own. She had also compelled several Union cruisers to be withdrawn from the blockade in a vain attempt to run her down—thus making it easier for a short time for Confederate blockade-runners to enter and leave Southern ports. Finally, she had won a vitally important diplomatic victory by inducing British authorities to clarify the practical consequences of their neutrality policy and to deny any Union attempt to declare Confederate naval vessels to be outlaws.

Bulloch in the meantime succeeded in reaching Great Britain and contracting for the construction of two raider cruisers that would eventually become CSS *Florida* and CSS *Alabama*. North, however, failed miserably in his assignment. Specifically instructed to purchase or have built a broadside ironclad of the *Warrior* type in Britain or of the *Glorie* type in France, he apparently did little or nothing to accomplish his mission besides touring the *Warrior* and rejecting her out of hand due to her deep draft. With the apparent failure of North's mission, Mallory recalled Bulloch, appointed him an officer in the Confederate navy with the rank of commander—thus outranking the seniority-conscious Lieutenant North to his immense chagrin—and placing all financial disbursements in Bulloch's hands.

This activity incensed North, who purloined £30,000 intended as a payment for the *Alabama* and placed an order in a Scottish shipyard for the construction of a broadside ironclad similar to the *Warrior*. North had been accidentally given the money by a clerk at the firm of Fraser, Trenholm, and Company—the Liverpool branch of the Charleston-based firm of John Fraser and Company—which served as the Confederate government's financial agents in Britain. North believed that the money was part of a two-million-dollar appropriation that had been promised to fund the purchase or construction of ironclads in Britain. Bulloch, upon his return to Britain, decided to overlook North's actions since the money had been used to order the construction of the South's first European-built ironclad. Bulloch also brought back with him plans for two more ironclads and placed orders for them to be built at the John Laird and Sons shipyard at Birkenhead. This was the shipyard that was building the *Alabama*. Later, Bulloch ordered two more ironclads to be built in French shipyards. He did this while arranging for the fitting out, escape, arming, and commissioning of the *Florida* and *Alabama*, both of which were highly successful raider cruisers.

Back in the Confederate States, after the apparent failure of North's mission, Mallory began considering the construction of ironclad ships inside the Confederate States. He contacted ordnance expert John Mercer Brooke, asking him to prepare some preliminary calculations. Mallory then assigned John L. Porter, a specialized naval constructor, to assist Brooke. Also called in was Confederate Navy Department engineer in chief William P. Williamson. On June 23, 1861, Porter and Williamson met with Mallory and Brooke. Brooke and Porter displayed their sketches and calculations. Porter also produced a model. Apparently he was thinking along the lines of the floating batteries used by the French in the Crimean War, while Brooke was seeking to build a true warship. The final result was a combination of the two proposals and a forced collaboration between Brooke and Porter that was presided over by Mallory.

Porter's proposal was accepted only in general outline. This included an ironclad casemate with its sides inclined at an angle of thirty-five degrees from the deck to deflect enemy fire. The design also called for the lower parts to be submerged, with the hull ending abruptly at both ends of the casemate. Brooke's contribution was the proposal that the bow and stern of the hull be lengthened beyond the casemate and that the bow and stern be formed like any fast vessel. To protect the bow and stern from enemy fire, Brooke suggested that both ends of the ship should be submerged under two feet of water. Brooke believed this arrangement would guarantee good speed and buoyancy while reducing the necessary armor protection. Decreasing the necessary armor protection would in turn reduce the vessel's weight. Thus the design demonstrated for the first time the compromise between firepower, speed, and protection necessary for the construction of any successful modern warship. Unfortunately, Confederate-built warships hardly ever managed to reached their designed speed since effective engines were simply unavailable.

By a stroke of luck, the Confederate navy had a chance to get a head start in constructing an ironclad, it was hoped before the Union navy would have a chance to react. In the aftermath of the surrender of Fort Sumter and Lincoln's call for troops to put down the "rebellion," four more states—Virginia, Arkansas, North Carolina, and Tennessee—joined the Confederacy. The secession of Virginia led to the Confederacy's obtaining the Gosport Navy Yard at Norfolk, Virginia, and inheriting the steam frigate *Merrimack,* which became the basis of Mallory's first ironclad, the CSS *Virginia.*

The loss of the navy yard and the *Merrimack* was a Union naval disaster of the first magnitude. The events surrounding the loss also helped to demonstrate that Mallory had been right in seeking to abolish the tradition of promotion by seniority.

AT THE time of the secession crisis, command of the navy yard, which lay opposite Norfolk on the west bank of the Elizabeth River, rested with sixty-eight-year-old Com. Charles S. McCauley. He was a staunch Unionist, although in the coming crisis he would prove himself to be timid, vacillating, and according to historian Ivan Musicant, somewhat too fond of the bottle. In addition, most of his officers and practically all of the workmen at the navy yard favored secession. In the spring of 1861 the Gosport Navy Yard was the largest naval arsenal and reserve store of guns in the entire country. Nearly two thousand pieces of heavy naval ordnance were stored here. Some of these guns dated back to the War of 1812, but many were modern smoothbore and rifled cannon. The yard also contained one of only two granite masonry dry docks in the entire country. This dry dock could berth any ship in the navy and probably any ship in the world.

Also present were a number of warships laid up in "ordinary," that is, mothballed. These included the sailing sloops of war *Germantown* and *Plymouth* and the tiny brig of war *Dolphin*. Also present were three obsolete ships of the line (*Pennsylvania*, *Columbus*, and *Delaware*) as well as three obsolete sailing frigates (*Raritan*, *Columbia*, and the *United States*, which had been originally commissioned in 1797). Finally, there was the pride of the U.S. Navy, the steam frigate *Merrimack*. Like the others, *Merrimack* was not in commission. Her guns were unshipped, and her engines were dismantled, having been deemed inadequate. These engines were the reason why *Merrimack* was in the navy yard in the first place, since they were scheduled to be replaced.

One of the few Unionist officers in the yard, chief engineer Robert Danby, was desperate to get *Merrimack* out of the navy yard and safely into Northern waters. McCauley, however, was influenced by the unfaithful Secessionist officers constantly obstructing Danby's way. Danby responded by contacting the U.S. Navy's engineer in chief, Benjamin Franklin Isherwood, who brought the situation to the attention of Gideon Welles. The secretary of the navy issued secret orders to McCauley, as commandant of the navy yard, that the *Merrimack* should be made ready for sea immediately, but Welles made the mistake of adding instructions that no steps be taken that would alarm Virginia authorities who were teetering on the brink of secession.

McCauley complied with the order, but due to protests from Norfolk's Secessionist elements, he soon halted the work. When Welles was informed of this, he immediately dispatched Isherwood and Cmdr. James Alden to Norfolk. Isherwood's mission was to prepare *Merrimack* for sea, while Alden would take command of the ship and get her to Philadelphia. Welles also ordered the East Coast stripped of every idle sailor with these men to be sent to Norfolk to crew the *Merrimack*. The first contingent was being prepared when the Confederates fired on Fort Sumter.

When Alden arrived at Norfolk, he found that his orders were general knowledge and that all of the civilian workmen had deserted the navy yard. Isherwood on his arrival inspected the *Merrimack* with Danby, and they estimated the engines could be put back together enough for her to leave Norfolk within three days.

To prod McCauley along, Welles also sent the senior officer in the Navy, Com. Hiram Paulding to Norfolk.

The crew problem was solved with the arrival of the sailing frigate *Cumberland,* whose captain was instructed to provide the men needed to get *Merrimack* to sea. She would be safe if she could at least be moved to Fort Monroe at the tip of the peninsula formed by the James and Elizabeth Rivers. On his arrival Paulding met with navy yard officers, all Southerners, who assured him they would defend the public property at the navy yard. Later, however, one of them pleaded to be relieved. Upon Paulding's return to Washington, Lincoln ordered that all of the officers at the navy yard be replaced with Northerners.

Before action could be taken, however, Virginia seceded and all of the officers at the navy yard promptly resigned their commissioners as McCauley shrank from any confrontations. Another factor weighing on McCauley was the gathering of Virginia militia troops outside of the navy yard who were intent upon taking the yard by force. On April 17 Isherwood and Danby reported to McCauley that *Merrimack* was ready to leave. McCauley declined to authorize her immediate departure deciding that "tomorrow" would be soon enough. The next day McCauley, paralyzed with indecision, according to Isherwood, would not give the order for *Merrimack* to cast off. Instead he ordered that her boilers be shut down. McCauley told Isherwood he was retaining the ship for the defense of the navy yard.

Although Alden would have been amply justified in ignoring the order, he accepted it and returned to Washington.

Too late Welles issued orders relieving McCauley of command and naming Paulding to succeed him, but command of the yard would not change hands until Paulding arrived and officially relieved McCauley. In the meantime, Welles also attempted to rush reinforcements to Norfolk. Paulding's orders instructed him to repel any attempt by Secessionists to take over the yard. If that should become impossible, he was to destroy the navy yard. Paulding and his reinforcements were dispatched aboard the steam sloop of war *Pawnee,* which arrived at the navy yard on April 21. To his horror Paulding discovered that all of the ships at the navy yard, including *Merrimack,* had been scuttled on McCauley's orders.

The *Merrimack*'s sea cocks had been opened, and she had sank to the bottom of the harbor before any action could be taken to stop it. Paulding's primary mission had been foiled by McCauley, leaving him with just two options. The first was to attempt to hold the navy yard. For that task Paulding had on hand only about one thousand sailors and marines. He could also utilize the heavy guns of the *Cumberland* and *Pawnee* until reinforcements were available. His only other option would be to accept the situation as hopeless and evacuate the navy yard, destroying anything that might be useful to the Secessionists. That included the ships scuttled by McCauley. Paulding decided he simply did not have an adequate force to defend the navy yard in the face of the gathering Virginia militia. Therefore, all of the scuttled ships were ordered burned (only the rotting hulks of *Delaware* and *United States* were spared). Finding themselves unable to destroy the three hundred Dahlgren smoothbores at the navy yard, these guns were spiked and dumped into the river (they were later retrieved by the Confederates and repaired). All of the buildings at the navy yard were packed with gunpowder and slow-match fuses were laid. The great stone dry dock was mined with two thousand pounds of gunpowder and prepared for destruction.

The tug *Yankee* towed the *Cumberland* out of the Gosport Navy Yard, and a signal rocket was fired as she and *Pawnee* departed. Shore parties then lit the fuses and the fires aboard the scuttled ships. A few moments later the entire area of the yard and the *Merrimack* were covered by a sheet of flame. Although they awaited the massive explosion that would mark the destruction of the dry dock, it failed to explode. Even today no one knows why.

Once the Confederate government took possession of the navy yard from the state of Virginia, the wreckage of the *Merrimack* was examined and it was decided that it could be salvaged. The hull was accordingly raised and towed into the massive stone dry dock. A lot of materiel was also captured or otherwise salvaged, including practically all of the heavy naval cannon of all types stored there. Where possible many of these guns were rifled and used to arm Confederate warships and coastal fortifications all over the South.

Aside from the hull, it was also decided that *Merrimack*'s original engines could still be utilized. Even though the engines had been scheduled for replacement as inadequate and their submersion in the James River had certainly not improved their condition, they were better than no engines at all. The hulk was cut down to the gun deck, an armored casemate was built atop the hull, and a total of ten guns were fitted, including two 7-inch Brooke rifles.

CONVERSION OF the *Merrimack* into the *Virginia* alone took practically all of the resources of the infant Confederate Navy Department and the resources of one of only two navy yards taken intact from the Federals. The other navy yard in Confederate hands was at Pensacola, Florida, and was practically useless because it was dominated by Fort Pickens, which remained in the hands of the Union government. If any more ironclads were to be built in the foreseeable future, they would have to depend upon individual private enterprise. And that is exactly what happened. Four other ironclads soon began construction. Two of these, *Louisiana* and *Mississippi,* were built at New Orleans. Another two, *Tennessee* and *Arkansas,* began to take shape at Memphis, Tennessee. They were the brainchildren of individual shipbuilders who either came to the attention of or sought the attention of Mallory.

The Memphis ironclads were begun on the initiative of Memphis resident John T. Shirley. He proposed the construction of two ships as a defensive measure against the anticipated Union strategy of advancing down the Mississippi River. His proposal was quickly approved, spurred on by the fact that the Federal government had already contracted for the construction of a number of ironclads for use on the Mississippi. John L. Porter, however, prepared the designs and specifications of the two Mississippi River ironclads named *Arkansas* and *Tennessee.* Asa and Nelson Tift of Key West, Florida, who were well known to Mallory, proposed building an ironclad at New Orleans, which was to become the *Mississippi.* They proposed to use the principle of a self-supporting hull structure in shipbuilding that within the next century would be widely accepted. The second New Orleans ironclad, *Louisiana,* was proposed by E. C. Murray, an able shipbuilder from Kentucky. The overly optimistic schedule called for *Arkansas, Tennessee,* and *Mississippi* to be completed by the end of December 1861 and *Louisiana* to be completed a month later.

A sixth ironclad, CSS *Eastport,* was originally a river steamer that was purchased on October 21, 1861, and placed under conversion as an ironclad by Maj. Gen. Leonidas K. Polk, then commander of Confederate troops in West Tennessee. The ship was towed to Cerro Gordo, Tennessee, for the conversion, and the work was placed under the supervision of Lt. Isaac N. Brown of the Confederate navy.

Mallory planned to use these ships to break the blockade and to stop the Northern advance down the Mississippi River. *Virginia* was to be aimed at the Union naval concentration at Hampton Roads, which was busy preparing to support Maj. Gen. George B. McClellan's Peninsula campaign. *Louisiana* and *Mississippi* were to be given the task of smashing the blockade of the Confederacy's gulf coast and seizing full control of the Mississippi with the assistance of *Tennessee* and *Arkansas* (along with *Eastport*). As it turned out, only *Virginia* and *Arkansas* were able to attempt to carry out their part of Mallory's naval offensive.

To arm these and other Confederate warships, Mallory turned again to the resourceful Lt. John Mercer Brooke, whose 7-inch Brooke naval rifle became the standard naval armament of the Confederacy. Mallory was convinced that rifled cannon should be used on naval warships because they had longer range and more hitting power than smoothbore guns of similar size. Unfortunately, the secretary's thinking was ahead of the technology of his day. Long-range naval gunnery—firing effectively from a moving platform on a moving target—was not perfected until forty years after the Civil War.

The Union navy chose to go in the opposite direction, in that most Union naval officers and officials favored massive-caliber smoothbore guns. Federal naval officials figured that since the shorter the range the more accurate the cannon fire, it would be better to get as close as possible (depending upon armor, if any, and maneuverability to protect the warships from enemy fire), then to sledgehammer the enemy with their massive smoothbore guns.

The Confederate ironclad construction program was not particularly secret. The *Philadelphia Inquirer* published a story on October 5, 1861, which stated in part: "The *Merrimac* [a common misspelling] is still in dry-dock, and it is expected that she will be ready for service by the first of the coming month. Some of the mechanics in Norfolk have expressed an opinion that, in consequence of the large amount of iron on her upper works, she will be so top heavy as to be unmanageable."

In the meantime, the Southern navy pursued another technological innovation whose initiator may well have been Mallory himself. This was the creation of submarine warfare designed to strike even the best-protected warship at its weakest point, below the waterline. Mallory created the Torpedo Bureau, and despite the rancor between the two men, he placed Matthew Fontaine Maury in charge.

Maury was much more a scientist than he was a man of war, but under his direction land and sea mines were developed by the Confederate navy. The stationary torpedo (or naval mine) had been originally developed during the Crimean War by the Imperial Russian Navy, which eventually became quite expert in their use. For the Confederate navy, mines made a great deal of sense. There were two reasons for this. First, they succeeded in sinking more than forty Union warships and support vessels of all sizes during the war. Second, even when they were not present, the mere suspicion that the Confederates could have laid fields of stationary torpedoes often was enough to stop Union shipping in its tracks.

Before Mallory's naval strategy could reach its full potential, he still had a bureaucratic battle to fight: the struggle against the entrenched rule of seniority. Mallory had fought this battle in the U.S. Senate when he had championed the Naval Retiring Board. Due to the controversy over Maury, he eventually lost that struggle. Ironically the old problem had also been inherited by the Confederate navy.

When the Confederate States seceded, a number of overage senior naval officers resigned from the U.S. Navy (which due to its unofficial retired list was in most cases not employing them anyway) and offered their services to the Confederate navy. Thus the Southern service started the war with an excess of these older senior officers. Some like Buchanan, Maury (whose effectiveness was limited by the feud with Mallory), and Semmes were able men. Most, however, such as Com. Victor Randolph of Alabama, the original Confederate naval officer in charge of the defenses at

Mobile Bay, turned out to be slow, lacking in imagination, opinionated, dull, and incapable of understanding—if not openly hostile to—the technological innovations in which Mallory believed lay the only hope of the Confederate navy. Eventually, Mallory tried several possible solutions to this problem.

First, in 1862 Mallory obtained from the Confederate Congress a law that allowed him to commission two captains, five commanders, and fifty lieutenants for the duration of the war and without regard to seniority. Mallory used this law to make his chief procurement officer in Europe, James D. Bulloch, a commander over the head of James H. North and a number of other officers. Another law stipulated that a substantial number of officers would be commissioned or promoted only as a reward for gallantry during the war.

His final solution to this problem was not achieved until May 1863 when the Confederate Congress—due to his constant prodding—created the provisional navy. Its genesis could be seen in the act of the previous year, which had created the volunteer navy that had been aimed at absorbing the former privateers into the regular navy. According to the provisional navy law, all personnel and ships of the regular navy could be transferred back and forth between it and the provisional navy at the discretion of the president as commander in chief. Officers would be transferred to the provisional navy in the number considered necessary. Once they were part of the provisional navy they could be commissioned and promoted without any consideration as to age, time in grade, or seniority as "the needs of the service" demanded.

Although the provisional navy was intended to exist only for the duration of the war, should the Confederate States win their independence, the ranks would be reexamined and possibly confirmed. By this means Mallory finally managed to replace—if only for the duration of the war—the seniority system with one based on both merit and demonstrated skill.

3

Anaconda and Ericsson

GIDEON WELLES NEVER HAD the scope of strategic planning that was made available by circumstance to his Confederate counterpart, Stephen R. Mallory. Welles had to subordinate his plans to the Union's national strategy, the so-called Anaconda Plan. (The name was coined by the Northern press early in the war, basing it on George B. McClellan's derisive nickname for the strategy—the "boa constrictor plan.") Although this plan, or blueprint, was never officially adopted, nonetheless it shaped the conduct of the war.

At the beginning of the conflict, practically no one foresaw what the war would become. Although responsible leaders in Richmond and Washington did not expect a short war, they had not perceived that it would be fought for total ends (either the North would conquer the South or the South would win its independence) and would therefore become a total war, requiring the total mobilization of men and resources. The South's objective, the political independence of the Confederacy, never wavered. At first, however, the Union fought not to conquer the South but to simply suppress the "insurrection" and win back what was believed to be the latent loyalty of the people of the seceding states. This false perception prevailed until it was realized that Southern Unionism was mostly illusion.

Future Union general in chief Ulysses S. Grant also held this opinion until the April 1862 battle of Shiloh. In the aftermath of Shiloh, which included some of the bloodiest fighting of the war to that point, Grant said that he realized that the Confederate soldiers who had fought so doggedly would have to be truly conquered before they would surrender.

Bvt. Lt. Gen. Winfield Scott was the Union general in chief at the beginning of the war. He had served in the army since 1808 and had become a general during the War of 1812. Scott's finest hour was in the Mexican War, when he demonstrated military genius in his campaign to take Mexico City (which served as a training ground for most of the prominent generals of the Civil War). Scott was a Virginian, but he remained loyal to the Union. He did not want a war of conquest. He felt that such a war would only "produce 15 devested provinces [the slave states] not to be brought into harmony with their conquerors, but to be held for generations, by heavy garrisons, at an expense quadruple the net duties or taxes which it could be possible to extort from them." Rather then invading the Confederate States, Scott proposed to envelope the South with a blockade by sea and a fleet of gunboats supported by soldiers along the Mississippi River. He suggested that the army conduct a holding operation in the East until the Mississippi had been cleared.

Scott believed that the Confederacy, thus sealed off from the outside world, would suffocate economically and the Federal government would then be able to bring the rebellious states to terms with less bloodshed then by direct conquest.

Scott's plan, however, would take time. The U.S. Navy would need time to obtain enough warships to make a blockade of the Southern seacoast effective. Time was also needed to build the gunboats necessary to support an army advancing South down the Mississippi. Scott estimated that his plan would require two hundred thousand men and take about three years. It was upon all these factors that the plan nearly foundered.

Public opinion—inflamed by newspaper editors who knew next to nothing about the military realities—urged that an immediate thrust be made upon the city of Richmond, which had become the capital of the Confederacy since the secession of Virginia. The city made an attractive target because it concentrated in one place the Confederate government, a goodly portion of the South's extremely limited industrial base, and a major transportation and communications hub. Therefore, it is likely that the editors were correct in assuming that the fall of Richmond would have doomed the Confederacy at almost any time. The Confederate leadership also grasped this fact and would for the better part of four years successfully defend Richmond.

The second major flaw of the Anaconda Plan was that it made no attempt to answer the question, then what? This was the question the Union would have to answer when the sweep down the Mississippi was completed and the Confederacy failed to collapse. Eventually the question would be answered by Ulysses S. Grant and the ubiquitous William Tecumseh Sherman. The answer was to adapt Scott's limited war strategy to meet the new conditions of total war that existed by the summer and fall of 1863. After Grant had secured Chattanooga as a base, Sherman launched his Atlanta campaign, which was quickly followed by his March to the Sea and his March Through the Carolinas, which finally—along with Robert E. Lee's surrender at Appomattox—brought the war to an end.

It was not until after the disaster at the battle of First Bull Run (or Manassas, as the South called it) in July 1861 that the Union government dusted off Scott's Anaconda Plan and adopted it in everything but name. The first portion of the plan had been put into effect even before the battle, when Lincoln proclaimed the blockade on April 19, 1861. Thus the main strategic problem faced by Welles was how the U.S. Navy would enact its part of the national strategy.

In 1861 the U.S. Navy was woefully unprepared for the task that faced it. Out of a total strength of just ninety ships only about half, forty-two ships, were in commission when the secession crisis began. Of those ships only twenty-four were steam-powered vessels, and eighteen of these were scattered on foreign stations from the East Indies to Brazil. When Lincoln was elected in the fall of 1860, just three modern steam-powered wooden warships were available in Northern waters: the *Mohawk* and the *Crusader* at New York City and the *Pawnee* at Washington, D.C.

The first thing that Welles did was to begin the greatest period of expansion the U.S. Navy had ever known, up to that time. The result would be an increase in the paper strength of 90 ships to a peak strength of over 670 ships. New ships were immediately placed under construction. In addition, anything that could float, mount a few guns, and make its own way South was purchased and dispatched to establish the blockade. Even so, given the magnitude of the problem of patrolling a coastline of thirty-six hundred nautical miles closely enough to choke off most, if not all, imports, it is not surprising that it took Welles three and a half years of building up the navy before he could establish an efficient blockade of the Gulf and Atlantic ports of the Southern states.

The blockade managed only to restrict—not cut off—the flow of supplies into the Confederacy from overseas. In his book *King Cotton Diplomacy*, Prof. Frank L. Owsley estimated that the Union navy was able to destroy or capture one in ten blockade-runners in 1861; one in eight in 1862; one in four in 1863; one in three by the late spring of 1864, and did not achieve two of three until January 1865. By that time the war was practically over.

By happy accident Welles also managed to create the doctrine of unified command. This was an idea that the Confederates (except for P. G. T. Beauregard) would never fully master. It occurred because Welles believed that the Anaconda Plan's projected Mississippi River operations were purely to be the responsibility of the army. Jack Coombe notes in *Thunder Along the Mississippi* that Welles stumbled upon the concept when Flag Off. Andrew Foote took command of naval operations along the western rivers. Foote's written instructions from Welles and Fox included the caveat that these naval operations were to be under the direction of the War Department, thereupon officially establishing the principle of a unified command. Welles instructed all of the naval officers who succeeded Foote in operating along the Mississippi that all movements on the river and its tributaries were to be under the control of the army. Even when the navy took complete control of the operations of its vessels on the inland waterways, the principles of cooperation and unified command were continued unofficially through the actions of the army and navy officers on the scene. This cooperation between Maj. Gen.

Ulysses S. Grant and Rear Adm. David D. Porter would be an important factor in the successful conquest of Vicksburg in the summer of 1863.

With the principle of unified command established along the Mississippi River, it was also carried out unofficially in the combined operations along the Atlantic and Gulf Coasts. This was done through the establishment of well-defined areas of responsibility. The naval commander had total control of naval operations; the army commander had similar control over army operations once the troops had been landed. Until the soldiers were landed, the naval commander was in command of the operation.

Once these preliminary steps were fully under way and firmly in hand, the strategic ball was now entirely in Welles's court. He had to decide how he could best employ the rapidly expanding fleet to enforce the fledgling blockade. He would do what he always did when in doubt: form a board of experts to study the problem. Thus was born the Blockade Strategy Board.

It was immediately recognized that detailed information about the coastline would be the key to the blockade. The first and most obvious appointment to the board was therefore Alexander Dallas Bache, a great-grandson of Benjamin Franklin, who was the superintendent of the U.S. Coast Survey. His agency was an independent civilian operation that reported directly to Congress and was responsible for the ongoing charting of the country's coastline. The job required a large number of surveyors, including dozens of naval officers, and thus Bache was well known to the navy's officer corps and was much admired and respected.

Other members of the board were Capt. Samuel F. Du Pont and Cmdr. Charles H. Davis, both of whom were serving naval officers; Maj. J. G. Barnard of the Army Corps of Topographical Engineers; and the new assistant secretary of the navy, Gustavus Vasa Fox.

The board met several times a week at the Smithsonian Institution, of which Bache was a regent. The members concerned themselves with the changing technology, which tended to complicate the problems faced by the blockaders. The primary change was the use of steam, instead of the wind, for propulsion. Steam had freed warships from their dependence upon winds and tides; however, it tied them to refueling bases. Maintaining an effective blockade called for the blockaders to keep up a head of steam, ready to pursue any blockade-runners, but this strained the ships' already limited fuel supplies. This condition of readiness increased the number of ships that would be needed to keep a reasonable number on station. Unless nearby refueling and supply depots were established, ships would be forced to undergo long voyages and use additional tons of coal traveling to and from their blockade stations and their refueling and supply depots. Such voyages would also greatly reduce the number of blockaders that could be kept on station.

The board studied charts, coastal survey reports, currents, weather, and distances. Eventually it produced five reports that became the basis for the blockade effort. In addition, these reports also marked the birth of the navy's amphibious operations and tactics that, in conjunction with input from the Marine Corps, would be refined and perfected over the next century.

One problem was the lack of a force specifically trained for amphibious operations that could spearhead such assaults. The Marine Corps was too small to be entrusted with this responsibility. Just prior to the Roanoke Island operation in the winter of 1862, a division of volunteer troops was specially organized and trained in that role, but it soon joined the main army as the nucleus of the Ninth Corps. The problems stemming from the absence of an adequately trained amphibious force were not resolved until the Marine Corps assumed the responsibility for amphibious operations prior to World War II.

The board's first report was presented to Welles on July 5, 1861. Its focus was Fernandina, an island town just off the Atlantic Coast of Florida at the mouth of the St. Marys River. The town was at the northern end of Amelia Island and had been a haven for freebooters and pirates. The board suggested that the island was an ideal place for a secure supply depot that could service the southern end of the Atlantic seacoast's blockading force. In this instance, the board failed to consider the larger scheme. The viewpoint expressed in the report was strictly naval and failed to consider the possibility of moving inland from this enclave.

A second report followed eight days later, on July 13. This one concentrated on approximately one hundred miles of coastline in South Carolina and placed particular emphasis on three locations: Bulls Bay, north of Charleston; St. Helena Sound, between Charleston and Savannah; and Port Royal Sound, slightly north of Savannah. All three sites would make excellent bases for blockading warships, but the board believed that Bulls Bay and St. Helena Sound were better options than Port Royal Sound, which the members were convinced would be too strongly held to be easily occupied.

Three days later, on July 16, a third report was delivered to Welles. A key recommendation was that the Atlantic Coast be divided into two. The first half was to extend from Cape Henry to Cape Romain, a total of 370 miles, while the second was to extend from Cape Romain to St. Augustine, a distance of 220 miles. The basis for dividing the Atlantic blockade in two was that the northern and southern sectors had radically different geographical features. The northern sector featured narrow belts of sand that separated large inland waters from the ocean, divided at irregular intervals by openings or inlets through which ocean tides ebbed and flowed and access was obtained to the enclosed sounds. The southern sector was distinguished by ordinary ports and bays.

The board recommended different tactics in the two sectors. In the northern section it advocated obstructing the passages through the sandbars by sinking hulks. What made the proposal attractive were the area's small tides, slow currents, and shallow channels. Although the currents and tides would likely open new channels, these could be blocked as they occurred. Thirteen specific blocking sites were specified in the report, along with recommendations for the appropriate means for blocking each location.

Among these potential blocking points was Hatteras Inlet, which provided access to both Albemarle and Pamlico Sounds. These two sounds formed North Carolina's principal outlets to the sea. If Hatteras Inlet could be blocked or held by Union forces, most of the coast of North Carolina could be closed to the Confederacy, leaving the port of Wilmington as the state's only remaining practical outlet to the sea.

A separate plan for the southern section was outlined in the board's fourth report, which was delivered on July 26. In this case the southern sector was divided into three subsections. The first extended from Cape Romain to Tybee Island off Savannah; the second from Tybee Island to Cumberland Sound, which was the mouth of the St. Marys River at Fernandina; and the third from Fernandina to Cape Florida, being the east coast of Florida.

Since the July 13 report had already dealt with the northernmost of the three subsectors, the remainder of the report concentrated on the middle and southern portions. The board deemed the coast of Georgia to be especially important. It took note of the inland passage available from Savannah to the St. Marys River, which offered a highway for relatively shallow-draft steam vessels. Board members compared this area to the coasts of Holland and Belgium, pointing out the similar protected coastlines with frequent openings to the sea. They warned: "A superior naval power must command the whole of this division of the coast. It will be occupied by the party or nation, whichever it may be, that chooses to place armed steamers of suitable draft in its interior waters, and fortifications of sufficient strength at the mouth of its inlets. And the naval power that commands the coast of Georgia will command the State of Georgia."

The eventual development of the Confederacy's coastal defense policies later in the war would make it appear that both Mallory and a certain Confederate general had also read this particular report.

The third subsector, although the longest, was found to be the simplest to blockade because of its barrenness. Only St. Johns and St. Augustine were considered of interest and were to be blockaded in the "usual manner," by ships standing offshore on a regular basis. The remainder of the Florida coastline, the board felt, could be watched by as few as two patrolling steamers.

The fifth and final report, delivered to Welles on August 9, was the lengthiest. It dealt with the Florida keys and reefs; the West Coast of Florida from Cape Sable to Cedar Key; the northern division of Florida from Cedar Key to the Perdido River; the coasts of northwestern Florida, Alabama, and Mississippi from the Perdido River to Ship Island (which included Mobile Bay and the Mississippi Sound with its numerous and very important subsidiary bays and dependencies); the coast of Mississippi and Louisiana from Ship and Cat Islands to Atchafalaya, Cote Blanche, and Vermilion Bays; and the whole coast of Texas from Grand Pass, Vermilion Bay, to the mouth of the Rio Grande.

The fifth report did not dwell on a possible policy or strategy for the entire coastal area it covered, concentrating primarily on New Orleans with some brief remarks concerning Mobile Bay. The remaining area was virtually ignored, because the board considered it too remote and inaccessible to be of any significance. Due to Bache's input, the report included a considerable amount of hydrographical and topographical information about the diverse geography of the New Orleans area. Such a depth of information indicates that the board had access to people with intimate knowledge of the area, most likely merchant captains or naval officers who had run in and out of the port on cotton packets or participated in coastal survey work before the war.

Concerning New Orleans itself, the board recommended:

> The question is, whether the present plan of proceeding should embrace the conquest of this city or sealing up its trade and navigation. We regard its conquest as incompatible with the other nearer and more urgent naval and military operations in which the Government is now and will be for some time hereafter engaged. It is an enterprise of great moment, requiring the cooperation of a large number of vessels of war of small class, but of formidable armament, a great many troops, and the conduct of sieges, and it will be accomplished with slow advances.
>
> We recommend, therefore, that the subject of the capture of New Orleans be deferred for the present; be deferred at least until we are prepared to ascend the river with vessels of war sufficiently protected to contend with the forts now standing and the temporary fortifications which, in the event of invasion would be established at every defensible point.

Although somewhat cavalierly dismissing the importance of New Orleans, the report called for the targeting of Ship Island in the Mississippi Sound as the best base for blockaders and suggested that it be taken and fortified as quickly as possible. Mobile Bay was dealt with in five paragraphs, compared to the eleven pages devoted to New Orleans.

Most of the board's recommendations were sound, and they were eventually carried out. Yet the series of reports had shortcomings as well. The chief among these were their limitations to closing various Southern ports and seizing sufficient coastal enclaves to support the blockading fleet. No mention was made about the possibility of exploiting successes and moving farther inland, since such operations required complete army cooperation. It took awhile for the Union navy—and the Lincoln administration for that matter—to realize the simplest, best, and most effective way of closing a port was to capture it.

Mobile proved to be an exception. Once Farragut's fleet established its control of Mobile Bay, the capture of the city proved to be unnecessary and it could be left to wither on the vine and finally surrender to Union troops about a month after the surrender of Lee's Army of Northern Virginia at Appomattox Court House.

Another problem was the fact that the board members subscribed to the opinion that "a ship is a fool to fight a fort." This assumption grew out of the members' experience that failed to take into account the changes wrought by steam-powered warships. These vessels were also armed with massive rifled and smoothbore guns. Thus the advantage had shifted from the land-based, immobile forts to the steam-powered warships and their increasingly formidable mobile firepower. If these steam-propelled gun platforms also happened to be ironclads, so much the better.

It was another of Welles's special boards, the Ironclad Board, that proved Mallory's delusion that ironclad steam vessels were the nineteenth-century's ultimate weapon. The problem with Mallory's theory was that any weapon is an ultimate weapon if only one side is so equipped. Mallory failed to consider fully the North's huge industrial advantage and what would likely happen once the Union navy and government realized the immense possibilities that were represented by steam-powered ironclads.

Although Welles had at first discounted the use of ironclads, he changed his mind once it became known that the Confederates were converting the *Merrimack* into such a vessel. Welles and Fox soon agreed that the North needed an ironclad warship to match the *Merrimack/Virginia,* but senior naval officers remained unconvinced. In addition, John Lenthall, chief of the Bureau of Construction, Equipment, and Repair, was openly hostile to the idea, calling ironclads "humbug." Instead of challenging the prevailing naval opinion, as Mallory might have done, Welles passed the matter on to Congress, which responded with a bill calling upon Welles to appoint a board of naval officers to investigate possible plans and specifications. Notices were placed in various newspapers to solicit plans for the construction of ironclads for the Ironclad Board. The members of this board were Com. Joseph Smith, Com. Hiram Paulding, and Cmdr. Charles H. Davis, who also served on the Blockade Strategy Board.

The board quickly adopted two fairly conventional designs. One became the USS *New Ironsides,* which was basically a broadside ironclad or armored steam frigate of the *Warrior* or *Glorie* type being built in Great Britain and France. The second design was for a stream-powered armored gunboat designed by Cornelius Scranton Bushnell, a Mystic, Connecticut, friend of Welles. His ship, the *Galena,* was much smaller than *New Ironsides* and was of a design that was at the same time both novel and conventional. Board members, however, were concerned about her stability since she carried considerable top weight in armor and heavy guns. Bushnell also utilized an armor system that sought to provide adequate protection with a lighter and less expensive armor shield.

Bushnell decided to consult John Ericcson, a Swedish immigrant engineer and naval architect in New York City. Ericsson had invented the screw propeller, which was in the processing of replacing the paddle wheel as the primary means of moving a steamship through the water. Ericsson was also persona non grata with the U.S. Navy over an earlier affair. He had designed and built the USS *Princeton* in partnership with Capt. Robert F. Stockton, an ambitious naval officer. Aside from her screw-propeller propulsion system, Ericsson had also designed a 12-inch smoothbore naval gun that had been built in Great Britain. During a demonstration cruise of the vessel, a second 12-inch smoothbore—which had been designed by Stockton—burst while firing a salute, killing or mortally wounding seven and injuring twenty dignitaries. Two of the fatalities were Secretary of State Abel P. Upshur and Secretary of the Navy Thomas Gilmer. Stockton was among the wounded. President John Tyler narrowly escaped injury and possibly death as he had gone below with his fiancée just prior to the explosion. Stockton blamed the entire affair upon Ericsson, who was never paid for his work on the *Princeton.*

Ericsson reviewed Bushnell's design and specifications of the *Galena* and assured him that the ship would be seaworthy. He also noted that the *Galena*'s armor would be sufficient to withstand shot and shell fired from a 6-inch gun, provided the gun was fired from a respectable distance. Later events proved Ericsson correct in this assessment, unfortunately in every detail.

After completing his evaluation, Ericsson asked his visitor if he would like to see his plans for a "floating battery absolutely impregnable to the heaviest shot or shell." He had the plans and a model of a vessel like nothing Bushnell had ever seen before. It appeared to be a raft with a tower on top. Ericsson's design was a shallow-draft flat-bottomed vessel. The deck was flush, the freeboard almost nonexistent. There were only two structures on the deck. One was a revolving turret that contained the ship's armament. He explained that while the armament would be only two guns, they would be of the heaviest caliber available. Forward of the turret was a squat structure that served as the ship's pilothouse when she was in action.

After leaving Ericsson, Bushnell immediately rushed to Washington and took Ericsson's plans and model to Welles. Although the deadline for design proposals had passed, Welles was sufficiently impressed by Ericsson's vessel and Bushnell's endorsement that he agreed to submit the vessel to the board. Bushnell also showed the model to Lincoln, who said he was reminded of the girl who stuck her foot into her stocking: "It strikes me there is something in it."

The board members, however, were not impressed. Charles H. Davis summarized the general opinion of the board when he paraphrased Exodus 20:4 by saying, with a sweeping gesture aimed at Ericsson's model, "You may take the little thing home and worship it; it would not be idolatry, since it was made in the image of nothing that is in heaven above, or that is in the Earth beneath, or that is in the water under the Earth."

Despite this outright rejection, Bushnell managed a reprieve, provided that Davis could be convinced of the proposed vessel's stability and of Ericsson's reliability. Bushnell realized that only Ericsson could be persuasive enough to get beyond the impasse. He returned to New York on the first available train to convince the Swede to go to Washington. Aware of Ericsson's temper, Bushnell knew that he faced no small problem in getting the inventor to address the Ironclad Board. So he decided to lie.

He told Ericsson that his ship design had been accepted pending some technical explanations. An elated Ericsson agreed immediately to allay anyone's concerns about the ship.

Upon his arrival in the capital, the inventor was closeted with Welles and the board members. Immediately he learned that instead of answering a few technical questions, his design had been rejected. On the point of withdrawing in a huff, Ericsson simply asked why.

Joseph Smith announced that the main concern lay with the suspected instability of the shallow-draft ship. Somewhat insulted, Ericsson dug into his plans and specifications and proceeded to prove mathematically that the craft would be stable. "She will float upon the water and live in it like a duck!" he exclaimed. After considerable and eloquent argument, the board relented and awarded a third contract for an ironclad.

One factor that worked in favor of the board's approval of Ericsson's vessel had to do with time. Washington officials were receiving constant reports about the progress being made at Norfolk in the conversion work on the *Merrimack/Virginia*. The North had nothing that could be ready in time to meet the Southern ironclad. The conventional nature of the designs for the *New Ironsides* and the *Galena* meant that neither would be ready in time to confront Mallory's creation. Ericsson, however, claimed he could build his ship within one hundred days, which would be barely enough time to engage the *Merrimack/Virginia*.

Work began on the Ericsson ironclad before the final contract was signed. To speed construction along, much of the work was subcontracted in what amounted to an early attempt at modular construction. Continental Ironworks of Green Point, New York, built the hull; the New York firm of Delamater and Company built the engines; and Novelty Ironworks, also of New York City, built the turret. The ship's keel was laid on October 25, 1861. From there the naval arms race between the Union and Confederacy to see who would build and fit out an ironclad first was on. As his masterpiece took shape, Ericsson eventually suggested a name for the vessel:

In accordance with your request, I now submit for your approbation a name for the floating battery at Green Point. The impregnable and aggressive character of this structure will admonish the leaders of the Southern Rebellion that the batteries on the banks of their rivers will no longer present barriers to the entrance of the Union forces.

The ironclad intruder will thus prove a severe monitor to those leaders . . . I propose to name the new battery *Monitor*.

Ninety-seven days after her keel was laid, she was launched on January 30, 1862, fitted out, and hurriedly dispatched to Hampton Roads to meet the *Virginia*. The shipbuilding race turned out to be something of a draw, with perhaps a slight edge in favor of Mallory and his collaborators since they did not wait until their *Virginia* was fully completed before committing her to action. The construction of the *Monitor*, however, boded ill for Mallory's hopes that Confederate ironclads could break the blockade and even establish control of the seas along the Atlantic or Gulf Coasts, even for a temporary period. Once the North flexed its industrial might and began producing ironclads of its own, the South had no chance to achieve naval supremacy.

4

First Strikes from the Sea

THE NAVY DEPARTMENT ACTED quickly upon the initial reports presented to Welles by the Blockade Strategy Board. It was decided to follow the main recommendation and to block and/or seize certain points along the Confederate coastline and establish the coaling and supply depots necessary to support the blockade.

Chosen as the first target was Hatteras Inlet on the coast of North Carolina. This attack was to have several repercussions, one of which would lead to the eventual reassignment of Matthew Fontaine Maury to Europe as a form of exile. Thus Mallory was able to eliminate his most outspoken critic and closest possible rival and/or replacement.

Maury already hated Mallory for his role in the Naval Retiring Board before the war, which had threatened to force Maury's retirement from the old navy. Maury was also the leading proponent of what was dubbed the Mosquito Fleet strategy, which differed radically from the ironclad scheme that had been adopted by Mallory. By championing a vastly different approach from Mallory's, Maury set himself up—in the eyes of his supporters in the Confederate Congress—as an alternative to Mallory. In the aftermath of the loss of Hatteras Inlet, either Mallory or Maury had to go—and it was not going to be Mallory.

Maury believed the South's best hope in the naval war was to use its limited resources to build or convert large numbers of small fast gunboats instead of a limited number of large expensive ironclads, which Mallory championed. Thomas Jefferson had favored a policy similar to Maury's strategy during his administration, but the War of 1812 had proved its fallacy. Maury revived the idea, pointing out that steam power had changed the equation. Each of the Mosquito Fleet gunboats was to be equipped with at least one large pivot-mounted gun. Clusters of these smaller vessels were to swarm like mosquitoes around their larger and slower opponents and overwhelm them with their greater speed and numbers.

It was decided to use the Hatteras Inlet area (where the Pamlico and Albemarle Sounds come together) as a test site for Maury's proposal. With support from his political backers in Virginia and North Carolina, Maury managed to get legislation passed by the Confederate Congress authorizing the construction or conversion of one hundred gunboats with a one-million-dollar appropriation for financing the endeavor. The gunboats were intended for use in North Carolina's offshore sounds, which were of considerable strategic importance since they connected with the Dismal Swamp Canal that served as the back door to the Confederate naval base at Norfolk, Virginia, the home of the *Virginia*. When the Union blow fell upon Hatteras Inlet, there had only been time enough to complete six of the projected one hundred gunboats.

The task of taking control of the inlet had been given to Maj. Gen. Benjamin F. Butler, commandant of Fort Monroe, and Flag Off. Silas H. Stringham, commander of the Atlantic Squadron. Butler was given about 1,000 troops—860 infantry and a company from the Second U.S. Artillery taken from the Fort Monroe garrison. The mission of the joint army-navy force was to capture Forts Clark and Hatteras, which guarded the inlet.

When Stringham was informed of the proposed attack at a conference in Washington, held on July 25, 1861, he assumed that this would be a typical army-navy assault. The naval guns would be used to suppress the land-based fortifications, doing as much damage as possible, while the actual capture of the forts would be done by the troops landed from the fleet. Butler's troops were to travel light, with just ten days' rations and 114 rounds of ammunition per man. Supplies were kept at a minimum because the intent was to hold the forts only long enough to bring in stone-laden hulks with which to block the channel through the inlet. In short, the operation was planned as a raid, not a full-scale invasion.

Following a brief delay caused by a strong east wind, the attacking force left Hampton Roads on August 26, 1861. Stringham and Butler were aboard the steam frigate USS *Minnesota*, which served as the expedition's flagship. She was accompanied by the steam gunboats *Monticello, Pawnee,* and *Harriet Lane* and the sailing corvette *Cumberland.* The expedition's troops were aboard the chartered transports *Adelaid* and *George Peabody.* Several of the ships towed surf boats to be used in the assault.

The attack was scheduled to be launched at noon, August 27, 1861, so the troops were wakened at 4 A.M. and Stringham gave the signal for the debarkation to begin at 6:45 A.M. Butler planned to land the main portion of his force on a beach three miles north of Forts Clark and Hatteras. At the same time Stringham planned to use his warships to bombard the forts. Because heavy seas and green troops have a tendency not to mix well, the landing took more than four hours. As they approached the shore, the heavy surf smashed the surf boats onto the beach. Thankfully the water off the beach was not deep, and the soaked soldiers managed to drag themselves ashore. By early afternoon Butler had managed to land only about 318 wet, tired, and thoroughly terrified soldiers.

On Stringham's end, things went much better. The *Minnesota*, with the *Cumberland* in tow, steamed toward the two Confederate forts at 8:45 A.M., and by 10 A.M. they were close enough to open fire. At 11 A.M. they were joined by the newly arrived steam frigate *Susquehanna.* Stringham ordered his ships to adopt an elliptical pattern, with each of the warships firing on Fort Clark whenever their guns bore upon the fort at the end of each circle. Because of the distance offshore the Union ships' draft forced them to accept, they concentrated on Fort Clark, which was the only one of the two Confederate strongholds within range. By 12:25 P.M. Fort Clark's garrison evacuated the position and retreated to Fort Hatteras. Shortly thereafter what few troops Butler had managed by that time to get ashore entered the abandoned fort.

Stringham then ordered the *Monticello* to enter the channel near Fort Hatteras and attempt to outflank it. A withering fire from the fort, however, forced the gunboat to retreat. Then the heavier Union vessels moved in around 4 P.M. and began a bombardment. When the falling tide forced them to move out of range, the shallow-draft ships—*Pawnee, Monticello,* and *Harriet Lane*—remained inshore during the night to provide Butler's troops at Fort Clark with close artillery support in case the Confederate garrison decided to attack. In the morning the heavier ships moved back in and began raining explosive shells upon Fort Hatteras that wreaked heavy damage, caused numerous casualties, and forced the fort to surrender about two hours later.

Com. Samuel Barron, Confederate commander of the Mosquito Fleet force defending the coasts of Virginia and North Carolina, was rowed out to Stringham's flagship. He was petitioned by the army officers on the scene to negotiate the surrender. Once Barron boarded the *Minnesota* he surrendered himself, Fort Hatteras, and the inlet to Stringham, whom he had known in the old navy, because he refused to deal with the likes of Butler and the Union army.

Although the six gunboats of the Mosquito Fleet had attempted to intervene during the action, they were outnumbered, outgunned, and outclassed. The result was inevitable, given the circumstances. They were easily brushed aside and defeated, retreating to the Roanoke Island area to the north. Barron agreed to Stringham and Butler's demand that the surrender be unconditional a good six months before Brig. Gen. Ulysses S. Grant gained fame for making the same demand at Fort Donelson, Tennessee. Barron spent the next two years as a prisoner of war before he was exchanged.

Although Stringham and Butler had intended to conduct just a raid, they changed their minds once the two forts had fallen. As the commanders on the scene, they now urged that the forts be retained. Welles was the first Washington official to concur, and he persuaded Lincoln and the cabinet to agree to the occupation. Although it was a halfhearted decision, the occupation closed Pamlico Sound to the Confederacy. Through inaction, Stringham missed the chance to use his gunboats to take control of both the Pamlico and Albemarle Sounds as well as the surrounding area.

To do so, however, would have required additional troops, which Washington was reluctant to provide.

The most direct outcome of the Hatteras Inlet debacle for the Confederate navy was that instead of building the large number of gunboats that Maury had advocated, the Mosquito Fleet plan was abandoned. Maury claimed that the battle of Hatteras Inlet was not a proper test, since the invaders were not met by the number of gunboats that his plan had originally required. Fair test or not, Maury was soon relieved of his responsibilities as head of the Torpedo Bureau and was dispatched through the blockade to join Bulloch as a naval purchasing agent in Great Britain. It was also announced that Maury would continue his experiments with underwater explosives, using the much better facilities that were available in Britain. Maury spent the rest of the war in Europe as a direct consequence of his intellectual incompatibility with Mallory.

The battle of Hatteras Inlet also resulted in a number of changes on the Union side. Stringham and Butler were later criticized in the press for their failure to take advantage of the victory. Both of the commanders had seemed more concerned with besting the other's claim to the victory laurels, because the two men had quickly departed the scene of the fighting in order to race each other to Washington to take credit for the victory. Few would have expected anything else from Butler, but Stringham opened himself up to intense chiding for this unseemly race. Stringham was also denigrated for operating a lax blockade and soon was forced to retire from the navy.

Stringham's forced retirement opened the way to divide his command and form the North Atlantic Blockading Squadron under the command of Com. Louis M. Goldsborough, to cover the Virginia and North Carolina coastlines, and the South Atlantic Blockading Squadron under Flag Off. Samuel F. Du Pont, erstwhile chairman of the Blockade Strategy Board, to cover the coastlines of South Carolina, Georgia, and eastern Florida.

THE USE of stone-filled ships purposely sunk to block access into Confederate harbors was tried once and was such an ignominious failure that the tactic was abandoned.

A so-called stone fleet was fitted out at the old whaling ports of New Bedford, Massachusetts; New London, Connecticut; Sag Harbor; and New York City. Twenty-five vessels were loaded with seventy-five hundred tons of stone and dispatched to Charleston. Two of them accidentally sank soon after they arrived, one was sunk to serve as a breakwater, two were used to form a wharf to facilitate the landing of troops at Tybee Island, off Savannah, another four were transferred to the quartermaster's corps, and one was used as a naval stores ship. The remaining fifteen were turned over to Cmdr. Charles H. Davis, who directed their scuttling in the harbor's main ship channel on December 19 and 20, 1861.

A second stone fleet of fourteen vessels was sunk on January 25 and 26, 1862, in Maffitt's Channel, a secondary entrance to Charleston Harbor. While it was hoped that these block ships would close Charleston as a blockade-runners' port, the opposite happened. The hulks became infested with toredo or marine worms, which later in the war would cause the sinking of the Confederate ironclad *North Carolina* at her moorings in Wilmington, North Carolina. In less than three months the worms caused the wooden hulls of the hulks to break open, leaving piles of stone on the bottom of the main ship channel. The flow of water around the piles of stone scoured out a passage several feet deeper than had previously existed.

Welles and Fox eventually ignored the fiasco. Welles himself never even mentioned the stone fleet and the attempt to block Charleston Harbor in his 1862 departmental report. Everyone else followed the secretary's example and evaded any discussion of the affair.

PORT ROYAL SOUND in South Carolina became the next target.

Responsibility for reducing it fell to Du Pont's South Atlantic Blockading Squadron. The Port Royal attack led to the establishment of Du Pont's independent command, as had been recommended by the Blockade Strategy Board in one of its earliest reports to Welles. Taking control of Port Royal Sound was considered one of the best means to strengthen the blockade in that area, because the sound was one of the best of the few deep-water ports in the South. On October 16, 1861, Du Pont's squadron departed from New York City. Commanding the army contingent was Brig. Gen. Thomas W. Sherman.

Beaufort, South Carolina, was near the sound. It had a population of two thousand, and if the Old South of myth and legend ever actually existed, it was in Beaufort. France, Spain, and the infant United States had all failed in their attempts to fully defend the sound. The problem lay in its vast anchorage, the entrance alone being two and a half miles wide, too broad for the protection of most artillery. In addition, the defenders did not have the newly developed heavy-caliber rifled guns that could have, just barely, covered the mouth of the channel leading into the sound. Therefore, all an attacker had to do to avoid heavy fire from the defenders was to stay in the middle of the channel.

Du Pont's squadron consisted of more than seventy ships. These included fourteen warships, thirty-one transports to carry Sherman's thirteen thousand troops, and two dozen schooners that served as supply ships to support the armada. The Confederate defenses consisted of Fort Beauregard on Phillips Island and Fort Walker on Hilton Head Island. Also assisting in the defense was a Mosquito Fleet flotilla, known as the Savannah Squadron, commanded by Com. Josiah Tattnall. After Tattnall had received intelligence reports that the Yankees were about to attack Port Royal Sound, he had gathered every gunboat he could find in Savannah and Charleston and had sent them to Port Royal. In addition, the Confederates also removed all navigational aids.

Du Pont and Sherman's combined force arrived on November 3. Sherman had lost many of the surf boats for landing his troops in a storm that the fleet encountered while approaching Port Royal Sound, so he decided not to land until the guns of the two forts were silenced.

On November 5, after the sounding and marking of the harbor entrance by the coastal survey vessel *Vixen* that had accompanied the fleet, Du Pont dispatched seven shallow-draft gunboats into the sound under the command of his aide, Cmdr. John Rodgers. This small force was immediately attacked by Tattnall's makeshift flotilla, which moved out of its protective anchorage at Skull Creek at the northwest end of Hilton Head Island, about four miles up the sound from Fort Walker. The gun duel, in which both forts joined, continued for several hours. Tattnall soon realized that his small gunboat force could not seriously threaten Rodgers's gunboats, and he eventually withdrew.

With Tattnall's ships no longer a factor, Rodgers turned his full attention to the forts. The falling tide required Rodgers to withdraw, however. That night, under cover of darkness, Confederate volunteers in longboats ventured out and removed the marker buoys that Du Pont had ordered placed by the *Vixen*. In the morning Tattnall attempted another attack on the Union warships. He planned to lure the Union ships onto the shoals, where they could then be pounded by the Confederate shore batteries.

It almost worked.

Du Pont's flagship, the steam frigate *Wabash,* ran aground on a sandbar while attempting to close with Tattnall's gunboats. He managed to pull his flagship off the sandbar by ordering full steam astern on his engines before the Confederate gunners in the forts managed to find the range. Realizing that his ruse had failed, Tattnall was forced to break off his attack.

Du Pont's squadron thereupon crossed the bar and on November 7 began anew the bombardment of Forts Walker and Beauregard. Du Pont repeated Stringham's tactics and poured thirty-five hundred shells into the Confederate shore positions. The bombardment forced the surrender and/or evacuation of the two forts after a cannonade of several hours. Casualties at the battle of Port Royal were fairly light on both sides. The Union had eight dead and twenty-three wounded while the Confederates in the forts reported losses totaling forty-eight killed.

Thus Du Pont gained for the Union navy an excellent base deep within the heart of the South. From Port Royal Sound his squadron could both closely blockade and threaten Charleston and Savannah. In addition, the entire coastal area from North Edisto, a few miles south of Charleston, to Ossabaw Sound, south of Savannah, was largely abandoned by Confederate forces.

After the fall of the forts, Sherman's troops improved and then manned the fortifications, establishing additional landward defenses and an important refueling, supply, and repair depot. Neither Du Pont nor Sherman, however, realized that the whole interior of South Carolina and Georgia now lay completely open to them, a situation that would be quickly corrected. Had the Union commanders known that and entertained the inclination to move inland, they did not have the necessary manpower to make any such movement, nor were additional troops forthcoming.

If a full-scale invasion had been launched, it is possible that the war would have ended years earlier than it actually did.

Even so, some subsidiary operations continued. On November 24, 1861, attention was turned to the Confederate port of Savannah. In an amphibious operation Union troops seized Tybee Island, near the estuary of the Savannah River. Using this island as a base and coaling station, Union blockaders moved ahead to choke off Savannah as a blockade-runners' port. With Tybee Island as a coaling station, the blockaders were able to remain on station and maintain their patrols far longer than they had previously been able. With the addition of heavy guns placed on the island to bombard Fort Pulaski, Federal forces soon closed the Savannah River estuary to all blockade-runners.

Although the Federals had seized the island, most Confederate army and naval officers believed that the port itself was safe since it was defended by the massive masonry structure of Fort Pulaski. The fort had walls seven and a half feet thick, mounted forty-eight large-caliber guns, and had been designed and built by Robert E. Lee when he was a young officer in the U.S. Army Corps of Engineers. Conventional military wisdom said that such a formidable fort was impregnable. Another engineer, Union Brig. Gen. Quincy A. Gillmore, was determined to prove the conventional wisdom to be wrong.

Gillmore made his move on April 11, 1862, when he oversaw the mounting of several batteries of massive rifled cannon on Tybee Island and began a long-range pounding of Fort Pulaski. The fort's walls were unable to withstand the power of Gillmore's guns, and he proceeded to prove that he could eventually pound the fort to pieces. The garrison quickly surrendered. Although the fall of Fort Pulaski closed the estuary of the Savannah River to blockade-runners, the approaches to the city through Wassaw Sound and the Ogeechee River remained open. They were protected by an earthen fort known as McAllister, which was to eventually prove that earthworks were a better defense than masonry against modern cannon.

Fort McAllister's original purpose was to allay the fears of local rice planters and to protect a vital railroad upstream. With the fall of Fort Pulaski, however, the mouth of the Ogeechee River at Ossabaw Sound became a back door into Savannah, and the fort's new mission was to keep this door open. It was first bombarded on July 29 and November 19, 1862, by wooden gunboats belonging to Du Pont's South Atlantic Blockading Squadron. In January 1863 the wooden gunboats were joined by the *Monitor*-type ironclad *Montauk*. It carried out a bombardment on January 28, 1863. A second bombardment in which the *Montauk* participated occurred on February 1, 1863, and a third on February 23, 1863. It was during the third bombardment that the Confederate raider cruiser *Nashville/Rattlesnake* was destroyed by *Montauk*'s guns. A fourth bombardment occurred on March 3, 1863, and this time *Montauk* was joined by the ironclads *Patapsco, Nahant,* and *Passaic,* all of which were known as *Passaic*-class monitors. For their attack the ironclads were joined by two mortar schooners and two wooden gunboats. After an eight-hour bombardment, the Union flotilla withdrew when the fort refused to surrender.

Although damaged to varying degrees during the various bombardments, the fort was quickly repaired between shellings. The fort's earthen walls absorbed much of the power of the various bombardments rather than shattering as the masonry walls of Fort Pulaski had done. The fort eventually fell, but not to naval bombardment. It was overwhelmed by William Tecumseh Sherman's troops at the end of the March to the Sea in December 1864.

During March 1862, Du Pont and Thomas W. Sherman had moved on to Fernandina, which fell without a shot being fired since the Confederates, realizing they could not stop Du Pont's ships, had already abandoned it. Like Port Royal Sound and Tybee Island, Fernandina became a major Union base supporting the blockade. Additional operations resulted in the captures of St. Augustine and Jacksonville, Florida, along with Brunswick, Georgia.

After the fall of Port Royal, Tattnall was ordered to send his borrowed gunboats back to Savannah and Charleston. Command of what remained of the Mosquito Fleet in North Carolina waters was placed in the hands of Com. William F. Lynch, and Tattnall returned to his command of Confederate naval forces at Savannah.

The next operation was to be Roanoke Island. It was selected as a target by Maj. Gen. George B. McClellan, now wearing the two hats of general in chief and commanding general of the Army of the Potomac. McClellan had replaced Scott, who retired to West Point. The Roanoke Island operation was to be a subsidiary action to his Peninsula campaign. McClellan was well aware of the *Virginia,* and he feared that she might attempt to disrupt his ambitious amphibious campaign aimed for the quick and hopefully bloodless conquest of the Confederate capital at Richmond. McClellan intended this operation to force open the back door to the Confederate naval base at Norfolk, Virginia. If Norfolk could be captured in this way, then the *Virginia* could be easily eliminated as an obstacle to his plans.

McClellan had no difficulty obtaining Welles's approval and endorsement, particularly since the operation was among those already recommended by the Blockade Strategy Board.

Chosen as commander of the army contingent was Maj. Gen. Ambrose E. Burnside, who gathered fifteen regiments that were specially recruited for and trained in amphibious warfare. Later these troops formed the bulk of the army's Ninth Corps. Com. Louis M. Goldsborough, as commander of the North Atlantic Blockading Squadron, decided to take charge of the supporting fleet for the operation and left his primary station at Hampton Roads in the hands of subordinates.

Burnside had no experience with amphibious operations and gathered an assortment of transports of varying drafts, which would later become a problem since they were to operate in the shallow waters of the North Carolina sounds. The variety of the vessels assembled to transport and support the army troops frustrated any attempts at coherent planning for the landing itself. The expedition was to be launched from the Union base at Hatteras Inlet, which was finally reached by all the participating ships on January 13, 1862. For a variety of reasons, mostly weather related, it took almost a month for the invasion fleet to make the short hop to Roanoke Island, the expedition's first objective.

The attack came on February 7, 1862. It began at noon as the Union gunboats concentrated their fire against Fort Bartow, which they bombarded for six hours. William F. Lynch's Mosquito Fleet tried several times to draw the fire of the Union squadron away from the fort, but the firepower of Goldsborough's ships was so overwhelming there was little Lynch's flotilla could do. One of the Confederate gunboats was smashed by a 100-pound shell, and another was disabled. The Confederates in the fort could do little but duck and return fire whenever they could. The Union fleet's biggest worry was its dwindling supply of ammunition. Burnside put his troops ashore about 3 P.M. as Goldsborough's worries about his ammunition supplies mounted. There was no opposition to the landings, and Burnside's troops soon brought an end to the fighting, which petered out the next day.

Lynch and his remaining gunboats withdrew to Elizabeth City, North Carolina, where he hoped to replenish his ammunition, return to Roanoke Island, and resume the battle. He soon realized there was practically nothing he could do.

Once again the Federal commanders failed to follow up their victory, and after a few subsidiary operations they rested upon their laurels. These other operations included seizing the coastal towns of New Bern and Plymouth, along with a February 10 strike at Elizabeth City, which was at the southern end of the Dismal Swamp Canal that connected with Norfolk. This canal was the vulnerable back door to Norfolk, and it was here that the remnant of Lynch's Mosquito Fleet was concentrated in a desperate effort to defend the vital waterway.

After a short, sharp battle with a detachment from Goldsborough's squadron, four of the Confederate gunboats were sunk or captured and the town surrendered. The remaining gunboats— *Appomattox*, *Raleigh*, and *Beaufort*—were driven up the canal. *Raleigh* and *Beaufort* retreated all the way to Norfolk, where they became consorts of the ironclad *Virginia*. *Appomattox*, however, was five inches too wide to enter the canal lock thirty miles above Elizabeth City. Lynch elected to destroy the gunboat and the canal lock so as to deny the use of the canal to the Union navy if the decision were made to pursue the fugitives. The *Appomattox* was filled with explosives, rammed into the canal lock, and blown up, destroying herself and the lock.

This act of desperation succeeded in defeating the primary mission of the Union force's attack on Roanoke Island and its vicinity, namely, gaining control of the Dismal Swamp Canal and using it to approach Norfolk and eliminate the *Virginia*.

Nevertheless, these coastal victories demonstrated the Union navy's mobility and muscle. The bases and depots established along the coast of the Confederacy allowed Union blockaders to occupy vantage points from which they could sweep the coast, blockade the various ports, and thus strangle the economic lifelines of the South, or so it was believed at the time. The problem with the blockade was that while it could and did restrict Confederate access to overseas markets and suppliers, it never completely severed these shipping lanes and approaches. In and of itself, the blockade could never have brought about the collapse of the Confederacy.

This string of Federal victories, however, served to offset the effects of some of the early Union disasters like the battle of First Bull Run and the loss of the Gosport Navy Yard practically intact into Confederate hands. They also discouraged and alarmed the Southern populace and leaders. In addition, these operations caused a backlash against Mallory while, at the same time, discrediting Maury's Mosquito Fleet, which had been the only alternative to Mallory's comprehensive naval strategy. The Southern secretary of the navy was also learning from these defeats. They forced him to realize that coastal defense was of supreme importance, even more vital to the survival of the Confederacy than the attempts to break the blockade itself. If the Yankees were to follow up on these successes, they could open up additional fronts and draw off badly needed troops, which could in turn cause a general collapse. Mallory's challenge was to find a way to counter the amphibious tactics and operational strategies that the Union navy was rapidly developing and executing.

As successful as they were for the Union, these same coastal operations all suffered from the same problem. At Hatteras, Port Royal, and Roanoke, the Federal commanders failed in each and every case to fully exploit the navy's initial victories. These new coastal enclaves gave the Union the opportunity to establish new fronts deep in the South against which no real defenses had as yet been erected. The window of opportunity for such advances, however, was rapidly closing with each day. Because there was no follow-up, the only strategic results of these limited attacks were to awaken Mallory to the danger poised by the Union's amphibious operations. Eventually the Confederate navy's proudest boast would be that it was able to stop any further incursions along the Southern coastline until it too was caught up in the final collapse of the Confederacy in the spring of 1865.

Another factor in the Union failure to fully exploit its advantage at sea was that the army had lost interest in the strategic uses of sea power after McClellan was removed as general in chief so that he could concentrate on his duties as commander of the Army of the Potomac. His replacement, Maj. Gen. Henry W. Halleck, won his post because he was Ulysses S. Grant's immediate superior. Halleck was able to bathe in the reflected glory of Grant's successes at Forts Henry and Donelson and, at the same time, avoid any blame for the vast Federal loses at the April 1862 battle of Shiloh. Halleck also succeeded in promoting his snail's-pace march on Corinth, Mississippi, and its evacuation by the Confederates into a major victory. Unfortunately, although he took full advantage of the mobility that Union naval superiority on the inland rivers gave him, Halleck had absolutely no understanding of the role the navy could play on the East Coast by opening up new fronts from which to menace the Confederacy. As the war dragged on, it would become more and more difficult to pry troops loose from the army for what the army leadership considered to be peripheral efforts of little real value.

5

Attack of the Ironclads

ON MARCH 8, 1862, Confederate Flag Off. Franklin Buchanan ordered the CSS *Virginia* to raise steam and took Confederate Secretary of the Navy Stephen R. Mallory's ultimate weapon down the Elizabeth River and into the Federal anchorage at Hampton Roads. His target was the concentration of Union warships and other ships that were blockading Southern access to Chesapeake Bay while also preparing to support Maj. Gen. George B. McClellan's projected Peninsula campaign. The Federal warships and other vessels were based at Fort Monroe and nearby Newport News, Virginia.

McClellan had originally planned to land his Army of the Potomac at the mouth of the Rappahannock River and march from there on Richmond—avoiding the Confederate defenses at Manassas Junction, then under the command of Gen. Joseph E. Johnston. McClellan believed that he could march from his landing point to Richmond within two days—long before Johnston's troops could be moved to confront him. McClellan also believed that his plan could break the back of the rebellion with one swift blow. The problem was that McClellan was not the man to strike that blow.

The Federal commander was a splendid strategist, organizer, and motivator of troops, but he was not suited for a field command. It would have been far better if he had remained in Washington as general in chief. As a field general, McClellan was far too cautious. In the field he was also obsessed with the belief that he was greatly outnumbered. Although his chief of intelligence, detective Allan Pinkerton, had at first endeavored to provide honest reports, Pinkerton soon realized that McClellan was not really interested in honest reports. Thereupon, Pinkerton gave McClellan the information he wanted, which only served to reinforce McClellan's native caution at a time when his army considerably outnumbered the Confederate forces initially commanded by Johnston and later by Robert E. Lee.

Pinkerton's reports eventually credited the Confederates with having as many as 150,00 to 200,000 troops opposing McClellan. At the most, just prior to the Seven Days' battles, which ended the Peninsula campaign, Confederate troop strength reached a peak of about 85,000.

McClellan's final weakness was that he so loved his creation, the Army of the Potomac, he could not stand to see it bloodied.

In order for McClellan's plan to have any chance of success, the North had to maintain absolute control of the logistical line of operations along the James River at Newport News. The town itself was protected on the seaward side by the sailing sloop of war (or corvette) *Cumberland* and the sailing frigate *Congress*, whose guns covered the approaches to the town. Moored near Fort Monroe, at the tip of the peninsula formed by the York and the James Rivers, were the supporting steam frigates *Minnesota* and *Roanoke* (sister ships of the *Merrimack*) along with the sailing frigate *St. Lawrence*. On that particular Saturday the rigging of all of the ships was festooned with the crew's clothing as they did their laundry. Awaiting Buchanan at the mouth of the James River to support his attack were the auxiliary cruiser *Patrick Henry* and the small gunboats *Teaser* and *Jamestown*. Accompanying *Virginia* were the gunboats *Beaufort* and *Raleigh*, which had escaped through the Dismal Swamp Canal from the Union naval forces that had seized Roanoke Island and Elizabeth City, North Carolina, the southern terminus of the canal.

Although *Virginia* was operational, she was not yet fully completed. Among the items left behind were the shutters needed to close her gun ports. Buchanan knew the Union was racing to complete and send its own ironclad, Ericsson's *Monitor,* to the area. (In fact, the *Monitor* would nearly be sunk in a storm while being towed to Hampton Roads.) Therefore he was resolved to attack first; whether or not his ship was fully prepared for battle was immaterial. He decided that she was ready enough.

The sea conditions were calm, which was of utmost importance to the successful operation of the *Virginia.* She had a draft of twenty-two feet. Her speed was only a cranky five to eight knots. Her turning circle was enormous, taking between thirty and forty minutes for her to make a complete 360-degree turn. There was no way that the Confederate ironclad could possibly leave the sheltered waters of Hampton Roads and make for the open sea. Still a historic confrontation was about to occur. "The whole world is watching you today," Buchanan told his crew as he ordered the attack on the Union fleet.

When the *Virginia* reached the mouth of the Elizabeth River, she had to call upon the *Beaufort* to help her to turn 90 degrees. Once the turn had been completed at 12:30 P.M., she made directly for the mouth of the James River. Just fifteen minutes later the sailors aboard the Union fleet sighted her as their drummers sounded "Beat to Quarters." Federal seamen compared the Confederate ironclad to a house or barn sunk in the water up to its eaves and roof gutters. Dense smoke poured from her single funnel as she offered battle to the Union ships at Hampton Roads. The *Cumberland* and *Congress* cleared for action. Meanwhile, the *Minnesota, Roanoke,* and *St. Lawrence* made for the approaching *Virginia. Minnesota* advanced under her own power; *Roanoke* (due to inoperable engines) and *St. Lawrence* were towed into position. The three Union warships only managed to get within eight miles of the battle area when all three ran aground. *Cumberland* and *Congress* would have to face the smoke-belching monster alone.

The two Federal ships opened fire first—to no apparent effect. *Virginia* continued her creeping advance without bothering to return their fire. Finally, at a range of fifteen hundred yards, her forward pivot-mounted 7-inch rifle opened fire. This first shot struck the *Cumberland,* knocking her stern-mounted 10-inch pivot gun and its crew out of action. As the *Virginia* passed the

Congress, the Union warship opened fire with a full broadside. The ship's guns scored a number of hits on the armored bulk of the *Virginia,* all of which bounced off like so many rubber balls. *Virginia* answered with a broadside of her own, her point-blank fire having a devastating effect on the wooden-hulled *Congress.* Many of the Federal sailors were killed or wounded, numerous guns were dismounted, and several fires broke out and were quickly extinguished.

Ignoring the impotent *Congress, Virginia* maintained her steady approach upon the *Cumberland* as the two ships poured shot and shell upon each other. The *Cumberland*'s fire was as ineffectual as that of the *Congress,* but the *Virginia*'s return fire smashed into the Union warship, covering her decks with dead and wounded. Abruptly the crew of the *Virginia* felt a shock as if she had run aground. The Confederate ship rammed the *Cumberland*'s starboard side, just aft of the bow. The ram broke through the anti-torpedo obstructions surrounding the Federal warship (showing that even at this early date the Union navy feared Confederate torpedoes) and struck the wooden hull with a rumble that was heard above the crash of the guns on both sides. Although the *Virginia*'s ram broke off inside the *Cumberland,* it opened a hole large enough to drive a wagon through it. *Cumberland* took on a forty-five-degree list and quickly sank, her crew continuing to man and fire her guns at the assailant until the water reached her upper decks. Within minutes the Union ship was resting on the bottom of the roadstead with only the tops of her masts—their still-defiant flags fluttering from them—being all that could be seen above the water.

In her death throes the *Cumberland* managed to score the only damage to be suffered by the *Virginia* that day. Not only did the Confederate ironclad's ram remain embedded within the Union ship, causing some minor leaks in the *Virginia*'s bow, but the *Cumberland*'s guns knocked out two of *Virginia*'s broadside guns and repeatedly struck her funnel, causing the casemate to fill with smoke and reducing her engines' draft, thus diminishing what little speed she had.

After the *Cumberland* sank, the *Virginia* steamed several miles up the James River, knocking out a number of Union artillery batteries and destroying two transports with her guns. Then joined by her gunboat cohorts, *Virginia* turned back to the *Congress.* Hurriedly, the crew of the Federal warship called for the tug *Zouave* to tow the ship into shallow water so she could be beached to keep the *Virginia* from ramming her as she had the *Cumberland.* Buchanan brought his ship up on the *Congress* while continuing to pound her with his guns. The captain of the *Congress* was ashore, and her executive officer was killed along with more than one hundred other casualties. The remaining officers decided to surrender and hauled down the ship's flag.

Buchanan quickly ordered the *Beaufort* and *Raleigh* to go alongside the Union frigate, receive her surrender, and evacuate her wounded. As the two gunboats attempted to do so, they were fired upon by two companies of soldiers and a section of field artillery from the shore. Several of the gunboats' officers and crew were killed or wounded as the *Beaufort* made off without orders. Highly incensed, Buchanan climbed up on top of *Virginia*'s casemate. When his flag lieutenant was wounded, Buchanan in a rage ordered the *Congress* to be destroyed with red-hot shot and incendiary shells. He lingered on top of the casemate to watch and was seriously wounded in the leg by Union small-arms fire from the shore. Command of the *Virginia* now devolved upon her executive officer, Lt. Catesby ap Roger Jones.

The time was now 5 P.M., and Jones turned the *Virginia* toward the grounded *Minnesota.* Fortunately for the crew of the *Minnesota,* the ironclad was unable to close with the Union ship due to her deep draft and the falling tide. Jones nevertheless directed a brisk and accurate fire upon the stranded Federal vessel. This fire caused considerable damage and even started some fires, which were quickly extinguished. Finally, due to her pilots' fear that the Confederate ship would run aground as the tide went out, Jones ordered the *Virginia* to break off the action, mooring for the night near Sewell's Point.

The Confederate ironclad had just handed the U.S. Navy the worst defeat in its history to date. Three ships had been sunk and a fourth set afire and turned into a gigantic pyre. Another ship, the *Minnesota,* was crippled and aground. Two other ships— *Roanoke* and *St. Lawrence*—were also aground and helpless. An estimated three hundred men were dead. The remaining Union ships fled the scene, clearing out of Hampton Roads.

The U.S. Navy would not see such a disaster in battle again until December 7, 1941, when the Pacific Fleet was caught at its anchorage at Pearl Harbor by Japanese carrier aircraft in the attack that precipitated U.S. entry into World War II.

Meanwhile, in Hampton Roads, at 9 P.M. the USS *Monitor*—her way lighted by the burning *Congress*—arrived. The Union iron-clad tied up alongside the grounded *Minnesota* just as the flames reached the magazines of the *Congress,* which exploded with a reverberating roar. The *Monitor* had proved herself to be not quite as seaworthy as Ericsson had assured the Ironclad Board. She had to be towed from New York to Hampton Roads and had nearly been lost in a gale. But she was here now and her commander, Lt. John Worden, understood that his mission was to protect the wounded *Minnesota* from the monstrous Confederate ironclad.

It was 6:30 A.M. the next day when the *Virginia* was ready to move on the rising tide. As the second day of the battle dawned, Jones directed his helmsman to make straight for the *Minnesota.* He would destroy her in the same way the *Virginia* had already destroyed the *Congress.* Yet as the Confederate ship approached to within two thousand yards of the *Minnesota,* the *Monitor* appeared. She rounded the *Minnesota,* and the two ironclads simultaneously opened fire on each other. Witnesses on shore were convinced that the little *Monitor* did not stand a chance against the massive *Virginia.*

Worden steered the *Monitor* upstream, against the tide, for better control. The ship's turret turned and her two 11-inch Dahlgrens opened fire as they bore. *Virginia* fired a full broadside, which "rattled our iron decks like hailstones," recalled paymaster William Keeler aboard the *Monitor.*

Aboard the *Virginia,* Jones was frustrated on a number of fronts. His objective was to destroy the *Minnesota,* and he thought his pilots were too timid and overly wary of sandbars, not letting him approach closer than a mile from the Union warship. Jones also had difficulty keeping track of the *Monitor*'s guns since the turret containing them revolved so rapidly. Of particular distress to Jones was the fact that his shells appeared totally ineffective against the Union ironclad. In fact, when Jones asked his gunnery officer why he had temporarily ceased fire, the officer replied that he found that snapping his fingers at the Union ironclad every five minutes seemed to be as effective as firing *Virginia*'s guns at her.

Then *Virginia* ran aground.

Hurriedly Worden took advantage of his adversary's problem and positioned the *Monitor* off *Virginia*'s stern quarter, blasting away at her, seeking to disable her propeller or rudder.

Jones ordered his engineer to lash down the safety valves and to heap quick-burning combustibles into the ship's furnaces to redline the boilers. As the power to her propeller increased, it churned up mud furiously, but *Virginia* failed to move. Now *Virginia*'s engineer piled on cotton waste, splints of wood, anything that would burn faster than coal. Slowly she managed to haul herself off the sandbar by the strength of her engines.

Now Jones decided to ram his smaller, nimbler opponent. It took him half an hour to get *Virginia* into position for the attempt, but she only managed to score a glancing blow that spun the *Monitor* around like a top. It had little or no effect on the ship, which got off another shot as soon as she stopped spinning.

Virginia had yet to suffer any major damage from the projectiles fired by the *Monitor*'s two big guns. Ericsson later blamed this on the navy's leadership. Ever since the *Princeton* incident, standing orders limited the amount of gunpowder to be used in naval cannon to just fifteen pounds. The navy's ordnance experts refused to permit Worden to double-shot his guns, fearing they might burst. Ericsson, however, knew that 11-inch Dahlgren smoothbores would not rupture because of the reinforcing bands that had been added when the guns were cast. If the guns had been double-shotted, Ericsson was convinced that they would have broken through *Virginia*'s armor.

Although the *Virginia* had not suffered any gunnery damage from the *Monitor*'s guns, her grounding had reopened the leaks in her bow originally caused when she had lost her ram inside the *Cumberland*'s hull. Jones now decided to try to board his small adversary.

Worden apparently read his mind and allowed his ship to drop astern of the *Virginia*, frustrating any attempt at boarding.

With the *Monitor* falling astern, Jones redirected *Virginia*'s fire against *Minnesota*. A hit caused a small fire amidships on the steam frigate, but that was quickly extinguished. *Monitor* responded by moving back between *Virginia* and *Minnesota*, thus obstructing the Confederate's line of fire.

As the two ships maneuvered around each other, the *Monitor* passed so close to *Virginia*'s stern that she almost struck the other ship's propeller. In the process Jones decided to aim at *Monitor*'s pilothouse. A direct hit upon the low-lying boxlike structure was decisive. The hit dislodged the iron logs sheltering the pilothouse and carried away part of *Monitor*'s steering gear and some signal apparatus. Worden, who had been looking through the eye slits at the front of the pilothouse when the shot hit, was stunned and blinded; eventually he lost all sight in one eye. Command of the *Monitor* was now thrust upon her executive officer, Lt. Samuel Dana Greene.

Greene directed *Monitor* toward the shallows that *Virginia* could not enter while he ascertained his ship's damage and checked his ammunition reserves. Discovering that *Monitor* was not severely hurt and that she had plenty of ammunition, Greene ordered her to reenter the battle. Jones, in the meantime, had decided to finish off the *Minnesota*, but it was now nearly noon and the tide was falling fast. Once again the pilots feared that the falling water might prevent *Virginia* from returning to her base. Jones allowed himself to be persuaded that the *Monitor* had broken off the battle, so he decided to return to Norfolk.

Just as Greene was bringing *Monitor* back into action, the *Virginia* withdrew. Thus both sides were convinced they had driven the other warship off. Both sides also quickly claimed victory in the two-day battle, but the events of March 9 (the day of the duel between the *Monitor* and the *Virginia*) were anticlimactic. The actual strategically decisive portion of the battle had been the previous day, March 8. If the *Virginia*'s objective on March 9 had been to destroy the *Minnesota* and the *Monitor*'s objective had been to save the *Minnesota*, then the *Monitor* won a tactical victory on March 9. The far more important strategic victory, which had been won on March 8, belonged to the *Virginia*.

First, the Union fleet had suffered crippling losses and had been forced to abandon the roadstead. It would not return while the threat of the *Virginia* remained. Even the *Monitor* never again risked battle inside the roadstead against the *Virginia*. The primary strategic result of the battle was that the vital line of operations along the James River was now closed to McClellan.

The battle of Hampton Roads and Joseph E. Johnston's decision to move his army closer to Richmond caused McClellan to change his objective to landing on Union-held territory guarded by Fort Monroe at the tip of the peninsula. Debarking his troops in late March and early April, McClellan succeeded in drawing Johnston after him—but not immediately. McClellan faced a small covering force behind a fortified line that stretched across the peninsula. The Federal commander was unable to turn this position by landing troops behind it because the navy feared to attempt passing the batteries placed by the Confederates at the mouth of the York River or risk possible intervention by the *Virginia* on the James River. McClellan, therefore, decided his only option was to besiege the area and open the mouth of the York River to the navy, which could then force the Confederates back by threatening to land troops behind the Southerners' fortified line.

In addition, McClellan was forced to use the much less promising line of operations along the York River. In particular, McClellan found himself forced to move all of his supplies by land, rather than by water as he had intended, because the Union navy denied McClellan any naval support on the York River, except for a token force of two ships. Instead the navy concentrated its ships to oppose the *Virginia* if she should ever come out again, which she never did.

The battle of the ironclads was equally disastrous personally for Com. Louis Goldsborough, commander of the North Atlantic Blockading Squadron. First, Goldsborough was not present when the battle occurred since he opted to take command of the naval forces involved in the subsidiary operation aimed against Roanoke Island. Goldsborough received considerable criticism for focusing his attention on a sideshow when, in the opinion of his critics, he should have remained at Hampton Roads since it was to be the site of the primary operation and of his main responsibilities. What Goldsborough could have done if he had been on the scene is debatable. Eventually he would be replaced by Rear Adm. Samuel P. Lee.

Buchanan was rewarded with promotion to the rank of admiral, and Jones was advanced to the rank of commander. Buchanan thus became the highest-ranking officer in the Confederate navy.

Mallory was certain that the battle had demonstrated that the Confederacy had the ultimate weapon. Unfortunately the secretary missed the significance of the presence of Ericsson's *Monitor*. Buchanan, the venerable sea dog, did not. In his euphoria Mallory went so far as to write to Buchanan and suggest that the *Virginia*, on being repaired and refitted, should now attack New York City, ignoring the likelihood that she would probably founder if she ever entered the open sea.

From his hospital bed, Buchanan responded but also dampened the secretary's enthusiasm. First, he underscored that the *Virginia* was still an experimental warship, that she had not shown herself to be invulnerable in battle, and that the Union's *Monitor* was at least her equal. He also noted that *Virginia* could not possibly leave Hampton Roads for the open sea. Even if she did not founder, she would still have to face the fire of some of the heaviest and most powerful coastal defense guns in the world, which were emplaced at Fort Monroe and covered the only exit to the open sea. In addition, *Monitor* and other heavily armed Union warships would probably follow her, battering her nonstop with their heavy guns. Further he noted that it would likely be impossible to find adequate pilots to take her to New York. Then there would be the difficulty of entering New York Harbor, if she got there at all, in the face of the heavy fire that could be expected from the harbor's defending fortifications. All in all he agreed that if *Virginia* could reach New York City and enter the harbor, she could cause immense damage, but the Yankees would most likely bottle her up within the harbor, where she would be lost.

Buchanan then offered Mallory some strategic advice: "I consider the *Virginia* the most important protection to the safety of Norfolk, and her service can be made very valuable in this neighborhood, rather than taking the opportunity to make a bold dash at some other point."

While the South experienced elation, the North was seized with an unreasoning panic. It was immediately decided that the *Monitor* should be prepared for a deadly fight against the *Virginia,* but she must not be exposed to undue risk since she was the only Union ironclad then available. The *Virginia,* meantime, was placed in dry dock, where repairs were made along with a number of improvements that increased her capabilities as a fighting ship. One of these improvements was the addition of special armor-piercing shells to her magazine. When she finally left dry dock on April 4, *Virginia* was much more formidable in both appearance and actuality than she had been during the March 8–9 battle at Hampton Roads.

With Buchanan bedridden from his wound and likely to be incapacitated for several months, it was decided that a new commander was needed for the *Virginia* and the James River Squadron. Mallory had been encouraged by the initiative shown by Com. Josiah Tattnall in attempting to stop the Union amphibious operation at Port Royal Sound, and it was therefore decided that he would succeed Buchanan.

Under Tattnall's command, when *Virginia* attempted to induce the *Monitor* to accept battle, the Federal vessel refused. Tattnall in turn refused to stick his own head into a Union trap, which included the guns of Fort Monroe and other Union ships, aside from the newly commissioned steam ram USS *Vanderbilt.* (The ship had been donated to the navy by Cornelius Vanderbilt, a New York City shipping and railroad tycoon.) It was decided by Mallory to maintain the stalemate until another ironclad, CSS *Richmond,* then under construction at Norfolk, could be completed and join the *Virginia.*

This failure by Tattnall to force a confrontation with the *Monitor* may have been the beginning of Mallory's misgivings about Tattnall's perceived lack of dash and determination, which eventually led to his being removed from command. Mallory later limited Tattnall to command of the naval station at Savannah and placed command of the warships with other officers who were perceived as being more willing to strike a blow. These actions by Mallory also led directly to the loss of the ironclad CSS *Atlanta.*

Thus the *Virginia* alone took on the strategic role of a fleet of one, which she maintained even after Johnston had pulled back from his lines at Yorktown and had retreated into the vicinity of Richmond on May 3. The withdrawal totally uncovered Norfolk, which soon fell to McClellan's advancing army. Johnston did not bother to notify Tattnall at Norfolk that he was abandoning the positions that covered the landward approaches to the Confederacy's most important naval base.

Nevertheless, navy yard personnel were able to save the *Richmond*, evacuating her to her namesake city where she was eventually completed. All alone, the *Virginia* covered the evacuation of Norfolk and then tried to slip up the James River to Richmond. Her deep draft defeated her, however, and Tattnall was forced to scuttle her. On May 11 the mighty ship was blown up.

6

Southern Debacle at New Orleans

J UST ABOUT SEVEN WEEKS after the euphoria of the *Virginia*'s victory at Hampton Roads came the Confederate disaster at New Orleans. On April 29, 1862, Union Flag. Off. David G. Farragut conquered the port of New Orleans. His achievement was the seizure of the most important port and shipbuilding center in the entire Confederacy. In a single blow he dashed whatever real hope the Confederacy had to prevail against the sea power wielded by the North. And it was done by disregarding the Anaconda Plan.

Winfield Scott's Anaconda Plan had called for a blockade of the Southern ports and a combined army-navy advance down the Mississippi River that was to climax at New Orleans.

Closing the Gulf of Mexico to the Confederacy was crucial to a successful conclusion of the war. The area involved was immense. It is fifteen hundred miles from Key West, Florida, to Matamoros on the Mexican side of the Rio Grande. Blockading this entire coast—given the demands of the blockade along the Atlantic seacoast of the Confederacy—would have been almost impossible. But a full blockade was not necessary.

Florida to the east and Texas to the west were of minimal importance. With the exceptions of Galveston in Texas and Tampa in Florida, there were almost no good harbors along either end of the extensive coastline.

Although Tampa, Galveston, and Brownsville (just across the Rio Grande from neutral Matamoros) remained in Confederate hands practically throughout the war they were so far removed from the major theaters of action as to be practically useless. Moving material north from Tampa or across Texas from Galveston or Brownsville was difficult, time consuming, and hazardous. Good inland roads were nonexistent and the two major Confederate armies, those of Northern Virginia and Tennessee, required water transportation and rail networks to move the volume of materials they needed.

What became known as the "Cotton Road" soon became a fragile lifeline for the Confederacy. It stretched from the southern terminus of the Houston and Central Railroad at Alleyton, thirty-five miles west of Houston, to Matamoros. There were no signs to mark the road; cotton lint snagged on cactus spines and tree branches indicated that there was a trail. The first or northern half of the route passed through southeast Texas and ended at the huge King Ranch, owned by Richard King (present-day Kingsville). At the King Ranch, eastern and western traffic merged with the northern traffic for the move south.

The southern half of the road stretched 125 miles to Brownsville and Matamoros. "It became a broad thoroughfare along which continuously moved two vast, unending trains of wagons; the one outward bound with cotton, the other homeward bound with merchandise and Army supplies," according to John Warren Hunter, a fourteen-year-old who worked as a teamster on the road.

After the closure of the Mississippi with the fall of New Orleans, Vicksburg, and Port Hudson, the supplies brought into Matamoros and moved over the Cotton Road benefited only the Trans-Mississippi Department of Gen. Edmund Kirby Smith, which consisted of Texas, Arkansas, and most of Louisiana, all of which was on the western side of the great river.

There were only two ports that had any real military or strategic importance, having the requisite water transportation and rail networks. These were New Orleans, at the mouth of the Mississippi, and Mobile, which was served by the protected harbor of Mobile Bay in Alabama.

New Orleans was the South's largest seaport, the Gulf region's largest city, and the sixth largest city in the country, North and South. It owed its importance to its position at the mouth of the Mississippi River. Whoever controlled New Orleans was well on the way to controlling the Mississippi.

During the early history of the United States, the Mississippi had formed a natural highway for moving the produce of the old Northwest Territory to market and tying what would later become the Midwest to the South. The development of canals and later railroads, however, worked to eventually shift economic ties between the sections. Thus the agricultural production of the Midwest came to be linked more and more to markets in the industrial Northeast. Thus was created what would become the economic-political coalition in the North that prior to the war had so frightened the South.

Assisting in the defense of the city of New Orleans was the fact that it is not directly at the mouth of the river but relatively far from the waters of the Gulf of Mexico. After passing the city, the Mississippi meanders another one hundred miles before it finally empties into the Gulf. A considerable distance before it enters the Gulf, the river makes a sudden turn to the east. At this bend in the river were Fort Jackson on the south bank and Fort St. Philip on the north bank. They were positioned to be able to pour a crossfire into any naval squadron attempting to force its way past and onto the city.

During the War of 1812 Fort St. Philip alone had been enough to stop and/or deter the British from attempting the direct route along the river when they attacked New Orleans during 1814–15.

Another twenty miles downstream the river changed again, at what was called Head of the Passes. At Head of the Passes the river branched off into three navigable channels. There was Pass a L'Outre, which led to the east, South Pass, and Southwest Pass, all of which had sandbars offering varying obstructions to navigation. Pass a L'Outre had at that time a depth of seventeen feet over its sandbar and was suitable for large vessels. South Pass could offer only six feet of clearance, and Southwest Pass offered thirteen feet. Originally the Union had been content, in accordance with the Anaconda Plan, to simply block access to the city by attempting to control Head of the Passes.

Meanwhile, the Confederate Navy Department was very busy at New Orleans. Confederate Secretary of the Navy Stephen R. Mallory envisioned New Orleans as the place where ships could be built or otherwise obtained to provide cruisers for commerce destroying and ironclads to break the blockade along the Gulf Coast and control the Mississippi River. Already the former merchant ship *Habana* had been converted into the raider cruiser *Sumter.* At least one other cruiser, CSS *McRae,* and a number of gunboats were built or converted. In addition, since September 1861 two huge and powerful ironclads, *Mississippi* and *Louisiana,* had been under construction at New Orleans.

The Union navy planned to do no more than place a battery at Head of the Passes and thus close all three passes. On October 12, 1861, a flotilla of warships was sent to Head of the Passes to erect this battery. They included the steam corvette *Richmond,* the sailing sloops of war *Vincennes* and *Preble,* and the small steam gunboat *Waterwitch.* The senior Union naval officer present was Capt. John Pope of the *Richmond.* Unfortunately for his flotilla, Pope neglected to post pickets, and he had no warning that Confederate Com. George N. Hollins had decided to attack.

Hollins, who eventually would command all naval forces on the river, was in command of the naval station at New Orleans and the warships defending the city. (At that time these included, aside from *McRae,* the gunboats *Ivy, Jackson, Maurepas,* and *Tuscarora.* His flagship was the chartered privateer *Calhoun.* There was also one other naval asset available, the first ironclad to be built in the Confederacy, the privateer *Manassas.*)

A converted tug, *Manassas* was one of the oddest looking warships ever built. When it was decided to convert her into an ironclad she had been cut down, losing her upper works. A framework was constructed and covered with a twelve-inch-thick convex deck of oak covered with one and a half inches of armor plate. Her bow was filled in solid with timber to create a twenty-foot ram. She also carried at this time a 9-inch Dahlgren smoothbore which fired through a small gun port that allowed no lateral training. The gun port was fitted with a hatch that automatically closed when the gun was run in for reloading. There were two other hatches on her curved deck, and a number of special steam hoses to be used to repel boarders had also been installed as part of the conversion. When the transformation was completed, she was fifteen feet lower in the water and her hull was five feet wider. The conversion had also caused her draft to be increased by four and a half feet, and she resembled nothing so much as a huge cigar floating in the water or a submarine minus the conning tower.

Hollins wanted her as part of his attack force, and on October 11 he seized her from her owners. She was later officially purchased by the Confederate government.

The next night Hollins's little squadron approached the Union flotilla. Although Hollins was a somewhat elderly senior officer, he was no Charles McCauley. Instead he was one of the most combative naval officers of the war in either navy, Union or Confederate. A confused battle followed, with more than a little comic opera thrown in on the Union side.

The action began when *Manassas* rammed *Richmond*. The blow was not serious since it had been deflected by a coal barge that had been moored alongside the *Richmond*. The damage was soon patched, but above decks there was pandemonium. The *Richmond*'s crew fired her guns at shadows, hoisted signal lights, set off rockets, and abandoned their posts. With *Manassas* in pursuit, *Richmond* fled down Southwest Pass without informing the other Union warships what she was doing.

Not knowing what else to do, the other ships followed. As they fled they approached the sandbar that *Preble* and *Waterwitch* had floated over with ease. *Richmond* and *Vincennes,* however, both ran aground. For the next several hours the Union and Confederate ships exchanged ineffectual gunfire.

At about 9 P.M. the captain, Cmdr. Robert Handy, and the crew of the *Vincennes* took to their boats and rowed to the *Richmond*. When Handy boarded *Richmond*, Pope demanded to know what was going on. Handy, looking somewhat ridiculous by having wrapped his ship's flag around his middle, announced that he had received a signal ordering him to abandon his ship. Pope roared he had made no such signal and ordered Handy and his crew to return to *Vincennes*. Handy said that was impossible because he had set a slow fuse to his ship's magazine.

Fortunately, incompetence—or maybe even common sense—saved the day. The slow match that had been set to blow up the ship's magazine went out. A veteran sailor had been given the responsibility to light the slow match, and it has been suggested by several historians that the match may have been put out intentionally, if it had been lighted at all.

Eventually *Vincennes* was refloated after she was reboarded by the sheepish Handy and his crew, but only by dumping all of her guns overboard. Pope also eventually refloated *Richmond,* although she managed to keep her ordnance. Following the fiasco, Pope asked to be relieved. Handy's career was over.

To say that Union Secretary of the Navy Gideon Welles was incensed would have been putting it mildly. The Federal navy had been humiliated. Welles commanded that if New Orleans could not be sealed off from the rest of the world, then the city must be seized and occupied. Thus he abandoned—for the moment—the Anaconda Plan.

During its operations along the Confederate coastline at Hatteras Inlet, Port Royal Sound, and Roanoke Island, the Union navy had learned it was possible for a naval force of steam-powered warships to conquer land-based fortifications, particularly if the ships were equipped with heavy rifled cannons and/or shell guns. This capability would be a vital factor in any attack on New Orleans since the Union army could not be expected to spare a large number of troops from the main theaters of war, especially since McClellan's Peninsula campaign was just getting under way.

If a fleet could run past Forts Jackson and St. Philip and brush aside the Confederate warships, the rest would be relatively easy because all of the city's remaining defenses were positioned to repel an attack from the north. Confederate President Jefferson Davis was even in the process of stripping the city of regular troops—leaving mostly militia—in order to concentrate troops for Gen. Albert Sidney Johnston's proposed offensive at Shiloh. Apparently, Davis believed the main threat to New Orleans was from an advance down the Mississippi, which Johnston's attack, if successful, would help to thwart. Thus the shift in Federal planning paid off, because most of the Confederate military and political leaders, including Secretary of the Navy Mallory, shared

Davis's belief that the Union would follow Scott's Anaconda Plan, of which they had been fully informed by Northern newspapers. Scott, being a soldier, had not considered the possibility of the North's launching an amphibious attack aimed at closing the mouth of the Mississippi at New Orleans. Thus the decision by Welles to attack the Crescent City directly from the Gulf enabled the North to achieve a strategic surprise. This in turn allowed a relatively small number of troops to march in through the back door, once the navy had prepared the way, to tie off one of the Confederacy's most important economic and industrial arteries.

If—that is—the Union navy could deliver.

Welles and Fox began planning the operation. As part of the process they called in Cmdr. David D. Porter, who had considerable experience and knowledge of the conditions at New Orleans. This was done in spite of Porter's earlier action that had deprived Fox's Fort Sumter expedition of its most powerful asset, the *Powhatan*. In his memoirs Porter also claimed to have offered advice for the next step, which was to name a commander for the effort. At this time the three most prominent officers of the Union navy were Samuel F. Du Pont, Louis M. Goldsborough, and Charles Wilkes. Du Pont already commanded the South Atlantic Blockading Squadron, Goldsborough commanded the North Atlantic Blockading Squadron, and Wilkes commanded the West Indies Squadron, which was specifically targeted against Confederate cruisers, privateers, and blockade-runners that were making use of various Caribbean ports, mostly British.

Thus all three men already held vital commands from which none of them could possibly be spared for the attack upon New Orleans. What Welles wanted was to find an American Horatio Nelson to command the attack. What he got was an elderly and undistinguished senior captain named David G. Farragut.

Farragut was a Southerner, born in Tennessee. By virtue of his marriage and his residence in Norfolk, Virginia, he was a Virginian before the war. When the critical moment came and Virginia seceded, he remained loyal to the Union. To Welles's disappointment, however, Farragut was no Lord Nelson. He lacked dash, eloquence, and style. In 1810, at the age of ten, he had been the youngest person ever appointed to be a midshipman in the U.S.

Navy. Farragut's naval career by 1862 had spanned fifty-two years, most of it relatively solid but undistinguished service. During that time he had managed to develop moral courage, the endurance required to resist strain and fatigue, imagination and creative powers for his strategic and tactical plans, and above all else, he was a fine seaman.

Ironically, if it weren't for nepotism, Farragut might never have joined the navy in the first place, nor would he have been given the command in the Gulf, for there were thirty-five other names ahead of his on the captain's list.

Farragut was made a midshipman upon the application of his foster father, Capt. David Porter. Knowing the boy's ambition to join the navy, Porter had him named a midshipman on his own ship, the frigate *Essex*, so he could keep an eye on him. Half a century later the captain's own son, Farragut's foster brother, David D. Porter, claimed that he had suggested Farragut's name as a possible commander of the expedition. In his memoirs, Porter claimed he insisted that his foster brother was the best officer to command the expedition. Welles and Fox listened to Porter despite his overambitious nature, in part because of the great respect both men had for Porter's father and Farragut's foster father. So Porter was sent to New York City to meet with Farragut and sound him out about commanding the assault.

For this task of taking New Orleans, the existing Gulf Blockading Squadron was divided and Farragut was given command of the new West Gulf Blockading Squadron.

After accepting the assignment, Farragut assembled an attack fleet that consisted of the old steam frigate *Mississippi*; the steam corvettes *Hartford, Brooklyn, Richmond,* and *Pensacola*; two cruisers, *Oneida* and *Iroquois*; and the steam gunboats *Varuna, Cayuga, Katahdin, Kineo, Wissahickon, Pinola, Kanawha, Itasca, Winona,* and *Kennebec*. Supporting this force was a flotilla of mortar schooners under Porter's command, which were towed into position by the steam gunboats *Westfield, Owasco, Miami,* and *Harriet Lane*. To actually occupy the city the Union army contributed eighteen thousand troops under the command of Maj. Gen. Benjamin F. Butler, who was chosen because of his previous experience in commanding the landing force in the amphibious operation that had conquered Hatteras Inlet the previous summer.

Under the Federal command structure it was clear that Farragut was in charge, at least until the city surrendered. This was when Butler and his troops were supposed to take over. The Confederate lines of authority were considerably more blurred.

Command of the city of New Orleans itself was in the hands of Maj. Gen. Mansfield Lovell. He had been born in Washington, D.C., and was a graduate of West Point. Before the war he had been a New York City businessman and then went South. Lovell's authority, however, did not extend beyond the city limits. The outer defenses, including Forts St. Philip and Jackson, were the responsibility of Maj. Gen. Johnson Kelly Duncan. Lovell and Duncan disagreed about how best to defend the city. Duncan put his faith in the forts. Lovell believed that the forts alone would not stop the Union navy, and he wanted obstructions placed in the river. Eventually Duncan permitted the stretching of a chain of hulks across the river, but it was a case of too little too late.

Command of the Confederate naval forces at New Orleans was also something of a muddle because between August 1861 and February 1862, command responsibility was held by no less than four commodores or flag officers. They were Lawrence Rousseau, George N. Hollins, William Whittle, and John K. Mitchell. They all attempted to make New Orleans a strong, safe base for naval operations; however, none of them received precise instructions from Richmond, except for constant complaints that they were spending too much money. The problem was that the Richmond government was reluctant to invest scarce cash in the Confederate navy.

Hollins, the most capable of the naval commanders, unfortunately clashed with Mallory. The root cause of the clash was that Mallory shared with President Davis the belief that the main threat to New Orleans was from the north. Furthermore, he was greatly alarmed by the fall of Forts Henry and Donelson and Island No. 10. Both Davis and Mallory also believed that it would be impossible for a Union fleet to successfully pass Forts Jackson and St. Philip.

Therefore, Mallory ordered Hollins to take the bulk of the naval forces at New Orleans north to counter this threat.

Hollins, on the other hand, believed that the real threat to New Orleans lay with Farragut's West Gulf Blockading Squadron and the formidable task force assembling in the Gulf. Thus Mallory made the grave mistake of second-guessing the commander on the spot.

Mallory was never quite able to overcome this failing, particularly if he suspected that the commander on the scene lacked daring and dash and especially if he considered the senior officer to be overage or to have spent too long in grade before the war in the old navy. Mallory's problem regarding Hollins and other commanders was entrenched in his experience with the Naval Retiring Board in the 1850s.

When Hollins, without permission, took the *McRae* back to New Orleans, he also telegraphed Richmond, begging Mallory for authorization to attack Farragut's ships in the same way he had attacked Pope's at Head of the Passes. Mallory refused permission for such an attack. He ordered Hollins to Richmond to serve on a board examining midshipmen at the Confederate Naval Academy, which had been established aboard the cruiser *Patrick Henry*, positioned outside the Confederate capital at Drewry's Bluff on the James River. In addition to the *Patrick Henry*, additional barracks to house the midshipmen had also been constructed there. In Hollins's stead, Com. William F. Lynch was transferred from his North Carolina post to command all Confederate naval forces on the Mississippi River. At this time, command of the naval forces at New Orleans passed from Whittle to Mitchell.

When Farragut launched his attack, the Confederates at New Orleans scraped together a naval force that included the ironclads *Manassas* and *Louisiana*, which was not quite completed but could be used as a floating battery; the cruiser *McRae*, after Hollins had sent her back to the city; the gunboat *Jackson;* and the steam rams *Governor Moore, General Quitman, Defiance, General Breckinridge, General Lovell, Resolute, Stonewall Jackson,* and *Warrior.* The mighty ironclad *Mississippi* was launched as Farragut began his attack; however, her armor and guns were not yet installed and her engines were not fully assembled. It was quickly realized that the *Mississippi* represented the only possible effective opposition to Farragut's fleet if his ships succeeded in passing the forts.

The Confederate navy proper was represented only by *McRae*, *Jackson*, *Manassas*, *Louisiana*, and *Mississippi*. *Governor Moore* and *General Quitman* were part of the Louisiana State Navy. Their captains, however, placed themselves under the command of Flag Officer Mitchell, whose pennant flew from *McRae*. Conflict between the Confederate navy and the Louisiana State Navy was avoided because the Louisiana State Navy's senior officer, Cmdr. Beverly Kennon, who commanded *Governor Moore*, was also a lieutenant in the Confederate navy and was serving without pay in the Louisiana navy. The other steam rams were under the direct control of the Confederate army and were thus commanded by Lovell.

Knowing that the Union fleet must not be allowed to get past Forts Jackson and St. Philip, the available Confederate naval forces were concentrated at the forts. Since *Louisiana* was immovable, she was moored as a floating battery about a mile north of Fort St. Philip. Each of the forts was manned by seven hundred militia troops and was well stocked with food, munitions, and other supplies in case they were cut off from the city. Fort St. Philip mounted fifty-two guns while the more modern Fort Jackson had seventy-four guns, including a 10-inch Columbiad (a weapon that combined the features of a gun, howitzer, and mortar). It was the heaviest coastal defense cannon available to the Confederates.

Worrying Farragut were the three Confederate ironclads known to be at New Orleans. His fleet had no ironclads, and when the expedition was being organized Farragut had not been convinced about the value of ironclads. His opinion had changed somewhat with news of the *Virginia*'s and the *Monitor*'s effectiveness at the battle of Hampton Roads. This early in the war, there were no Union ironclads available anyway. Therefore, Farragut decided to make do with what he did have and ordered the hulls of his wooden ships to be wrapped in anchor chains, thus providing in effect a makeshift chain-mail armor for his ships. This became the expedient to be used whenever the Union navy's wooden ships faced Confederate ironclads.

Then there was the chain of hulks with which the Confederates attempted to close the Mississippi to the Federal fleet as it approached the forts. This was the first obstacle that had to be overcome if Farragut were to claim a victory.

Cmdr. David D. Porter's flotilla of mortar boats commenced hostilities by opening fire on the forts on the morning of April 18. The plan was for the mortar boats to knock out both forts before Farragut made his advance. For six days the 13-inch mortars poured an accurate fire into both forts. The bombardment, however, was not particularly effective because of poor fusing, which caused most of the mortar shells to explode prematurely.

When Porter's ammunition began to run out, Farragut decided he could wait no longer to make his attack. On the night of April 20 the gunboats *Itasca* and *Pinola* in a daring raid broke the chain of hulks that had been stretched across the river between the two forts. At 2 A.M. on April 24, Farragut's fleet formed itself into three divisions and began to move past the forts.

The van, or first division, was led by the *Cayuga* and was followed by *Pensacola, Mississippi, Oneida, Varuna, Katahdin, Kineo,* and *Wissahickon*. The second division consisted of Farragut's flagship, *Hartford,* which was accompanied by *Brooklyn* and *Richmond*. The third division consisted of *Sciota, Iroquois, Kennebec, Itasca, Pinola,* and *Winona*.

The battle commenced as Porter's mortar boats opened fire on the forts. Farragut's ships opened fire as soon as the forts came into range. The forts opened fire on Farragut's ships, but the cannon and mortar fire created a great deal of smoke that made it difficult for the forts to see their targets well enough to respond adequately to the threat. At one point the *Hartford* ran aground and a fire raft was pushed under her port quarter. Farragut's well-trained fire-control party quickly eliminated the danger.

As *Hartford* reentered the battle, the Confederate ironclad ram *Manassas* attacked the Union steam frigate *Mississippi,* well ahead in the first division. Although *Manassas* rammed the *Mississippi,* the old frigate was too well built for the little ironclad to damage her severely. After being turned back by friendly fire when she tried to attack Porter's mortar boats, *Manassas* next attacked the *Brooklyn*. The Union ship, however, was well protected by the anchor chains draped along her hull, and she also suffered little damage from the Confederate ship's ramming attack. On Farragut's personal order *Mississippi* attacked *Manassas,* and her concentrated firepower was too much for the armor of the *Manassas*. In the words of her captain, *Manassas* was "shot through as though she had been built of thin plank, both in the bow and broadside, her smokestack was literally riddled."

Because of the damage his ship had sustained, the captain of the *Manassas* knew that she was foundering. To save the lives of his crew, he turned the bow toward the riverbank and then ran her aground. The crew quickly scampered ashore. The ironclad's stern filled with water, and the weight of the water caused her to slide off the bank and sink into deep water.

Although the heavy fire from the forts kept *Itasca, Winona,* and *Kennebec* of the third division from passing, the Union's major loss was the gunboat *Varuna,* which became the special target of the Louisiana State Navy's steam ram *Governor Moore.*

The *Governor Moore* first encountered the Union gunboat *Cayuga,* which fired upon the Louisiana gunboat from only a few feet away. Then a large Union frigate, most likely the *Mississippi,* appeared out of the battle's smoky haze and fired a hail of shells from small boat howitzers positioned in her top masts. These killed a number of *Governor Moore*'s men at her guns.

The Union gunboat *Pinola* positioned herself on the *Governor Moore*'s port quarter, and a broadside killed five more aboard the Lousiana ram.

The ram managed to shake off her tormentors, and shortly afterward her crew sighted a large steamer, the gunboat *Varuna,* pulling ahead of the rest of the Union fleet. The *Varuna* was the fastest ship in Farragut's fleet, but the large gunboat was not a true warship, only a merchant steamer that had been converted into a warship while still under construction. By pulling his vessel out of support range of the other Union ships, *Varuna*'s captain committed a terrible blunder. *Governor Moore* turned to pursue *Varuna* and was assisted by the fact that there was no light in the background, which made the Louisiana ship almost invisible as she bore down on *Varuna.* This allowed the *Governor Moore* to greatly close the range without coming under fire from the *Varuna*'s rifled guns.

Governor Moore tenaciously closed the range until she was finally spotted at practically point-blank range. The two ships opened fire simultaneously. *Governor Moore* was able to ram

Varuna twice, but the range became so close that she could not sufficiently depress her forward cannon to fire into the *Varuna*. Instead she fired through her own hull, using the resulting hole as a gun port thereafter.

The impact of the two hits scored by *Governor Moore*'s ram forced *Varuna* aground. Then she was rammed again, this time by the Confederate army steam ram *Stonewall Jackson*. The *Stonewall Jackson*, living up to her namesake, proved to be the scrappiest of the Southern army's steam rams.

As *Governor Moore* turned around to head back downstream, her decks and those of the *Stonewall Jackson* were swept by heavy cannon fire from the Union cruiser *Oneida*. Both rams were forced aground near the wrecked hulk of the *Varuna*, where they were abandoned by what was left of their crews. In the furious action about half of the *Governor Moore*'s crew were dead on her decks as the battle moved past her final resting place.

By this time the bulk of the Union fleet had passed the forts where they still had to contend with *Louisiana*, *McRae*, and what remained of the steam rams. During the resulting running battle, all but one of the steam rams with *McRae* were destroyed (mostly by their own crews). *McRae* herself was engaged by several of Farragut's ships, but she managed to extricate herself and limped, badly damaged, back to New Orleans, where she sank alongside a wharf. The only surviving steam ram, *Defiance*, fled the scene and was destroyed by her crew after New Orleans surrendered.

Just before Farragut began his run past the forts, Butler and his eighteen thousand troops arrived on the scene. After Farragut successfully ran past the forts, Butler decided to place a regiment aboard the gunboat *Miami*, which he borrowed from Porter. Over the next few days the troops were landed near Fort St. Philip, and Butler managed to get them into position behind the fort while sending a few companies to cut off Fort Jackson. The Confederate garrisons saw that the situation was hopeless. Defying their officers, they mutinied and surrendered during the early morning hours of April 28.

After the forts surrendered, the crew of *Louisiana*, which had fought doggedly in her role as a floating battery throughout the battle, decided to abandon and destroy their ship. Her guns were loaded and run out and combustibles were scattered about her gun deck. The crew abandoned her, set her afire, and cast her off downstream. Blazing from stem to stern, her guns exploding, and flames showing from every gun port and opening in her hull, *Louisiana* was carried downstream by the river's current. Finally, with a flash and a roar, she exploded and disappeared.

Farragut, who did not stop to wait for Butler, steamed on to New Orleans. Butler, as a politician, knew the importance of appearances, and he wanted desperately to participate in the surrender of New Orleans. Forced to scavenge for transportation, he followed far behind in Farragut's wake.

For Farragut the first item on the agenda was to find and take care of the Confederate ironclad *Mississippi*. She was without guns, ammunition, and armor, and her engines were still not yet assembled. Her captain was away from the ship, seeking a means to tow her to safety. As soon as Farragut's ships were sighted approaching her anchorage on April 25, her crew burned and scuttled her.

Once he reached the New Orleans waterfront Farragut ordered his senior captain to demand the surrender of the city. Accompanied only by a lieutenant, Capt. Theodorus Bailey braved a mob of civilians determined to prevent the surrender. The two officers made it to the city hall despite curses, verbal assaults, and threats of physical violence. Municipal officials, however, refused to surrender as the city was under martial law. Mansfield Lovell was asked to surrender the city, but he responded that all military personnel had evacuated the city and he was about to leave himself—which he did.

Lovell, along with John C. Pemberton (who would surrender Vicksburg to Grant on July 4, 1863), has been vilified in the South, primarily because Jefferson Davis allowed him to be used as a convenient scapegoat. By evacuating the city, Lovell actually saved it from the destruction a fight would have entailed, since only three thousand militia could not have defended it against Butler's eighteen thousand troops.

Over the next few days Farragut made no attempt to land in the city, but the townspeople occasionally gathered to stare at his ships. They flew the flag of Louisiana over the city hall and the customs house. On April 29, Farragut had had enough. He sent a detachment of sailors and a battalion of marines with two boat howitzers ashore to take possession of the city. Butler watched, but his troops did not arrive until May 1.

The capture of the port city of New Orleans, along with the closing of the mouth of the Mississippi to Confederate traffic, may have been the single most important contribution made by the Union navy to winning the Civil War. If Gideon Welles had decided to allow the Anaconda Plan to take its course, it is likely, since Vicksburg did not fall for another fourteen months, that the Confederate navy would have had time to complete the *Louisiana* and *Mississippi* and make them fully operational. In the book *Ironclads at War,* Jack Greene and Alessandro Massignani speculate that since no ironclads were available to operate in Gulf waters in 1862, that the *Mississippi* and the *Louisiana* could likely have dominated the Gulf for a summer and a fall. Moreover, the consequences of this naval supremacy could have been catastrophic for the Union cause. For one thing, these two ships could have made New Orleans and Mobile impregnable. Union naval operations on the East Coast could have been paralyzed as the Union navy scrambled to regroup to meet this threat from the Gulf coast. *Louisiana* and *Mississippi* could even have made a lunge at Pensacola and opened up the Pensacola Navy Yard to full use by the Confederacy.

With an aggressive commander such as Franklin Buchanan and some reasonable weather, Greene and Massignani reason it is conceivable that the Southerners could have won European recognition and intervention, which the Confederacy desperately needed to win the war. Farragut's victory at New Orleans made all of this impossible. Not only that, Farragut's victory made the seizure and control of the entire length of the Mississippi River inevitable.

Thus it seems only appropriate that Congress created the rank of rear admiral in recognition of Farragut's achievement. Welles and Lincoln immediately named him to be the first man to hold that rank in the U.S. Navy. Rather than being an American Nelson, Farragut was instead an American original.

According to historian Chester G. Hearn, author of *The Capture of New Orleans,* the Union victory was due to a combination of Farragut's personality and the soundness of the tactical plan that had been hammered together by Welles and Fox in Washington. "Welles and Fox," Hearn observed, "scraped together some of the best warships they had, but they knew nothing at all about the lower Mississippi. The thing that made it work was Farragut and his professional, evenhanded method of pulling together the ship commanders, many of whom were not eager to run that gauntlet [formed by Forts Jackson and St. Philip]."

Hearn has also noted that the Confederate defeat came not on the operational level but rather upon the executive level. Although Lovell originally believed that Farragut's entry into the lower river was a trick, thinking that the Federal attack was aimed at Mobile Bay, the Confederate commander changed his mind when Farragut got all of his ships into the river. He telegraphed the War Department, calling for reinforcements and guns to be rushed to the city. Instead, the Davis administration kept pulling regiments and guns out of the city, stripping Lovell of what he needed to adequately defend the city.

Thus Hearn blames the fall of New Orleans solely on Davis and Mallory for their inability to see the forest (represented by Farragut's fleet) because of their concentration on the trees (represented by the Union thrust down the Mississippi River that would not secure the city of Memphis, the next major objective below Island No. 10, until June). To a certain extent, the fall of Island No. 10 to Maj. Gen. John Pope's army and to Flag Off. Andrew Foote's river flotilla panicked Confederate officials in Richmond and those on the scene at New Orleans. The fall of Island No. 10, which focused the attention of Davis and Mallory north of New Orleans, also caused the evacuation of the incompleted ironclad *Arkansas* to Yazoo City and the premature abandonment and destruction of the ironclad *Tennessee* at Memphis.

Charles L. Dufour, in *The Night the War Was Lost*, also commented on the fixation of Davis and Mallory with the Union's combined army-navy campaign down the Mississippi River. Dufour, however, also cites the hopelessly divided and confused command situation that existed at New Orleans as a major cause of what was probably the greatest single defeat to be levied on the Confederacy during the course of the war.

Other factors contributing to the disaster included the delays in getting the *Louisiana* and *Mississippi* completed and fully operational. Aside from the materiel shortages, aggravated in part by transportation and communication difficulties, there were also labor problems as noted by Dufour, Greene, and Massignani. Greene and Massignani note in particular that often a democracy is faced with a daunting task of getting the people to lay aside their petty concerns in favor of advancing a national objective. These misguided strikers, motivated as they were by their own misguided and uninformed self-interest, must also carry part of the blame for the fall of New Orleans.

7

Triumph of the Arkansas

EVEN AS NEW ORLEANS was threatened, work on the two major Confederate Mississippi River ironclads—*Arkansas* and *Tennessee*—continued. The keels for the two vessels were laid at John T. Shirley's shipyard near Fort Pickering, twelve miles below Memphis, Tennessee. There was a severe shortage of skilled shipyard personnel as many workers had gone north to work in Yankee shipyards. In addition, a lack of resources caused Shirley to concentrate on one of the ironclads at a time rather than work on both simultaneously. He concentrated his efforts on the *Arkansas.*

That decision was made in March 1862, when Gen. P. G. T. Beauregard sent a naval officer, Lt. John J. Guthrie, to inspect the two incomplete ironclads and report on their status. Guthrie noted that it would probably take about six weeks to complete the hull of the *Tennessee* while the *Arkansas* would soon be ready for launching. Shortly after that launching came the news that Island No. 10 had fallen to Union Maj. Gen. John Pope on April 7. Three weeks later word arrived that the city of New Orleans had been captured.

A third Mississippi River ironclad, *Eastport*, had already been lost. When Fort Henry on the Tennessee River fell on February 6, 1862, a force of Federal gunboats had been sent upriver on a raiding expedition, and they found the *Eastport*. The ironclad was hastily scuttled and everything of value was burned or otherwise destroyed. *Eastport* was raised, completed, and commissioned as part of the Union navy in August. After striking a stationary torpedo on the Red River in April 1864, she was eventually blown up and destroyed to prevent her falling back into Confederate hands when receding water levels threatened to leave the damaged ship stranded deep in Southern territory.

In the spring of 1862, as a state of panic gripped the military and civil authorities at Memphis, the *Tennessee* was hurriedly destroyed on the stocks to keep her out of the hands of Union forces, which would not seize the city of Memphis and its environs until after the Confederate River Defense Fleet was destroyed at the battle of Memphis on June 6, 1862. Meanwhile, the hull of the *Arkansas,* under the command of Lt. Charles H. McBlair, was towed downstream by the civilian steamer *Capitol,* along with barges loaded with equipment to complete the ironclad. McBlair headed twelve miles up the Yazoo River to Greenwood, where he hoped to complete her. He, however, proved inept as a shipbuilder and left her moored in a severe state of disrepair. Engine parts, boilers, guns without carriages, and assorted equipment was left strewn about her decks, and her partly completed iron plating was badly rusted. The remainder of her armor lay on the bottom of the river aboard a sunken barge. *Arkansas* was little more than a floating wreck. Civilians in the area were so incensed about the ironclad's condition that they petitioned Secretary of the Navy Mallory to complete the *Arkansas.* Beauregard also urged that Mallory act.

The secretary chose Lt. Isaac N. Brown. He had been in charge of the conversion of the *Eastport* and later was supervising the shipyards at New Orleans at the time of Farragut's attack. A native of Kentucky and a twenty-eight-year veteran of the U.S. Navy before throwing his lot in with the South, Brown inspected the *Arkansas* on May 28. What he found so infuriated him that he considered having McBlair shot. Alarmed, McBlair departed hastily for Richmond to protest his treatment at Brown's hands. Nothing is known of the reaction to this grievance since McBlair simply disappears from the official records that still exist.

Brown's first act was to establish a headquarters at a nearby plantation and to requisition available area blacksmiths, carpenters, and machinists to work on the *Arkansas*. Next he secured a detachment of soldiers to raise the sunken barge containing the remainder of the armor plate needed by the *Arkansas*. Brown then had the vessel towed downstream to Yazoo City, where he established the Yazoo City Navy Yard.

The town had been founded in 1824 as Hanan's Bluff and was incorporated in 1830 as Manchester. The name was changed to Yazoo City in honor of the Yazoo Indians who had originally inhabited the region. By 1839 the town had one thousand inhabitants and was the largest marketing center in Mississippi. When Brown arrived, the people in the region gave their overwhelming support to the *Arkansas*. Blacksmiths were sent from the surrounding plantations, iron was hauled from a rail junction at Vaughan, and wagon masters at Jackson built gun carriages for the ship. Ordnance stores and munitions were obtained from Vicksburg. Round shot was forged in Jackson, and some gunpowder for her magazines was even made in Yazoo City.

Soon more than two hundred workmen were swarming over the hulk, and twelve iron forges were active around the clock. To protect the *Arkansas* while the work was under way, Brown placed a set of guns on a raft in the middle of the Yazoo River, a few miles downstream. It consisted of two 42-pounders crewed by militia. The makeshift gun platform was designed to forestall any Union excursions upriver aimed at the *Arkansas* and/or at the navy yard.

Eventually Brown and the *Arkansas* were joined by three refugees from the Confederate River Defense Fleet. The ram *General Earl Van Dorn* had fled from the battle of Memphis, where most of the Confederate fleet was destroyed, and the steamer man-of-war *General Polk* and the side-wheel steamer man-of-war *Livingston* had moved downriver after the fall of Island No. 10. Brown's authority did not extend to these other vessels. Com. William F. Lynch by this time had been transferred from North Carolina and had succeeded George N. Hollins in command of Confederate naval forces on the river. He summarily rejected Brown's suggestions about squadron operations by the four ships. When the Union steam ram *Monarch* came poking up the Yazoo on a reconnaissance, Confederate Cmdr. Robert F. Pinkney burned the three ships, leaving the *Arkansas* as virtually the only Confederate naval vessel on the Mississippi.

Meanwhile, after the fall of New Orleans and Memphis, the Mississippi River fortress town of Vicksburg seemed ripe for the taking. Rear Adm. David G. Farragut, the conqueror of New Orleans, turned his attention to it, but only because of orders from Washington. Left to decide the matter himself, he would not have considered it. Farragut had no desire to hazard his ships among the river's swift currents and shallow depths. In addition, summer was approaching, and the water level would soon be falling. Furthermore, the batteries protecting Vicksburg were emplaced on bluffs from which his ships would be subjected to plunging fire, and his own guns would be unable to elevate sufficiently to fire back. Furthermore, he commanded an entirely different kind of fleet from the one that was heading downriver under the command of Flag Off. Charles H. Davis, who had replaced Flag Off. Andrew Foote. Foote had died as a result of complications from a wound he had taken when his gunboats had attacked Fort Donelson. Unfortunately his earlier easy victory at Fort Henry had made him overconfident, and he had taken his gunboats too close to the much more formidable works of Fort Donelson. Farragut's ships were blue-water, wooden warships, not brown-water gunboats. Although they were powerful, they were not designed and were certainly never intended for riverine operations and combat.

Farragut, however, was not in a position to refuse. Since he had just won what was likely to be the most important naval battle of the war, he was considered something of a miracle-worker. The result was that he was now being ordered to take his oceangoing vessels upriver, deeper into enemy territory, during a hot Mississippi summer where they really had no business being. It would have been like demanding that Lord Nelson follow up his victory at the battle of the Nile by sailing his fleet upriver to the Sudan.

Farragut penned his doubts directly to Union Secretary of the Navy Gideon Welles, noting that he would infinitely prefer attacking the other major Confederate port on the Gulf Coast: Mobile. From New Orleans, Gen. Benjamin F. Butler wrote Welles concerning Farragut's apparent unwillingness to move upstream, which prompted other officials in Washington to worry about the willingness of their new naval hero to carry out orders. Several redundant dispatches were sent to Farragut. Like Mallory, Welles showed that he was willing to interfere with the decision-making of an officer in the field. In this case, Farragut was prepared to bend when he had to. The new admiral was soon advised that his position was being "misquoted." To somewhat placate Welles, Farragut made plans to move against the city of Baton Rouge, Louisiana, which could be seen as a preliminary move toward a strike against Vicksburg. On May 6 he sent the cruiser *Iroquois* to demand the city's surrender and supported the demand with the steam corvette *Brooklyn,* some gunboats, and troop transports.

There were no Confederate garrisons or batteries in or around the city. Although Baton Rouge was the capital of Louisiana, it had never been fortified because the Confederates believed that it was amply protected by the defenses of New Orleans to the South and Vicksburg to the North. With the fall of New Orleans it was only logical that the Southerners would try to turn Baton Rouge into a citadel to hinder Union control of the lower Mississippi. In response to the danger, the state capital was rapidly moved in succession to Opelousas, Alexandria, and finally Shreveport.

The *Iroquois* reached Baton Rouge on May 7, 1862, and anchored abreast of the city. The mayor was summoned to a conference on board, but he was "out of town" and therefore unable to surrender the city. The vice mayor, however, offered to come in his place. The captain of the *Iroquois* felt insulted and waited for the *Brooklyn* to arrive. He then sent a new message to city hall, demanding that the city capitulate immediately. When the mayor, who wasn't out of town after all, refused to do so, marines were landed and that was that.

From there the Union warships moved on to Natchez and took control of that city also.

Finally Farragut decided to take his squadron upriver to reconnoiter the Vicksburg defenses. He found the fortress city to be protected by heavy batteries to the north and south and a garrison of at least eight thousand troops. Deciding there was really nothing to be done, the fleet returned to New Orleans. There Farragut was greeted with another flurry of messages from

Washington, directing him to assault Vicksburg in coordination with Flag Off. Charles H. Davis and the river flotilla moving down from the north. By May 24 Farragut had returned to the vicinity of Vicksburg and once again deemed the defenses to be impregnable to an assault from the river. When his flagship, *Hartford,* was almost stranded at high water because of her deep draft, Farragut took his fleet back to New Orleans.

By now Confederate batteries covered the river from Port Hudson, north of Baton Rouge, to Vicksburg, and Farragut had to fight his way past the guns. In addition, the Southerners still controlled the Red River, which connected the eastern half of the Confederacy with Louisiana and Texas and over which flowed food, raw materials, supplies, and more than one hundred thousand recruits for the Confederate army.

While the merits of assaulting Vicksburg were endlessly debated, the city's defenders, under the command of Maj. Gen. Earl Van Dorn, were busy improving their defenses. The ongoing debate in the Union camp lost for the North a golden opportunity for an early seizure of Vicksburg at a time when Federal troops were available at Corinth, Mississippi, and at New Orleans, and when the Vicksburg garrison was seriously undermanned.

Finally, on July 1, 1862, the two powerful Union fleets—Farragut's from the south and Davis's from the north—were concentrated at a point above Vicksburg. The immediate result was that Van Dorn panicked. He insisted that *Arkansas* be completed forthwith, placed under his orders, and dispatched against the Union naval concentration. "It is better to die in action than be buried up at Yazoo City," he declared.

Eleven days after the Union fleets had completed their concentration, Isaac N. Brown decided that *Arkansas* was as ready as she would ever be and on July 12 he ordered her to sortie against the enemy. Receding water convinced Brown to act quickly or risk stranding the *Arkansas* at Yazoo City.

Under way at last, *Arkansas* resembled nothing so much as a house adrift on a raft. Her armament included four 7-inch Brooke rifles and six 9-inch Dahlgrens, but her most potent weapon was her ram bow. The ironclad's greatest weakness was her power plant; the engines had been salvaged from the sunken river steamer

Natchez. Making things even more interesting was the ship's lack of a rudder. She was maneuvered by twin screw propellers that operated independently.

She was forced to stop at Satartia when a broken stream line fouled her powder supply. The *Arkansas* moored alongside a sawmill while the powder was spread out on tarpaulins to dry in the sun. The powder was dried by nightfall, and *Arkansas* continued down the Yazoo River.

During the early morning hours of July 15, the *Arkansas* approached Old River, a channel that the Yazoo had once followed before changing its course many years before, and entered the Mississippi about twelve miles above Vicksburg. The crew were at battle stations, and the guns were primed and ready. The ironclad's smoke was spotted by a Union tugboat, which immediately turned about and fled downstream, blowing her whistle in warning.

Farragut was not overly concerned by a single Confederate warship. Therefore he dispatched the ironclad gunboat *Carondelet,* the steam ram *Queen of the West,* and the unarmored wooden gunboat *Tyler* to investigate the unknown vessel. While these three veteran warships moved upstream, the remainder of the two Federal fleets remained idle, conserving fuel at anchor. At 6 A.M. the Union and Confederate ships sighted each other. *Tyler* was the first to open fire at a range of about one thousand yards. *Arkansas* returned her fire. The captain of the *Tyler* stopped his engines, allowing his ship to drift downstream while maintaining a rapid rate of fire with his bow guns until he reached a position one hundred yards off the *Carondelet*'s bow. Together the two Union warships poured a withering volume of fire at the approaching Confederate vessel. But the *Arkansas* kept coming, Union projectiles bouncing off her armored casemate. Aboard the Southern ironclad her armor rang like a bell with each hit. Some of her armor shifted, but none of the Federal shells penetrated to the interior.

The *Arkansas* headed for the *Carondelet,* raking the Union gunboat and inflicting considerable damage. Brown then attempted to ram the vessel but missed. As *Arkansas* passed *Carondelet,* she fired a full point-blank broadside into her at the waterline. The resulting hits cut away *Carondelet*'s tiller ropes and destroyed steam gauges and water pipes. Her commander used the last of her forward momentum to run the ship aground on the riverbank to prevent her from sinking. The Union vessel suffered four dead, sixteen wounded, and ten missing. Several of the missing had jumped overboard and drowned.

The steam ram *Queen of the West* rapidly retreated back to the combined fleet anchorage. This left the gunboat *Tyler* alone as the *Arkansas* moved toward her. The Federal captain steered his vessel downstream, retreating ahead of the Confederate ram with his stern guns maintaining a rapid fire to match the fire from the bow guns of the *Arkansas*. The *Tyler* maintained a distance of about two hundred yards. Although *Tyler*'s guns repeatedly struck the *Arkansas,* they failed to do any appreciable damage. During the exchange, *Tyler*'s crew lost eight killed and eleven wounded, but the gunboat itself suffered little damage. In addition, one of her hits penetrated *Arkansas*'s armor and wounded Brown.

Arkansas chased *Tyler* and *Queen of the West* into the main channel where the Yazoo met the Mississippi and where the Union fleets lay sleeping at anchor. Suddenly the *Arkansas* found herself surrounded by more than thirty Federal vessels. The gunboats were anchored on the Vicksburg side, the rams were near the Yazoo, transports were off the Louisiana shore, and Farragut's fleet and mortar boats were downstream. Brown's options were limited since *Arkansas*'s funnel was riddled with hits, forcing her steam pressure to drop drastically to dangerous lows. He headed for his only refuge, under the guns of Vicksburg, his only path leading through the heart of the combined Union fleet. While doing so he decided to inflict as much damage on the Yankee vessels as he could.

By now the fleet was fully aroused. Among the first to respond was Farragut's steam corvette *Lancaster*. She moved out to challenge the *Arkansas,* but a lucky hit from the *Arkansas* pierced the *Lancaster*'s steam drum, scalding a number of her crew and knocking her out of the fight. Then the gunboat *Kineo* and Farragut's flagship, *Hartford,* challenged the Confederate ironclad. Gun smoke reduced visibility to almost nothing, forcing Brown's gunners to aim at the Union gun flashes. Brown suspected that the Federal steam rams were trying to get near enough to ram him, but he surmised they were being hurt as much by friendly fire as they were by the guns of *Arkansas*. The *Arkansas* did not escape without damage or casualties. One hit from the *Hartford* penetrated her armor, killing three of her crew and wounding three others.

As *Arkansas* passed the Union gunboats, she was confronted by the *Essex* and the *Benton*. As *Arkansas* attempted to ram the *Benton,* the Federal vessel sidestepped the effort, receiving instead a broadside from the Confederate ironclad. These were the last shots fired by the *Arkansas* as she emerged from the gauntlet and reached the safety of Vicksburg. Facing fire from both the *Arkansas* and the Vicksburg batteries, the Union ships withdrew out of range.

As soon as the *Arkansas* was moored to the Vicksburg wharf, Brown and his crew were greeted by Generals Beauregard and Van Dorn along with crowds of the city's cheering and celebrating residents. Meanwhile, Farragut and Davis were mortified. They had permitted a lone Confederate warship to simply blast its way through their combined fleet. That night the Union forces attempted a raid aimed at destroying the *Arkansas,* but Brown had moved his ship and the Federal vessels only wasted their ammunition. She was hit once by an 11-inch round that killed several crewmen and further disabled her engines. Fire from the *Arkansas* and the Vicksburg batteries damaged the gunboats *Sciota* and *Winona* along with the *Hartford*. Next Farragut tried shelling her with the 13-inch mortars of the mortar boats. They missed *Arkansas* entirely but showered her decks with dead fish. The bombardment continued for a week while Farragut and Davis planned another raid aimed at *Arkansas*.

This time the steam rams *Queen of the West* and *Sumter* were selected to spearhead the attack. They were to be supported by the ironclad gunboats *Essex, Benton, Louisville,* and *Cincinnati*. The timing was unfortunate for *Arkansas* since most of her crew were sick and one of her engines was not operating.

Essex made the first attack. The officers of the shorthanded *Arkansas* helped to man the guns along with those men who were still on their feet. *Essex* came at the *Arkansas* to soften up the Confederate ironclad for the two unarmored steam rams that were to follow her. Brown used his single operating engine to maneuver the ship so his bow faced the oncoming enemy vessel. As the distance closed between the *Arkansas* and the *Essex,* both ships blasted away at each other with their bow guns. *Arkansas* suffered eight dead. The *Essex* was damaged and blinded and went aground on the bank of the river. Every Confederate gun ashore and aboard the *Arkansas* fired on the *Essex*. Despite this intense cannonade, the Union crew managed to back the ship off the shore, although she suffered a dreadful beating. *Essex* was severely damaged and unmanageable; the only thing her crew could do was to drift downstream where she found safety among the Union fleet's mortar boats.

Next came the *Queen of the West*. The steam ram was "armored" with cotton bales piled around her machinery and other vital spots to absorb shot and shell. As the *Queen* headed for the *Arkansas,* she began taking hits from Vicksburg's batteries on the bluffs. On her first run the *Queen*'s captain overestimated her speed and missed the Confederate ironclad. This forced her to turn back and try again, against the current. This time the *Queen* managed to ram the *Arkansas,* almost sending her onto her beam, but the *Queen* ran aground on the bank and was raked by the stern guns of her intended victim. As with the *Essex,* the Federal crew managed to get their vessel off the bank, and she moved upstream to the safety of the main Union fleet anchorage.

After viewing the previous failures, the captain of the *Sumter* declined to move to the attack.

The river now became Farragut's main concern as he acknowledged that the *Arkansas* had withstood everything the combined Union fleets could throw at her. With the water level falling day by day, it was time for Farragut to withdraw his deep-draft vessels from Vicksburg before they were left high and dry. In addition, illness was running rampant throughout his ships. The *Brooklyn* had sixty-eight men on the sick list. In Davis's Mississippi River Fleet, a third of the gunboat *Louisville*'s crew were ill as was a quarter of the *Benton*'s crew.

Farragut began withdrawing his ships to New Orleans on July 24, 1862; Davis withdrew his ships to Memphis two days later. First though, the two fleet commanders dispatched four ships—the ironclad gunboat *Essex,* the gunboats *Kineo* and *Cayuga,* and the steam ram *Sumter*—to Baton Rouge. Also left at Baton Rouge were the troop transports and the soldiers of Brig. Gen. Thomas Williams, just in case the Confederates decided to send the *Arkansas* downstream or otherwise threaten Baton Rouge. By the end of the month, Federal forces had retreated from a two-hundred-mile stretch of the Mississippi between Vicksburg and Port Hudson. The fortress city and her ironclad protector were left without an enemy in sight.

Lt. Isaac N. Brown, the triumphant commander of the *Arkansas,* was ill and exhausted from his exertions. In addition, he remained weak from the wound he had taken from the *Tyler,* and fatigue threatened to incapacitate him. With great reluctance he decided to take a medical leave to Grenada, Mississippi, to recuperate. Command of the *Arkansas* devolved to his executive officer, Lt. Thomas H. Stevens. Before leaving his ship, Brown ordered Stevens not, under any circumstances, to leave the safety of Vicksburg.

With their success at Vicksburg, Confederate military authorities within the city began eyeing Baton Rouge. The city was important both for its proximity to the Red River as well as for its location on the Mississippi. Both made the city a strategically desirable prize. Van Dorn at Vicksburg decided that it was time for a counteroffensive and made the city his objective. His planned attack was aimed at reopening supply lines to Texas, Arkansas, and that portion of Louisiana remaining in Confederate hands on the opposite side of the Mississippi.

Van Dorn prepared a force of four thousand troops for the projected attack, but he realized that if the attack was to have any chance of success he needed the *Arkansas* to counter the four Union warships who had been left on the river. The only weak spot in the plan lay in the wretched state of the engines of the *Arkansas.* Van Dorn gave command of the expedition to Maj. Gen. John C. Breckinridge, a Kentuckian and a former vice president of the United States.

When Breckinridge reached Baton Rouge many of his troops were sick, putting his mission in doubt. Breckinridge persevered and requested naval support from the *Arkansas.* Although her engines desperately needed repairs and her crew, supplemented now with men from the artillery batteries at Vicksburg, was now largely inexperienced, great pressure was exerted on Stevens to disregard Brown's last order to remain at Vicksburg. Finally he received a direct order to sortie with the ironclad; he had no choice but to obey. Stevens sent a message to Grenada informing Brown he had been ordered to attack Baton Rouge. Brown hurried back to Vicksburg, arriving four hours after his ship had left.

On the way downriver to Baton Rouge, the engines of the *Arkansas* broke down after she had been under way for about twenty-four hours. Stevens was forced to anchor his ship while the engineers attempted to make repairs. Meanwhile, without waiting for the *Arkansas* to join them, Breckinridge's troops had begun the attack on Williams's garrison at Baton Rouge. As long as the Union warships remained in support of Williams, Breckinridge realized that his troops could only advance so far. He pulled back to the city's outskirts to await the arrival of *Arkansas*.

Stevens and his engineers managed to get the engines working, and *Arkansas* resumed her advance upon Baton Rouge. She was just four miles above the city when her starboard engine quit and the torque of the port engine forced her aground. After some further delay, the engines were put back into operation, the ship was worked off the riverbank, and *Arkansas* continued her journey.

When Stevens sighted the Union warships, the gunboat *Essex* in the lead, he decided to turn upstream slightly and get enough headway to allow *Arkansas* to ram *Essex*. Just as *Arkansas* was getting into position, both engines quit and the ship drifted ashore. Stevens immediately realized that the situation was desperate. The *Arkansas*'s engines had broken down completely, the ship had run aground, and four Union warships were now shelling her as she lay helpless. With great reluctance he gave the order to scuttle the ironclad and abandon ship. Her engines were broken up, powder and shells were scattered on the decks, and her guns were loaded and primed. Combustibles were strewn about the ship, and she was set on fire. The crew then leaped ashore where she had gone aground. Stevens was the last to leave.

In her death throes the *Arkansas* came free from the bank as her guns and ammunition exploded; the Union ships scrambled to get out of her way. After about an hour her magazines blew up with a thunderous explosion, which hurled parts of the burning ironclad all over the place. With no naval support, Breckinridge was forced to abandon his attack and withdrew his troops.

Although *Arkansas* was lost because of the extremely poor condition of her engines, a problem that plagued many if not most of the other Confederate-built ironclads, she—like *Virginia*—had won a great strategic victory. All by herself she had prevented the fall of Vicksburg and the final closure of the Mississippi River to the Confederacy. One of the factors in the final surrender of Vicksburg was the absence of the *Arkansas,* which was not there to again ravage the Union's riverine navy. Through the *Arkansas'*s efforts, the Confederates were able to take control of a 250- to 300-mile stretch of the river between Vicksburg and Port Hudson, and control of this section of the river allowed the Confederate government to maintain its communications with Edmund Kirby Smith's Trans-Mississippi Department.

With the loss of the *Arkansas,* Confederate naval operations on the Mississippi River to all intents and purposes came to an end. Although the deplorable conditions of her engines were the direct cause of her loss, there were other indirect causes. Most of the latter lie at the feet of Earl Van Dorn and William F. Lynch. Van Dorn knew next to nothing about naval operations, and therefore he should not have had any kind of command authority over the *Arkansas.* Through ignorance, Van Dorn threw away the only real naval asset the Confederates had on the river. Lynch carries some responsibility because he was apparently not on the scene at Vicksburg. As commander of all Confederate naval forces on the river, he could have used his authority to prevent Van Dorn's ordering the ship to join in the attack on Baton Rouge.

Arkansas should not have been squandered on an ill-advised offensive operation. Instead she should have remained in the vicinity of Vicksburg to defend the stronghold from further Union attacks. If she had been on hand, particularly if her engines had been repaired or replaced, she might have been able to disrupt David D. Porter's passing of the Vicksburg batteries and his ferrying of Grant's army from the western bank to the eastern bank of the Mississippi River below Vicksburg. This was the Union operation that finally broke the stalemate at Vicksburg and allowed Grant to set the stage for the siege that led to the final surrender of the fortress city.

In her short career, the *Arkansas*—like the *Virginia*—succeeded in proving the worth of the steam-powered ironclads. Their successes silenced once and for all those few remaining critics who still favored Matthew Fontaine Maury's discredited Mosquito Fleet proposal. The only problem was that the Union navy now also understood their worth and had already begun to utilize the North's infinitely greater industrial capacity to turn out ironclads rapidly and in numbers guaranteed to swamp the Confederate navy.

8

A Change in Strategy

BY THE SPRING AND summer of 1862 it had become apparent to Stephen R. Mallory that his comprehensive naval strategy was not working as he had planned. True, the success of the *Virginia* and *Arkansas* had proved that ironclads were the warships of the future. Although only two of his commerce-destroying cruisers (*Sumter* and *Nashville*) had gone to sea, they had already started the process of driving the Northern merchant marine from the world's oceans. The magnitude of their eventual success, however, was not yet apparent. In all other areas, Mallory's efforts and those of his department seemed to have brought about only great failures.

There were the Confederate naval disasters—and for the Union, the amphibious successes—of Hatteras Inlet, Port Royal Sound, Roanoke Island, and New Orleans. Even the *Virginia* and *Arkansas* were gone—scuttled and destroyed by their own crews to prevent their falling into enemy hands.

Even as Mallory was beginning to rethink his strategy, he was in danger of being dismissed as the scapegoat for the perceived failures of the Confederate navy.

By August 20, 1862, two full weeks after the *Arkansas* was scuttled, Charles M. Conrad, chairman of the Joint Committee on Naval Affairs and a political enemy of Mallory's, introduced a resolution to the Confederate Congress calling for consideration of the elimination of the Department of the Navy and the transference of all of its functions to the War Department. The other shoe was dropped when Rep. Henry Foote, a political opponent of both Mallory and President Davis, introduced a resolution calling for a vote of no confidence in Mallory as secretary of the navy.

Mallory and Davis moved to head off these efforts by having Rep. Ethelbert Barksdale, a supporter of Mallory and his department, introduce a resolution calling for an investigation of the navy department by a joint congressional committee. This resolution was approved on August 27, 1862. With the establishment of the investigating committee, it was clear that Conrad's and Foote's proposals could not be considered until after the investigating committee had completed its work. If the findings of the committee were favorable, the proposals to abolish Mallory's department and the no-confidence motion were both doomed.

Mallory was confident that the committee would eventually exonerate him. His confidence was borne out by the selection of the committee members, including both political friends and foes, which in turn attested to the committee's reliability since it was stacked neither in his favor nor against him. The committee delivered its report on March 24, 1863, vacating the charges that had been levied against both the secretary and his department.

It was during this period that Mallory dispatched his chief rival, Maury, to Europe. The Torpedo Bureau, which had been headed by Maury, was then split between the War and Navy Departments. The War Department's half retained the Torpedo Bureau name and concentrated on the use of torpedoes as land mines to obstruct the advance of Union troops, along with explosive devices for acts of sabotage behind Union lines. The portion retained by the Department of the Navy was christened the Submarine Battery Service and specialized in the development and placement of torpedoes as naval mines as well as the development of submarines and torpedo launches as delivery systems for the explosives. These represented attempts to make torpedoes mobile rather than stationary weapons.

Thus, at the same time that Mallory was endeavoring to adjust his strategy to meet the threat poised by the Union's innovative amphibious operations and tactics, he was forced to divert his attention by the necessity of putting together the records and witnesses to combat his enemies' insinuations and accusations before the joint investigating committee. Even though he was pulled into two diametrically opposing directions, Mallory managed to do both.

The genesis of Mallory's change in strategy had occurred in the late fall of 1861 when Robert E. Lee was named to head a new military department that encompassed South Carolina, Georgia, and the east coast of Florida. Davis created the department following Silas H. Stringham's and Benjamin F. Butler's amphibious assault on Hatteras Inlet on August 29, 1861. Lee was named commander of the new department on November 5, 1861, just as Flag Off. Samuel F. Du Pont's ships were approaching Port Royal Sound.

It is not known if Mallory conferred with Lee before the general left for his new headquarters in Charleston. There must have been some kind of communication between them either then or after Lee returned to Richmond, because Mallory soon put into effect a new combined army-navy coastal defense system that was first devised by Lee in his coastal department. Lee immediately realized the danger to the Confederacy posed by the Union's new amphibious operations and tactics, and the solutions he worked out became the blueprint for defending the entire length of the Confederacy's coastline—from the Virginia capes, around the Florida Peninsula, and to the mouth of the Rio Grande—from future Federal amphibious operations.

Upon his arrival at Charleston, Lee evacuated all but the most essential existing coastal fortifications, which in this department were the major port cities of Charleston and Savannah. He then pulled his troops and artillery inland, to a defensive line that was beyond the range of the superior heavy guns mounted on Union warships.

Once these steps had been accomplished, Lee decided to find ways to prevent Federal ships and troops from using the waterways leading inland from the coast. So he ordered the obstruction of all such waterway entries within his department. Mallory later ensured that this practice was repeated throughout North Carolina, Virginia, Alabama, Mississippi, Louisiana, and Texas. This prevented penetration by shallow-draft Union warships, the most effective of which were the double-ender gunboats that could change direction on narrow rivers simply by reversing their engines and engaging a rudder at the opposite end of the ship. These obstructions originally consisted of blocking the channels with sunken hulks or block ships and later the placement of stationary torpedoes along the most likely lines of approach. In addition, Lee ordered the construction of new fortifications along the Stono, Edisto, and Combehee Rivers. These new fortifications were to be armed with the heaviest available cannon. If the cannon he needed weren't available, Lee arranged to find them. These new fortifications were built well inland from the mouths of the three rivers, staying out of reach of the Union navy's heaviest guns, which of course were mounted generally on their heaviest warships and therefore were the least likely to be used in riverine operations.

Lee did not stop there, however. He ordered additional fortifications to be built in front of Hilton Head Island to bottle up the Union forces at Port Royal Sound. At the same time earthen forts were erected along the Broad and Salcatchie Rivers to protect Savannah by land. Lee also ensured that the railroad through Pocotaligo and Coosawhatchie, which linked the cities of Charleston and Savannah, was equally protected.

These measures—combined with additional steps taken by Mallory—so completely stalemated the Union's command of the sea and so inhibited its amphibious operations that it would prove practically impossible for direct amphibious assaults to compromise the new coastal defense system. The system did have one major weakness, however: It could stand defiant only as long as the landward fronts behind the coastal defenses stood firm. If those land approaches collapsed, it would allow for the coastal defenses to be attacked from the rear.

The Union planners were forced to unintentionally adopt the strategy that Alexander the Great had used against the Persian navy twenty-two hundred years earlier. In that ancient time, Alexander led his army against the Persian bases from behind and eventually denied his enemy's fleet access to them, thus eliminating the Persian ships as a threat to his forces.

Lee had barely begun to carry out his program when he was summoned back to Richmond after a command crisis forced the resignation of Judah P. Benjamin as secretary of war a few months later. When the uproar subsided, Lee had been named the president's senior military adviser, thus squashing demands that Davis either name a serving general as secretary of war or to name a general in chief. Although Lee now had a title, he had no real duties and thus his abilities were squandered.

After the April 1862 battle of Shiloh, P. G. T. Beauregard succeeded the fallen Albert Sidney Johnston in command of the Army of Tennessee. In June 1862 Beauregard was relieved and replaced by Gen. Braxton Bragg. In October, Davis transferred Lt. Gen. John C. Pemberton from command of Lee's former Atlantic coastal department to Vicksburg and named Beauregard as Pemberton's successor.

Beauregard's transfer was a highly popular move. The Creole had been in command of the batteries at Charleston that had forced the surrender of the Union garrison at Fort Sumter in 1861, which had started the war. Beauregard—with Mallory's assistance—built upon and expanded the coastal defense system devised by Lee. Mallory's naval commanders at Savannah and Charleston—Com. Josiah Tattnall at the former and Com. Duncan N. Ingraham, followed by Com. John Randolph Tucker, at the latter—had no problem working with the general. After the destruction of the *Arkansas,* Com. William F. Lynch was transferred to command Confederate naval forces in North Carolina. He would also work with Beauregard when the general took over the Department of Cape Fear and North Carolina.

Even though Lee, during his short tenure, had solved one set of problems, there remained others, such as the defense of the vital ports of Wilmington, Charleston, Savannah, Mobile, and even the Confederate capital at Richmond. It was in these areas that Mallory expanded on the foundation that Lee had established. Mallory knew that each of these cities represented a gateway to the interior of the Confederacy and that each one opened toward the sea, where the Union navy had proven its mastery in amphibious operations in 1861 and 1862 that climaxed with the fall of New Orleans.

Withdrawing from these cities was out of the question. To keep them open as lifelines to the rest of the world was a question of life and death for the Confederacy. Even if these ports could be adequately defended by land, they remained extremely vulnerable by sea. Since the primary threat was from the sea, as represented by the Union navy, Mallory reasoned that the primary responsibility of defending against that threat lay with the Confederate navy. Once Mallory reached that conclusion, he chipped away at the problem until he had formulated either new policies or adapted old ones to meet the changed situation.

The coastal defense strategy itself, as it was designed and perfected, was based upon recent naval events—both successes and failures. Perhaps the most influential event informing the secretary's thinking was the loss of New Orleans. The defense of the Crescent City had been disjointed and doomed because of a chaotic command structure. New Orleans, however, was not alone in this; each port city had a divided command—a commander of fixed land-based defenses and a commander of naval forces. Mallory's reformulated strategy required the complete and close cooperation of the Confederacy's land and naval forces. Under this scheme, a commanding general needed to obtain the cooperation of naval commanders and unify all his military resources under a single command. Unfortunately this kind of teamwork was achieved only with Beauregard, and the supply of Beauregards was very limited. Since Beauregard could be at only one place at a time, the most coordinated segment of the coastal defense system was at Charleston, which was where Beauregard had his headquarters. Mallory, however, could not lay all of the blame on the commanders in the field, because he never learned not to second-guess these men on the scene.

A cornerstone of the secretary's modified coastal defense scheme was a revised ironclad policy. Mallory was forced to admit that none of the Confederate-built ironclads had succeeded in breaking the Union blockade. Still the *Virginia,* by ruining the foundation upon which McClellan had based his Peninsula campaign, and the *Arkansas,* by single-handedly defying two Federal fleets and saving Vicksburg, had scored important and significant victories. Although the early success of the *Virginia* had given Mallory the illusion that he possessed the "ultimate weapon" in the naval war, the secretary's common sense soon made him aware of the hard facts. Although Mallory still held to the conviction that the blockade could be broken, he realized that the primary goal of the Confederate navy had come to be the defense of the coastline from Union amphibious assaults. Nevertheless, the navy still had the goal of breaking the blockade. Mallory decided that this could only be accomplished by a squadron of foreign-built seagoing ironclads that would break the blockade from the outside.

The early formulation of this part of Mallory's new strategic ironclad policy resulted in James D. Bulloch's being summoned back from Britain, where he had succeeded in contracting the construction of the cruisers *Alabama* and *Florida* in British ship-yards. Bulloch returned to Britain with an expanded mandate; he was also now the Confederate navy's chief European procurement officer. He soon arranged to have ironclad rams and additional cruisers and blockade-runners built for the Confederacy in both Britain and France. Mallory built upon Bulloch's work by sending Com. Samuel Barron and a staff to Europe to establish the command structure for this squadron of seagoing ironclads.

The secretary also realized that the loss of New Orleans had been a very close call. If the massive ironclad *Mississippi* had been completed in time, he believed that she could have emulated the successes of the *Virginia* and the *Arkansas* and would have turned back Farragut's assault.

Since the Confederate-built ironclads proved their worth by making a major contribution in checking the Union onslaughts at Hampton Roads and on the Mississippi River, Mallory decided that every important Confederate seaport must include in its defenses a squadron of Confederate-built ironclads. If they were not able to break the blockade by themselves, and Mallory never fully gave up hope that they might, they nevertheless remained a major component of Mallory's revised coastal defense scheme. The ironclads could still operate in coastal waters as mobile forts. Their presence in harbors, rivers, and roadsteads could still check the Union navy, which had already proven itself capable of simply steaming past immovable shore fortifications.

Together these elements show that Mallory's revised ironclad policy was based on twin goals. On the one hand, the ironclads built in the South had to counter the Union navy's amphibious

operations that threatened to open the Confederacy up to invasion from the sea. On the other hand, Bulloch's foreign-built
ironclads formed a second and complementary arm, and their
mission was to assail and smash the blockade from the sea.

For the homegrown ironclads there was yet another problem
that had to be addressed. If the Confederacy was to succeed in
building its coastal ironclads—which under Mallory's strategy
were intended to act as "fleets in being" to detour Union
amphibious operations aimed at the South's remaining port cities
and/or to combat successfully those operations that were
attempted—the building sites themselves had to be protected
while the ironclads were under construction.

Most of Mallory's "moveable forts," therefore, could not be
built in the few existing shipyards still within the South, as all of
them were exposed to Union attack. Of the first six Confederate-
built ironclads, one, the *Eastport,* was scuttled and later raised by
the Northerners and added to the Union Mississippi River Flotilla
and three were destroyed by the Confederates themselves to keep
them from falling into Federal hands when their shipyards either
fell or had seemed about to fall to amphibious or riverine operations. To be safe from these operations, the shipyards and other
naval plants would have to be moved inland since these Union
operations had turned all of the coastal zones into major or potential theaters of war.

Therefore, with Davis's full approval, Mallory set about relo-
cating these vital shipyards and naval plants in the interior. New
shipyards were established either in the deepest roadsteads or along
rivers as far as possible from their mouths to limit or eliminate
access by the Union navy. As a result, the ironclads *Albemarle* and
Neuse—which would challenge the North's control of the vital
North Carolina sounds that had seemingly been subdued at
Hatteras Inlet and Roanoke Island in 1861 and 1862—would be
built in former cornfields. Mallory also ordered the evacuation of
the Pensacola Navy Yard, which had become useless to the Confederate navy because of the blockade and because Fort Pickens in
the harbor remained in Union hands. These actions were not without a price, namely, the distances between the new production
centers and the places that the new ships were supposed to protect.

The next facet of Mallory's coastal defense strategy called for the placement of shore-based large-caliber rifled guns operated by trained gun crews. This also gave Mallory additional postings for his surplus naval officers.

The genesis of this idea had occurred during the May 1862 battle of Drewry's Bluff, which occurred shortly after the evacuation of Norfolk and the scuttling of *Virginia*. With the Confederate ironclad out of the way, and with her replacement, *Richmond*, still incomplete, a Union naval expedition, acting under the direct orders of Lincoln himself, was mounted against Richmond. Consisting of the ironclads *Monitor, Naugatuk,* and *Galena* and the gunboats *Aroostook* and *Port Royal,* the flotilla under John Rodgers advanced up the James River. With the James River under the control of the Union navy, the Confederate capital could be attacked from Fort Monroe, or the threat of bombardment from the river could force the evacuation of the city.

Drewry's Bluff is seven miles south of Richmond, on the right bank of the James River. The versatile Lt. John Mercer Brooke took it upon himself to rush eight Brooke rifles and a Columbiad to the heights. The hurriedly built gun emplacements were quickly christened Fort Darling, and the guns were manned in part by former crew members of the *Virginia*. In a deeply symbolic gesture, the *Virginia*'s flag—which had been saved by one of her crew when the ship was scuttled—flew over the position.

As the Union flotilla approached on May 15, 1862, the ironclads *Monitor* and *Naugatuck* had problems elevating their guns to reach the Confederate gun emplacements on the heights of Drewry's Bluff. They were forced to move farther away from the bluff, which adversely affected the accuracy of their gunfire. *Naugatuck* withdrew entirely from the action when her single gun, an 8-inch rifled gun, burst. *Galena,* however, did not have these problems and was anchored in the middle of the river and opened fire. This placed her directly under the guns on Drewry's Bluff. As a result, the inadequacies of her experimental armor system soon became apparent. She was hit twenty-eight times; eighteen penetrated her armor, one of which passed through the ship from one side to the other. Rodgers realized he could not move beyond the makeshift fort and eventually retreated to prevent the critically injured *Galena* from being sunk.

This was the first time Confederate coastal or riverine defenses had turned back a Union amphibious assault. Many on the scene immediately recognized, however, that if the Union flotilla had been accompanied by a few thousand troops (who could have taken the Confederate defenses from the landward side or rear of the position), the expedition might well have initiated the fall of Richmond. Once Mallory's revised coastal defense strategy was in place—in those instances when the Confederate army and navy worked cooperatively—practically all Federal amphibious operations, with one exception, attempted during the later half of the war were stopped dead in their tracks.

Mallory realized that there was nothing inherently wrong with the construction of the original Confederate fortifications, even though Fort Pulaski demonstrated that masonry forts had been overtaken by the technology of rifled guns. Rather, these forts were lost primarily because their weaponry was inadequate. Most of them had been armed with whatever cannon happened to be at hand when they were originally constructed and/or garrisoned, such as old small-caliber smoothbores and other obsolete guns. Practically all of these cannon had been of comparatively short range with only a modest throw weight and weak power of penetration. These factors, among others, including modified tactics that allowed attacking ships to move constantly, kept the forts from competing with the powerful ordnance carried aboard Union warships.

Mallory interpreted the action at Drewry's Bluff as a clear demonstration that the solution to this problem lay with the Brooke rifle. At his direction the Department of the Navy contacted the War Department's Ordnance Bureau and offered to provide Brooke rifles and trained gun crews in numbers sufficient to rearm all of the coastal fortifications and any fortifications that might be built in the future.

In addition, Brooke was at work refining the design of the heavy guns. Earlier 6.4-inch rifles were strengthened by double banding at the breech. The 7-inch rifle (Brooke's original invention) received double and triple banding. Brooke also turned out smoothbore cannon and Columbiads of 10- and 11-inch calibers that would produce ship-smashing firepower at shorter ranges.

Such guns were being manufactured by the Tredegar Iron Works in Richmond and the new naval cannon foundry at Selma, Alabama. The Selma plant was placed under the command of Cmdr. Catesby ap Roger Jones, formerly the executive officer of the CSS *Virginia*.

These production successes allowed the Confederate navy to provide its ironclads and other vessels and the coastal defenses with both heavy guns and Brooke's newly developed armor-piercing shells. Together these would deny the Union navy the easy successes it had enjoyed at Hatteras Inlet, Port Royal Sound, New Orleans, Forts Henry and Donelson, Island No. 10, and other locations.

The coastal defense system devised by Lee and Mallory proved itself on April 7, 1863, almost a full year after the fall of New Orleans. In an all-day battle, a Union ironclad flotilla under the command of Rear Adm. Samuel F. Du Pont, who had led the attack at Port Royal Sound, failed to similarly reduce the harbor defenses at Charleston. The objective—if the harbor defenses had been reduced—was to force the surrender of the city in the same way New Orleans had fallen. One of the attacking Union iron-clads was sunk (to add insult to injury its 11-inch Dahlgrens were salvaged and added to the Charleston Harbor defenses), and all of the other ironclads were damaged to varying degrees. Du Pont had not believed that the ironclads would force the surrender of Charleston by themselves. Although this failure proved his point, Welles, who had faith in the monitors and their inventor, would never forgive Du Pont. This failure marked the end of Du Pont's career, and he was soon replaced by ordnance expert and designer Rear Adm. John A. Dahlgren.

AT LEAST one other officer shared Du Pont's lack of faith in the monitors and their inventor. Capt. Percival Drayton was of the Charleston aristocracy, but he had remained loyal to the Union. In 1862 he was named captain of the monitor *Passaic,* the name ship of the class of monitors that succeeded the original *Monitor.* "I think that if Ericsson could only be persuaded to take a short cruise in one of his inventions, he would learn a great deal more of them then he ever will theorizing about them in his room," Drayton said.

Drayton soon formed the opinion that all of the optimistic expectations for Ericsson's creations—that they would demolish Confederate ironclads, forts, cities, etc.—were simply not going to happen. *Passaic* nearly sank on her first sea voyage as she moved to protect the new Union base at Port Royal Sound, South Carolina. Engine failure caused her to head for the Washington Navy Yard and an overhaul. Winter storms then forced her, leaking badly, into one of the newly seized North Carolina coastal enclaves for further repairs. At about the same time, Ericsson's original *Monitor* sank during a fierce gale off Hatteras Island on December 30–31, 1862.

Drayton blamed some of the problems aboard *Passaic* on the unseaworthiness of her design and to the poor workmanship of her construction. "I don't think we shall ever get things right until a contractor or two is severely punished as a reminder to his confreres that the country as well as the individual has rights and is entitled to a little consideration," Drayton said in a letter to a friend.

During Du Pont's battle in Charleston Harbor, the slow-firing Union fleet only managed to fire 139 rounds. Fifty of these struck or grazed Fort Sumter. The harbor batteries, however, fired 2,206 shots, 439 of which registered as hits on the various Union ironclads, mostly monitors, that participated in the assault. Ninety of these hits, including 19 below the waterline, were scored on the *Keokuk*. Hits on the *Passaic, Nahant,* and *Weehawken* jammed their turrets. Other shots smashed guns on the *Nantucket, Passaic,* and *Patapsco.* All the monitors were forced back to Port Royal for repairs. The only Union ironclads that remained at Charleston were the *Keokuk,* which subsequently sank, and the broadside ironclad, or armored frigate, *New Ironsides.*

Drayton believed that the best use of the ironclads would be to protect depots and the various coastal enclaves held by the army. He suggested that Port Royal Sound could not be held for a day without the ironclads, and without Port Royal Sound the entire blockade would unravel.

Later Drayton served as Farragut's flag captain when the admiral led his fleet into Mobile Bay. While Drayton shared Du Pont's view that ironclads, particularly monitors, were not a naval panacea, he also realized that, if properly employed, their presence could be decisive, as they proved to be at Mobile Bay in August 1864.

IN ADDITION to the heavy-caliber rifled guns, Mallory also encouraged the development of fixed torpedoes. The Confederate navy had started with a primitive system of fixed obstructions. To this the engineers of the Torpedo Bureau and later the Submarine Battery Service added explosive barges and finally devices with which to attach explosive charges directly against the hulls of Union warships. Electronic detonators were developed, perfected, and deployed so that torpedoes could be exploded from shore. Their most spectacular success occurred during the battle of Mobile Bay, when the ironclad *Tecumseh* sank when it apparently struck a torpedo.

One area of Mallory's original strategy that was not fundamentally changed, but rather strengthened, was the commerce-destroying campaign aimed at the North's maritime commerce. The cruises of the *Sumter* and the *Nashville* demonstrated the strategic viability of commerce destroying. By late August 1862 *Alabama* was at sea. Eventually she was joined by *Florida, Georgia, Rappahannock, Chickamauga,* and *Tallahassee/Olustee.*

Mallory resolved to further strengthen his efforts in this area by bringing what remained of the privateers fully under the control of the Navy Department. He accomplished this by establishing the volunteer navy.

Anyone who had already armed—or planned to arm—a "private" vessel and engaged in commerce raiding would be required to join the volunteer navy. Officers and petty officers of such ships would be given a "provisional" rank for the duration of the war. The officers and crew of such ships would wear naval uniforms, be paid by the government, and serve under all naval regulations.

At the request of Davis, the volunteer navy was created by an act of the Confederate Congress on April 18, 1862, by which time privateering had mostly ceased to exist. The volunteer navy remained apart from the regular navy but under the jurisdiction of the Department of the Navy.

In combination with the Submarine Battery Service, the volunteer navy also helped to provide the impetus for two new developments in naval warfare: the torpedo launch and the submarine.

The final facet of Mallory's revised coastal defense strategy lay in the opportunities offered by these two novel naval weapons. The torpedo launch offered a chance to resurrect Matthew Fontaine Maury's discredited Mosquito Fleet concept. Torpedo launches (instead of small gunboats) were ideally suited to the original concept in that it was obvious they would be most effective if they could be used in large numbers to overwhelm the Union blockaders. Unfortunately the adoption of torpedo launches and submarines as part of the coastal defense strategy proved to be too little too late since in the latter half of the war the Confederacy's already strained industrial infrastructure could not produce them in the numbers that would have been truly effective.

Torpedo launches were low-lying, almost submerged boats designed to be a mobile delivery system for torpedoes. The first torpedo launch was the CSS *Torch,* which was built at Charleston as a joint army-navy project. She was entrusted to an officer in the volunteer navy, Capt. James Carlin, a former blockade-runner, and a hastily recruited crew. The boat was dispatched to sink the *New Ironsides,* one of the most powerful Union ironclads used against Charleston. The *Torch* failed to accomplish her mission, but another torpedo launch, CSS *David,* succeeded. On October 5, 1863, the *David* drove her spar torpedo into the side of the *New Ironsides.* The big Union ironclad was so badly damaged that she was under repairs and out of the war for almost a year.

Mallory was so impressed with the performance of the *David* that he officially revived the Mosquito Fleet concept for the torpedo launches. He even turned to Bulloch's naval procurement operation in Europe to acquire more launches. The secretary reasoned that since the vessels were so small and unarmed—except for their spar torpedoes that could be added after the launches had been delivered—there would be no neutrality hurdles to overcome. Bulloch did the best he could, but he was simply overextended. If a cooperative effort could have been sustained between the many naval procurement agents then in Europe, something might have been done. As it was, Bulloch was a one-man band, incapable of coordinating such an effort. Besides obtaining ironclads, cruisers, and blockade-runners, he was now being asked to acquire torpedo launches. Although some progress was made in contracting them, not many European-built launches actually got through the blockade.

Confederate experiments with submarines, however, began in the summer of 1861 when the Tredegar Iron Works in Richmond contracted to build two such craft. One was a small, three-man iron boat designed by William Cheeney. It was intended to be operated by two of the men; the third man wore diving gear and was stationed in the bow in a special lookout chamber. When a target vessel came within range, the diver was to exit the submarine and attach a torpedo to the bottom of the enemy ship. He would return to the submarine, which would withdraw to a safe distance and detonate the torpedo with either a lanyard or a timing device. An unsuccessful submarine attack on the Union steam frigate USS *Minnesota* was actually attempted. Torpedo launches and submarines were eventually built in Richmond, New Orleans, Mobile, Savannah, and Charleston.

The most successful Confederate submarine was the *H. L. Hunley*. Built in the spring of 1863 at Mobile, *Hunley* was thirty-five feet long and was constructed from an old boiler that had been cut in half. A tapered bow and stern were added, along with two hatches sealed with rubber gaskets. A false keel of cast iron provided the main ballast. The crew consisted of an officer, a petty officer, and seven sailors. They turned a handcrank that powered her propeller. In her first trial the *Hunley* successfully sank a flatboat in Mobile Bay with a towed torpedo. It was found, however, that towing a torpedo could be dangerous in rough waters, so a spar torpedo was instituted.

Hunley was then transported by rail from Mobile to Charleston, where the submarine sank several times, each time killing all or most of her crew. On the night of February 17, 1864, *Hunley* attacked the steam gunboat USS *Housatonic*. *Hunley* rammed her torpedo into the Union ship, which sank in shallow water, but *Hunley* herself was also lost. A total of thirty-one men died during sea trials and in the actual attack.

As a result of the successful attack on the *Housatonic,* all Union wooden warships blockading the harbor were ordered to remain out of the area at night. This loosened the blockade to some degree and may have had the effect of making it easier for blockade-runners to slip in and out of Charleston during the final months of the war. Other than that, the successful attack had no other apparent effect upon the war.

The last recorded Confederate submarine action of the war is reported to have occurred on January 27, 1865, when the Confederate submarine *St. Patrick*—based at the still defiant city of Mobile—attempted an attack on the Union steam gunboat USS *Octorara* in Mobile Bay. Although the submarine's spar torpedo struck the Union gunboat, the attack failed when the torpedo did not explode.

9

More Southern Ironclads

MALLORY HAD NOT GIVEN up on breaking the blockade, and during 1863 there were two further attempts by the Confederate navy to do so. The first of these occurred at Charleston, the second at Savannah. The latter was an outright disaster for the Confederate navy, while the former appeared at first to be a success but in the end changed nothing and ultimately meant nothing.

While Mallory was adjusting his naval strategy, the second generation of Confederate ironclads was being constructed. Already the CSS *Richmond* was being completed in her name city. The next of the new generation ships was to be built in Charleston. Independently of the Navy Department, the city decided to build an ironclad to protect its port from Union incursions.

Funds for the construction of this ironclad were raised through popular subscription. Everyone contributed something, even small children and slaves. Among those who encouraged this effort were the commander of the Charleston Squadron, Com. Duncan N. Ingraham, and the local press. All were inspired by the achievements of the *Virginia*. The fund-raising drive was led by the *Charleston Daily Courier,* which had established a ladies' collection to raise the necessary funds to build an ironclad.

The keel of the subscription ironclad was laid in March 1862 at the Marsh and Son shipyard with considerable fanfare. News of the events at Hampton Roads was still reverberating across the

139

South and, for that matter, around the world, when Mallory announced that the Navy Department was willing to pay for its construction. Then it was immediately decided locally to construct another warship in the shipyard owned by J. M. Eason.

Work on the additional ironclad proceeded quickly, and it was launched seventeen days after the loss of the *Arkansas* on August 23, 1862. Christened the *Chicora*, she was fitted out in record time and commissioned in September. Construction of the subscription ironclad, to be named *Palmetto State*, proceeded at a much slower rate. She was finally launched on October 11, 1862. The two ironclads were of the same class as the *Richmond*, and each was armed with two 9-inch Dahlgren smoothbores and two 7-inch Brooke rifles.

The keel of a third ironclad, which was to be named *Charleston*, was laid in December 1862, and she was completed about nine months later. She suffered from the common complaint of Confederate ironclads, "enginitis." Although this resulted in some ships becoming little more that floating batteries, the engines of the *Charleston* were just barely good enough to save her from that fate.

Spurred to action by newspaper articles that described the Charleston Squadron as a "do-nothing fleet," Gen. P. G. T. Beauregard, the Confederate commander of the Coastal Department, prevailed upon Ingraham to order a sortie by the *Chicora* and *Palmetto State*.

The mission occurred on the night of January 30–31, 1863. It became one of the most successful sorties conducted by the Confederate navy, and its repercussions—which were the only practical effect of the affair—reverberated for months to come. The two ironclads moved out of Charleston Harbor in what was a major attempt to break the Union blockade. Thousands of soldiers in the harbor forts watched silently as the two ships, their lights out and their crews at general quarters, slipped over the bar at 4:30 A.M. on January 31.

Painted a dim gray-blue, the two ironclads were not sighted by the blockading Union warships until they had already attacked. The crew of the first target—the wooden gunboat USS *Mercedita*—did not see them until it was too late. She was struck by the *Palmetto*

State's ram, which tore a hole into *Mercedita*'s side while the Confederate's bow gun fired a shell that exploded in the Union ship's engine room, bursting a boiler.

Mercedita's captain, fearing that his ship was about to sink, lowered her flag in surrender. Two steamers were filled with Southern soldiers to take possession of any prizes, but they failed to cross the bar. Ingraham was forced to parole *Mercedita*'s crew and went looking for more Union vessels to attack.

The Confederates made no effort to take possession of the *Mercedita*, leaving her adrift instead. Eventually the Union crew found themselves alone, conducted repairs, and simply left the area. Confederate authorities later expressed considerable indignation that the ship had avoided capture in this way. To settle the matter, Samuel F. Du Pont ordered a court of inquiry to investigate the complaint. The court eventually found that although the captain and crew of the *Mercedita* had undoubtedly surrendered, the ship herself had not. Du Pont ordered the crew to take *Mercedita* home for repairs, but the captain and crew were bound by their parole not to engage in any hostile action against the Confederacy until they were officially exchanged. Once repairs were completed, the *Mercedita* returned to the blockade with a different crew.

Meanwhile, *Chicora* attacked the USS *Keystone State*, a former merchant ship that had been converted into a gunboat. During the action, *Keystone State* was set afire. The Confederate ironclad was, of course, impervious to the Federal ship's four relatively small-caliber smoothbore guns. As the one-sided fight continued, the *Chicora*'s shells created even more havoc aboard the *Keystone State*, disabling her engines and causing many casualties. Although her captain considered surrender, the *Keystone State* was able to limp away from the action with about twenty of her crew dead and as many wounded.

The rest of the Union blockaders scattered, but the two ironclads were not seaworthy enough to pursue them into unprotected waters and lacked the necessary speed to catch them. The alarmed blockaders only had to stay out of the way of the two ironclads until they returned to Charleston. Beauregard accepted the result as a complete victory. On the same day as the battle, he issued a proclamation declaring that the blockading ships had been driven off and the blockade at Charleston had been lifted. Included with Beauregard's proclamation were affidavits from the British and French consuls in the city claiming that they had left Charleston Harbor in a small vessel and steamed out to sea for a distance of five miles without sighting any Union blockaders. If this claim was accepted, under international law, the Federal forces would have to go through the formality of issuing new notices of blockade before it could be reestablished. Beauregard also claimed two Union ships had been sunk and five others damaged. Du Pont simply ignored Beauregard's proclamation, and his fleet resumed normal blockading stations.

Notwithstanding the statements of the British and French consuls, examinations of the blockading ships' logbooks reveal that any claim to have broken the blockade to be false. The captain of the USS *Housatonic* noted that his ship had fired upon *Chicora* as that Confederate ironclad retired to the safety of the guns of Fort Moultrie. Later *Housatonic*'s log noted the departure of the *Chicora* and *Palmetto State* back over the bar and into Charleston Harbor.

Once again Gideon Welles, as at the battle of Head of the Passes, was outraged by the Confederate sortie and ordered Du Pont to attack Charleston with all the ironclads he could gather. These orders became a major factor in the next Confederate attempt to break the blockade.

The genesis of this next effort to break the blockade dates back to the early summer of 1861 when the man who eventually became Mallory's chief naval procurement agent in Europe was introduced to a newly arrived purchasing agent for the Confederate army. Maj. Edward C. Anderson had been sent to Great Britain to investigate the activities of Maj. Caleb Huse, who was accused of a number of improprieties in the collection of military stores for the Confederate army. It did not take Anderson long to deduce that Huse was an honest patriot doing his best to accomplish a difficult mission. While waiting for an opportunity to return to the South, Anderson joined in Huse's procurement work. After being introduced to James D. Bulloch, Huse's naval counterpart, Anderson entertained Bulloch's suggestion that the army and navy share the cost of buying a fast steamer to be loaded with their joint war supplies and upon which they could make the trip back to the Confederacy.

Bulloch's chief contact in Liverpool was Charles K. Prioleau, an agent of Fraser, Trenholm, and Company, the Liverpool branch of the Charleston-based firm of John Fraser and Company. Through him, Bulloch and Anderson purchased the fast merchant steamer *Fingal*.

Bulloch, Huse, and Anderson's activities, however, had not escaped the notice of Thomas H. Dudley, the U.S. consul in Liverpool. With the cooperation of the U.S. minister to Great Britain, Charles Francis Adams, and his assistant, Benjamin Moran, Dudley put together a "wanted poster" that was given to the captains of all Union warships then in European waters. The poster included a woodcut picture of the *Fingal* and a detailed description of the ship and her cargo.

The cargo was truly impressive. It consisted of fourteen thousand British-made Enfield rifle-muskets for army use, another one thousand Enfield carbines with bayonets for naval use, several cannon (including two 2.5-inch and two 4.5-inch naval rifles with gun carriages and eight hundred projectiles), two million percussion caps, one million cartridges, five hundred revolvers with ammunition, a large number of swords, four hundred barrels of gunpowder, army and navy uniforms, and considerable medical supplies.

Bulloch had inadvertently given the Union cruisers looking for *Fingal* the slip when he failed to head, as expected, directly to a Confederate port. After departing from Greenock, Scotland, on October 10, 1861, the *Fingal* put in at Holyhead, where Bulloch and Anderson joined the ship. Upon boarding, Bulloch took command of the ship and steered his course for the Azores, spending considerable time exploring various islands, ostensibly looking for fresh water. He soon found what he was looking for at Terceira Island, a safe haven where he could eventually arm one or both of the cruisers (*Florida* and *Alabama*) that were then under construction in British shipyards.

From the Azores, Bulloch sailed to Nassau, the heart of the British-owned Bahamas. Nassau would soon begin a wartime boom as the port became the transfer point for cargoes to and from the Confederacy, Britain, and France. A great many of these ships would also be built in British shipyards. While *Fingal* was at Nassau, Bulloch picked up a pilot from Savannah who happened to have been dropped off by the CSS *Nashville*. From there Bulloch headed for Savannah, and since the blockade was not yet particularly effective, he had little trouble in reaching it. The ship was moored in the estuary of the Savannah River on November 12, 1861.

Upon his arrival, Bulloch headed to Richmond for a meeting with Mallory. When he returned to Savannah, his overseas mission had been enlarged to contract the construction of ironclads and blockade-runners as well as commerce raiders. Bulloch originally planned to return to Britain aboard the *Fingal,* but the ship was closely blockaded. He was forced to leave the *Fingal* behind and take passage on a blockade-runner operating out of Wilmington.

As the *Fingal* was trapped in Savannah, it was decided to use her hull and machinery for a new ironclad. The ship was purchased by the Confederate navy in January 1862, and the conversion project was contracted out to the Tift brothers, who had built the *Mississippi* at New Orleans. She was cut down to the waterline, and an armored deck was built that extended six feet beyond the original hull. The timber on the deck was three feet thick. Over this was built a slab-sided armored casemate covered with iron plates made by rolling out railroad iron. This armor was backed by strong bulkheads built of oak and pine.

Obtaining the iron for her armor had not been easy. President Davis was petitioned by forty-seven prominent citizens of Savannah who asked that the rails seized by the navy from the warehouses of the Georgia and Gulf Railroad be used to armor the ship. Davis turned the petition over to Mallory, who found that the armor of the vessel—now named *Atlanta*—required about six hundred tons of iron. The new ironclad was rather large, measuring 204 feet long and displacing 1,009 tons. She was armed with four Brooke rifles that had been cast in Richmond. Placed on her broadsides were two 6.4-inch rifles, and two 7-inch rifles were placed on pivots fore and aft. The *Atlanta* was also equipped with a spar torpedo on her bow. Her biggest shortcoming, however, was her seventeen-foot draft when fully loaded.

Confederate navy chief engineer James H. Warner was summoned from Richmond to oversee the work on her engines. Due primarily to a shortage of railroad iron for her armor, the conversion was not completed until August 1862, when she was formally christened and underwent her engine trial. Fitting out took another four months, and her commissioning occurred almost simultaneously with the completion of Mallory's revisions to his naval strategy. Although the ship appeared to be formidable to the untrained eye, the crew accommodations and living conditions aboard were poor because of leaks at the juncture between the new deck and the old hull and her shabby interior finishings.

By this time Josiah Tattnall was back in command of the naval squadron at Savannah, which in addition to the *Atlanta* included the ironclad *Georgia* that had been launched in October 1862. The latter was 250 feet long and carried ten guns. The ship was plagued with weak engines, which in *Georgia*'s case were so poor that the ship could not breast the current. Like the *Louisiana* at New Orleans, she was used as a floating battery. The *Georgia* was moored opposite Fort McAllister, downriver from Savannah. By crossing her fire with that of the fort, the ironclad provided the main obstacle to any Union attempt to attack Savannah simply by steaming up the river.

Upon completion of the *Atlanta,* it was decided that she would sortie as soon as possible in an attempt to break through the blockade at Savannah. *Atlanta*'s first attempt came on January 5, 1863, when Tattnall moved the ship downriver. The Confederate army corps of engineers, however, failed to open a passage through the river obstructions in time, and Tattnall was forced to turn back. He made a second attempt on March 19. His target was the Union naval base at Port Royal Sound. Knowing that the base was protected solely by wooden gunboats, Tattnall hoped that *Atlanta* could sweep through them like a hawk among a flock of chickens. The mission was canceled when two deserters warned the enemy. A third attempt on March 30 ended when *Atlanta* ran aground.

These tentative and abortive movements by the *Atlanta* began to worry Samuel F. Du Pont, who, as Tattnall well knew, had withdrawn his ironclads from Savannah as part of the preparations for the full-scale attack against Charleston.

Beauregard had quickly noted that all of the available ironclads in the Union South Atlantic Blockading Squadron were being concentrated off Charleston. Writing to Mallory, he pointed out that the gathering of ironclads left the Union blockaders between Savannah and Port Royal without any ironclad support at all. Upon receipt of this missive, Mallory immediately jumped at the "opportunity."

"Can you not strike the enemy a blow . . . while his ironclads are off Charleston?" Mallory telegraphed Flag Off. Richard L. Page, who had assumed command of the Savannah Squadron after Mallory, through the Office of Orders and Detail, had limited Tattnall just to simply command the naval station. Mallory again had second-guessed one of his commanders. As in the case of George N. Hollins—when Mallory became dissatisfied with Tattnall's aborted sorties—the secretary had replaced him with someone he believed would be a more active squadron commander. Mallory may have taken this action because of Tattnall's age. A native of Georgia, the sixty-eight-year-old Tattnall had been born near Savannah in 1795.

Tattnall, a former commander of the *Virginia* and something of an ironclad expert, informed Mallory that he feared *Atlanta* might not be able to face down Monitor-type ironclads, particularly in close action in shallow waters. Tattnall was concerned about the *Atlanta*'s seventeen-foot draft, because not only did her deep draft make steaming difficult in shallow coastal waters, it also adversely affected her steering. This message may have led Mallory to infer that the aging Tattnall was losing his nerve.

Then *Atlanta* developed trouble with her bow gun. This was particularly critical since the bow gun was considered to be the most important weapon for an ironclad in battle. A substitute was dispatched from Richmond, but the new gun would not arrive and could not be mounted until May, further delaying any possible missions against the blockade.

Meanwhile, Mallory was not happy with what he considered to be procrastination among the officers in command of the Savannah Squadron, and he made further changes in the command structure. After command of the squadron had been placed in the hands of Page as flag officer, Page's perceived inaction caused Mallory to name Cmdr. William H. Webb to command the *Atlanta* with discretionary authority to attack the enemy. At the March 1862 battle of Hampton Roads, Webb had commanded the gunboat *Teaser* and had shown himself to be a confident and daring naval officer.

The order was given on May 28, 1863, to open the obstructions to allow *Atlanta* to venture out against the Federal fleet. Webb began his sortie on May 30, 1863, confident of success. There were reasons for his confidence. *Atlanta* could make seven knots in good weather, which was good speed for an ironclad. Although she had her flaws, she was at that time probably the best warship in the South.

Aside from *Atlanta,* Webb took with him the gunboats *Isondiga, Oconee,* and *Resolute.* Because the Union seizure of Fort Pulaski had closed the front door to Savannah through the Savannah River estuary, the *Atlanta* was forced to use the back door through Wassaw Sound. To enter the sound, the Confederate ironclad had to pass through a tangle of canals that linked the Savannah and Ogeechee Rivers. Then the ship had to maneuver through the narrow and winding St. Augustine Creek to finally reach open water at Wassaw Sound. The trek took several days of toiling along shallow waters and narrow, winding canals to reach the sound, and valuable time was lost every time *Atlanta* grounded. In one grounding a boiler's valve broke and had to be replaced, causing several days' delay while a replacement part was fetched from Savannah and the necessary repairs were made. During this time, an unfortunate event and an unfortunate decision helped to doom both the sortie and the ship.

On June 12 five Confederate deserters drifted down the Savannah River and surrendered themselves at Fort Pulaski. They informed Federal officials that the *Atlanta* was coming. At that moment the Union navy had nothing in the area that could counter the threat as all of the ironclads were concentrated against Charleston.

Once Du Pont realized the danger represented by *Atlanta*'s mission, he decided to send two monitor-type ironclads, *Weehawken* and *Nahant,* to shadow the *Atlanta* and to intimidate the

Confederate navy at Savannah. Capt. John Rodgers, one of the best and most experienced ironclad officers in the Union navy, was placed in command of the two ships.

As events played out, Webb was too confident and too daring. Even though Federal ironclads had been dispatched to Savannah, Webb decided that he had to attack them. Many doubted his wisdom, and Mallory also wondered about his choice of commander. He telegraphed Webb, advising him to delay any action until the *Atlanta* could be joined by another ironclad then under construction at Savannah, CSS *Savannah II*.

Savannah was nearing completion when Webb began his foray against the Federal fleet. If he had waited another month for it to be completed, the odds would have been even and the two ironclads could have supported each other in case either should run aground. *Savannah* was armed, like the *Atlanta*, with four Brooke rifles, including two 7-inch and two 6.4-inch guns.

Webb rejected Mallory's urgent advice, demonstrating that he did not understand the strategic situation. He wanted to break the blockade between Savannah and Charleston, and he was willing to overlook his ship's defects, believing that the first step in accomplishing this goal was ridding the area of the two Union ironclads.

The *Atlanta* reached Wassaw Sound at the crack of dawn on June 16, 1863. Upon steaming into the sound, Webb immediately offered battle to Rodgers and the two Federal ironclads. As the Union vessels simultaneously closed, Webb targeted the *Weehawken*. Suddenly the *Atlanta* grounded and heeled over, making it impossible for her crew to bring any of her guns to bear on the enemy. Rodgers took immediate advantage of the situation. With *Weehawken* in the lead and the *Nahant* not far behind, he closed to within three hundred yards of the stranded Confederate ironclad. The two Union ships quickly positioned themselves to rake the *Atlanta* and opened fire.

Webb and his crew attempted to make a fight of it, but it was impossible. The battle—if such an uneven contest can be called a battle—lasted only a few minutes. *Atlanta* managed to fire a total of seven shots, none of which hit anything. Meanwhile, Yankee 11- and 15-inch Dahlgren smoothbores pounded the inert and immobile opponent.

The concussion from the first hit aboard the *Atlanta* threw down all of the Southern sailors. Bolts and splinters knocked loose from the blast wounded many. Much of the ship's interior oaken bulwarks were wrecked by the pounding. Another hit tore off the ship's pilothouse, mortally wounding two helmsmen. Quickly Webb realized there was nothing to be done and surrendered his ship.

News of the surrender of the *Atlanta* stunned the South. Among those who expressed astonishment was Franklin Buchanan in a confidential letter. By the time of the *Atlanta*'s sortie, he had assumed command of the naval defenses of Mobile Bay from Flag Off. Victor Randolph. Buchanan could not understand how Webb had managed to get himself into such a situation, because he had known him to be a competent and daring officer. Although he may not have realized it, Buchanan had pinpointed the problem. Webb's foremost virtue as a naval officer was also his greatest flaw: his daring was not complemented with good sense. For years Webb's performance at the battle of Wassaw Sound was criticized by fellow naval officers.

In Richmond all criticism, once again, was directed at Mallory. Perhaps in this instance, the criticism was warranted, for the secretary had once again failed in his judgment of a subordinate. For years Mallory had struggled to replace those whom he considered to be aged and worn-out officers with those whom he considered to be younger and more aggressive. In general, Mallory's assumptions were correct, but in this case, he had failed, as he had at New Orleans. He erred in replacing the experienced, battle-hardened Tattnall with a nonentity at first and then with an overaggressive officer who rashly threw away what could have been a formidable asset. Mallory failed to realize that combativeness needed to be tempered with some degree of prudence.

Although personally stung by this renewed criticism, Mallory carried on. More ironclads were ordered. Four were to be built in North Carolina, and the *Savannah* soon replaced the lost *Atlanta*. Additional ironclads were laid down in Charleston and Mobile. The new *Richmond* was commissioned and operated on the James River, protecting the Confederate capital. She was soon joined by the *Fredericksburg, Virginia II,* and *Texas.* Together the four vessels made up the James River Squadron, another fleet that permanently slammed shut the back door to Richmond. Ironically, while there would be several naval skirmishes along the James River, this squadron never fought a major battle. When the fall of Petersburg forced the evacuation of the capital, the squadron's ships were scuttled and destroyed by the Southerners themselves.

Thus the results of this latest attempt to break the blockade confirmed the events of 1862. As more and more Confederate-built ironclads were commissioned, they sealed off the remaining Southern ports from the Union navy—along with the inland and coastal waterways. They simply were unable to break the blockade, however. Whatever real hope remained of breaking the blockade now rested with the squadron of ironclads being built in Great Britain and France.

Yet one more try to break the blockade would be made in the spring of 1864. This was a coordinated operation conducted by the Confederate army and navy. It was not aimed directly at the blockading warships themselves. Instead it targeted the network of supporting bases along the North Carolina coast that had been originally set up in 1861 and 1862. These bases provided fuel, ordnance, and other supplies to the blockading warships; they were the infrastructure of the blockade. The Southern planners finally had realized that without these bases, the blockade of the Carolina coast could be seriously disrupted or even broken.

Interestingly, when the task was conceived, the motivation was more political than military because it related to the desperate national strategy then being followed by Jefferson Davis and Robert E. Lee. In this instance, it was surmised that the existing strategic stalemate would affect the outcome of the November 8, 1864, presidential election in the North. Davis and Lee hoped that the election would become a referendum on the war. If Lincoln could be defeated, they believed the next president could be induced to accept a peace of exhaustion that would recognize the independence of the Confederate States of America.

10

Resourcefulness in Europe

J AMES D. BULLOCH, THE chief naval procurement officer in
Europe, first arrived in Liverpool, England, on June 4,
1861. A true son of the South, he had been born in June 1823
near Savannah, Georgia. His father, Maj. James Stephen Bulloch,
had been a member of the company that owned the first
steamship to cross the Atlantic, *Savannah*, traveling between her
namesake city and Liverpool. He was also connected to high society in New York City through his half sister, Martha, who married
Theodore Roosevelt Sr. and was the mother of the future president. In 1839 Bulloch entered the U.S. Navy as a midshipman
and spent twelve years in the navy, advancing only to the rank of
lieutenant. He resigned in 1851 and became a maritime mercantile businessman in New York City, the financial and trading
center of the country.

When the bombardment of Fort Sumter occurred, Bulloch was
in New Orleans as the master of the merchant steamer *Bienville*,
and found himself in the middle of the national crisis. On April 13,
1861, when news of the surrender of Sumter reached New Orleans
by telegraph, the whole city literally went mad. The townspeople—
whose state had already seceded from the Union—demanded that
Bulloch turn his ship over to Louisiana or to Confederate authorities so that she could be converted into a warship.

151

Bulloch refused. He believed he had a duty to take the ship back to its owners in New York City. As it turned out, the ultimate defender of Bulloch and his refusal to surrender his ship turned out to be Confederate President Jefferson Davis. When news of the controversy reached his desk in the temporary Confederate capital at Montgomery, Alabama, the president had sent a telegram: "Do not retain the *Bienville*. We do not want to interfere with private property." Apparently Davis hoped that if the Confederacy respected Northern property, then the North would respect Southern property. Such property of course included the slaves on Southern plantations.

Bulloch took his ship back to New York City, turned her over to her owners (who then sold her to the Union navy), and returned to the South to volunteer his services to the fledgling Confederate navy. Mallory named him a civilian naval purchasing agent and sent him to Liverpool with orders to contract the construction of cruisers suitable for commerce destroying.

The day after his arrival in Britain, Bulloch called at the offices of Fraser, Trenholm, and Company. The firm, the London branch of the Charleston-based trading firm of John Fraser and Company, was headed by George Alfred Trenholm, who eventually became the Confederate secretary of the treasury. Trenholm and his companies had almost unlimited credit in Liverpool at the start of the war, and the Confederate government made extensive use of this boon when Trenholm patriotically donated his services and those of his various business interests to the South.

Long before the arrival of Bulloch and prior to the attack on Fort Sumter, Trenholm's Liverpool-based firm had worked with John Laird, a Birkenhead shipbuilder who sought to establish the Liverpool and Charleston Steamship Company. This projected firm required a capital outlay of £150,000, half to be raised in Charleston and half in Liverpool. Laird and his sons were to build three iron steamers for the new company. The plan foundered, however, after the fall of Fort Sumter, since it had been predicated on the peaceful establishment of the Confederate States of America.

On his arrival at the offices of Fraser, Trenholm, and Company, Bulloch met for the first time with Charles K. Prioleau. He used his contacts and the firm's credit to help Bulloch to negotiate the construction of two cruisers. The first, which was eventually to become the CSS *Florida,* was laid down at the William A. Miller and Sons shipyard in Liverpool. A British dispatch vessel served as the basic model for the projected raider since the plans were readily available at the shipyard, which had built a number of such ships for the Royal Navy. Modifications included increasing her length so that more coal could be carried, which also increased her speed. In addition, some changes were made to the rigging.

Prioleau next used his connections with Laird and Sons to contract for what was originally known simply as Hull No. 290 but eventually became the CSS *Alabama.* This was the most successful of the commerce-destroying raider cruisers to be commissioned for the Confederate navy. Although there were many delays in her construction, she became a splendid example of the shipbuilder's art. She featured abnormally tall lower masts that enabled her to carry large fore and aft sails. While her scantlings were light in comparison with other vessels, her clean lines allowed her to sail and steam extremely well. She was also fitted with a lifting propeller that could be raised in fifteen minutes; this feature eliminated the drag of an idle propeller while operating under sail alone.

Bulloch's work was not unchallenged. Almost from the moment he landed he faced considerable opposition from the U.S. minister to Great Britain, Charles Francis Adams. The diplomat was the son of former president John Quincy Adams and the grandson of former president John Adams. Of equal importance in the war of words, secrecy, and diplomacy that immediately began was Thomas H. Dudley, the U.S. consul at Liverpool, and Adams's chief assistant, Benjamin Moran.

The Lincoln administration maintained that the construction of a belligerent vessel fitted out for the purposes of war was outside the permissible acts that the subjects of a neutral nation could perform. This position was later encapsulated in the 1871 Treaty of Washington, which settled the U.S. government's "*Alabama* Claims" against Great Britain. During the war, the British government rejected the Union position that this rule was part of international law, but it was generally acknowledged and frequently cited by the neutrality laws of a number of different nations.

In Britain the law that was then in force was the Foreign
Enlistment Act, which had been approved in 1819. The original
intention of the law had been to prevent British subjects from
enlisting in Latin American rebellions against what had been at
that time a British ally, Spain. Over the years two opposing inter-
pretations of the law had developed. Was it a domestic law or was
it an international law?

If it was a part of international law, then it prohibited any
assistance to a belligerent power. Those in the British government who favored this interpretation realized that a great deal
had changed during the forty-plus years since the law had been
formulated. Most of these changes had been due to better communications. A sea voyage that had taken three months in 1819
had been reduced to less than three weeks by the 1850s. Every
action undertaken—or permitted to be undertaken—by a major
power, which Britain most assuredly was in the 1860s, ran the
risk of internationalizing any conflict. Thus what had begun as a
regional conflict could be unintentionally turned into a general
international war that would ultimately include all of the world's
major powers.

This fear of a worldwide war was a constant concern of most
British politicians throughout the second half of the nineteenth
century. Their wariness became a reality in 1914, but the American Civil War carried a similar potential fifty years earlier. Many
British leaders feared that the American conflict would be
extended, dragging themselves, France, and even Russia into a
global war.

If, on the other hand, the Foreign Enlistment Act was purely a
domestic law, then it was limited to preventing British subjects from
participating in a foreign war. In such a case, it could be argued, the
law did not prohibit ships from being built for the Confederacy as
long as the ships did not have any British arms, munitions, or
seamen aboard. This was the interpretation that Bulloch followed
in contracting naval construction and later was used by him and
other naval procurement agents to buy or have built additional
cruisers, ironclads, and blockade-runners for the Confederacy.

Nonetheless, Bulloch and the other naval procurement agents
permitted violations of the letter of the law when it came to enlist-

ing British seamen to crew the various cruisers. Bulloch also took advantage of the fact that the British ruling class, the landed aristocracy, would have been very happy to see the United States collapse. In addition, economic reasons also caused many to favor the South, since the blockade was causing British shipping interests to lose money. The threat of the end of Southern cotton shipments to British textile mills caused deep resentment in England's commercial circles, although the British working class to a large extent favored the North because of a strong antislavery bias.

To cover their tracks, the procurement agents pretended that they had no links with the Confederacy. Shipbuilders, such as the Lairds, pretended to be carrying out routine business orders for private individuals or companies with no knowledge of the nature or intended function of the ships being built at their shipyards. This ruse never fooled anyone. It certainly did not fool Adams, Moran, and Dudley, and it did not fool any of the ordinary citizens in Liverpool or Birkenhead for that matter. The only people who even pretended to be so ignorant were the shipbuilders and those Southern sympathizers who were part of the conspiracy.

As the keels of his first two cruisers were being laid, Bulloch was summoned back to the Confederacy after the failure of James H. North's mission became apparent. Bulloch had no objections to returning home, since it would be difficult in his absence for Adams, Moran, and Dudley to link him with the two ships under construction.

During his preparations for his return through the blockade to Great Britain, Bullock was joined by Confederate navy paymaster Clarence Yonge, who had been assigned by Mallory to serve as his assistant and clerk. Upon his return to Britain, Bulloch discovered that, taking advantage of his absence, fellow purchasing agent James H. North had diverted £30,000 intended for the *Alabama* to belatedly contract construction of an ironclad in a Scottish shipyard. Since it was now Bulloch's mission to have ships built for Mallory's projected squadron of seagoing ironclads, he decided to overlook North's actions. He immediately contracted the construction of Hulls No. 294 and No. 295 at the Laird shipyards. These two ships came to be known as the "Laird Rams."

Aside from their rams, their main feature was twin armored turrets amidships, carrying four 9-inch rifled guns.

At this time Bulloch may have also contracted with the Laird shipyard for the construction of the *Georgiana,* which eventually became known as the Confederate "ghost ship." Her construction was so secret it was not included in the record of ships built by Laird and Sons. This absence was a rather interesting clerical oversight since the *Alabama,* the Laird Rams, and various blockade-runners were all included in the company's official records in one way or another. The mystery ship left Liverpool for Charleston on January 22, 1863, with a scheduled stopover at Nassau. There the vessel was detained for some time before proceeding to Charleston, where she was intercepted by Union blockaders on the night of March 19–20, 1863, and ultimately destroyed.

Although no records are available concerning the construction of the *Georgiana,* it appears likely that she was ordered at roughly the same time as the Laird Rams. Apparently the intention was to use her first as a blockade-runner and then have her armed, equipped, and crewed as a commerce-destroying cruiser based out of Charleston. This ill-fated decision may have been forced upon Bulloch and Mallory by British pressure on Confederate operations in Europe after the launching and subsequent careers of the cruisers *Alabama* and *Florida.*

Other vessels built in Britain for the Confederacy were also to be sent to the Confederacy as blockade-runners and fitted out as warships upon their arrival, thus serving two purposes. These included the *Adventure, Enterprise, Hercules,* and *Ajax,* which were completed too late in the war to be of any real use to the Confederacy.

In addition, while Bulloch had been away, the cruiser under construction in the Miller shipyard in Liverpool had been launched and christened the *Oreto.* She had been given an Italian-sounding name because the cover story was that the vessel had been built for a buyer in Palermo, Sicily. When the fitting out of the ship was nearly completed, Bulloch decided that she must be put to sea as soon as possible.

Bulloch's instincts were correct. Although he did not yet know it, Thomas H. Dudley in Liverpool was already warning

Adams in London about his suspicions concerning the ultimate destination of the *Oreto*. In addition, Dudley was also becoming suspicious of Hull No. 290 under construction at the Laird shipyard. Adams and Dudley began doing everything in their power to have the *Oreto* seized by the British government or at least to delay her departure long enough to ensure that Union warships would be on station just outside of British territorial waters and ready to seize her whenever she appeared.

The British port authorities in Liverpool, in conjunction with the British Foreign Office, decided that the *Oreto* had the lines and look of a warship, but she had nothing on board that might be used for any war purposes. She carried no munitions or ammunition of any kind and was totally unarmed. This was where Bulloch's policy of not arming his cruisers paid off. Dudley was unable to secure, at the time, any proof that *Oreto* and Hull No. 290 were anything other than what Bulloch wanted them to appear to be—a pair of harmless merchant steamers.

On March 22, 1862—just twelve days after Bulloch had returned to Liverpool—*Oreto* left Liverpool under the command of a British master, John A. Duguid. She was supposed to be heading for her fictional Italian owners in Palermo. Also on board was a passenger named John Low. At Green Key, near Nassau, *Oreto* rendezvoused with the British steamer *Bahama,* which was supposed to be carrying everything necessary to make the *Oreto* into a warship.

Bahama transferred her cargo, and Mst. John Low of the Confederate navy took command. Once the transformation was completed, Low commissioned the ship as the CSS *Manassas,* after the Confederate army's victory of the previous year. He did not know that a CSS *Manassas* already existed at New Orleans. The ship then proceeded on to Nassau where Lt. John N. Maffitt took command. The ship, now recognizably a man-of-war, was detained and her crew deserted.

Maffitt did know that a CSS *Manassas* already existed, and he changed his ship's name to CSS *Florida* in honor of Mallory's home state. Once the Nassau authorities released the *Florida,* he recruited a tiny crew and proceeded to Mobile, Alabama. Low returned to Liverpool and rejoined Bulloch, who continued to use him as a troubleshooter. At sea, aboard the *Florida,* yellow fever broke out among the tiny crew of about thirty seamen. Although gravely ill himself, Maffitt managed to bring the ship through the blockade to Mobile on September 4, 1862, where she was immediately quarantined. Although damaged during her dash into the harbor, no repairs were started until she left quarantine on October 3.

The vessel's draft left her unable to reach the city itself, and she was forced to anchor twenty-eight miles away. Having to haul everything to and from the ship from that distance incurred a number of delays in completing her repairs and getting her ready to return to sea. Further delays were incurred because of a shortage of skilled workers and ordnance supplies; therefore, the ship was not ready to leave Mobile for her first raiding cruise until January 10, 1863. Using a storm as cover, the *Florida* slipped out of Mobile Bay and began her career as a commerce raider.

As Hull No. 290 finally neared completion, Bulloch expressed a desire to command her himself. Mallory, however, was not willing to forgo the services of his best purchasing agent. In addition, the perfect commanding officer became available when Cmdr. Raphael Semmes was forced to decommission and sell Mallory's first commerce-destroying cruiser, *Sumter,* at Gibraltar. Semmes realized that Bulloch wanted the command, so he declined it and made arrangements to return home to the South. When he arrived at Nassau, he was intercepted by a message from Mallory informing him of his promotion to captain and ordering him to take command of the new cruiser. So Semmes and his officers from the *Sumter* turned around and headed back to Liverpool.

Now that Hull No. 290 had a captain, Bulloch's next task was to get her armed and out to sea. It was here that his success in smuggling the *Oreto/Manassas/Florida* out of Liverpool came back to haunt him. Bulloch quickly demonstrated that he could rise to the challenge. When Hull No. 290 was finally launched on May 15, 1862—an event that was delayed by the Laird Brothers' fetish with perfection as they insisted that only the best materials and best workmanship were acceptable—she was christened the *Enrica.* The story circulated that Bulloch himself owned her and that she was to be a West Indies trading vessel. Matthew J. Butcher was hired as captain with the understanding that he was to take the vessel to the West Indies.

Enrica's fitting out was completed within a month and a satisfactory trial voyage was made on June 15. As soon as the trial voyage was completed, Bulloch ordered the ship to be coaled, provisioned, and otherwise prepared for a long voyage.

Adams, Dudley, and Moran, however, had not been idle. Adams and Moran anxiously read Dudley's dispatches as preparations to take the *Enrica* out to sea went forward. Alarmed, Adams began pestering Lord Russell, the British foreign secretary, with requests and then with demands that the authorities seize the ship. He accompanied these demands with evidence collected by Dudley that showed the *Enrica* was to be a Confederate cruiser and that Bulloch was violating the Foreign Enlistment Act in spirit if not in fact. Adams went so far as to engage one of the best attorneys in Britain who, on July 20, 1862, submitted a formal request to a court that the *Enrica* be seized.

Bulloch was not a man to be trifled with. First, through a tremendous stroke of luck, Lord Russell referred the court petition and Dudley's evidence to a legal officer within the Foreign Office who became ill. The papers remained on his desk in his home for four days before any action was taken. In addition, when Bulloch had first arrived in Britain, he had taken the precaution of recruiting an agent within the Foreign Office. This agent, whose identity has remained unknown to this day, warned Bulloch on July 26 that the *Enrica* had to leave Britain within forty-eight hours.

Shortly after his Foreign Office contact had warned him of the imminent seizure of the ship, another agent informed Bulloch that the Federal cruiser *Tuscarora* had arrived at Southampton. Bulloch immediately surmised that this arrival was no coincidence. Adams's alarm about the *Enrica* had influenced the Union assistant secretary of the navy, Gustavus V. Fox, to dispatch the ship to Southampton following her failure to intercept the Confederate cruiser *Nashville*.

Bulloch did not delay since his escape plans had already been laid. He immediately went to the Laird shipyard and announced that he desired to take the *Enrica* out for a second trial voyage to more fully test her engines. The vessel took on additional coal on July 27 and 28 and, during the early morning hours of July 29, she steamed out of Liverpool with a number of "guests" on board. Among them were Bulloch and the ubiquitous John Low. At the helm was Matthew J. Butcher.

At about the same time, another vessel, the bark-rigged merchantman *Agrippina,* also put to sea. There was no objection made to her leaving harbor since Adams and his cohorts did not know that she had been secretly chartered by Bulloch. Her cargo consisted of the ordnance and munitions needed to transform *Enrica* into a powerful warship. Among *Agrippina*'s passengers were Raphael Semmes and his officers.

On July 29, 1862, the British government decided to accede to Adams's demands and ordered *Enrica* to be seized. By then it was too late. She was already at sea.

Once at sea, Bulloch put most of his guests aboard the tug *Hercules* and sent them back to Liverpool. The *Hercules* soon returned with additional seamen and the news that *Tuscarora* had left Southampton and was on her way to the mouth of St. George's Channel. Bulloch took command from Butcher and turned the *Enrica* north, steaming around Ireland to avoid the Union cruiser and then setting his course for Terceira Island.

Upon arrival at the island Bulloch and the *Enrica* were met by the *Agrippina,* which had been able to steer a direct course to the island. The merchantman's cargo—ordnance, munitions, and other supplies—was hurriedly transferred to Bulloch's ship. Semmes, a native of Maryland who at the beginning of the secession crisis had moved to Alabama, boarded the *Enrica* with his officers, rechristened her the CSS *Alabama* after his adopted home state, and then persuaded the predominately British crew to serve aboard the new Confederate cruiser. In addition, Bulloch's clerk, Yonge, also joined the crew. Permitting Yonge to join the *Alabama* turned out to be a grave error.

Since the crew had been persuaded to stay with the ship, Semmes immediately began another raiding career. Bulloch boarded the *Agrippina* and returned to Liverpool. Upon his return he extended his charter of the *Agrippina* and loaded her with a cargo of provisions and various other supplies that would be needed by a ship on a long voyage. He then dispatched the merchantman to a predetermined rendezvous with the *Alabama*.

WITH *FLORIDA* and *Alabama* finally at sea, Bulloch turned his full attention to the next part of his mission—obtaining blockade-runners that were to be operated by the Confederate navy. He had begun this work soon after his return to Britain from his consultations with Mallory. Within a few days of his arrival he had purchased the fast steamer *Coquette* and dispatched her to the Confederacy with a cargo of naval supplies.

The Confederate army now had its own blockade-runners, and the state of North Carolina also sponsored its own blockade-runner. In a typical demonstration of states' rights run amok, the governor of North Carolina reserved the supplies brought in by his blockade-runner solely for North Carolina troops.

Meanwhile, Bulloch purchased four ships from the Liverpool shipbuilding firm of Jones, Quiggen, and Company—*Bat*, *Stag*, *Owl*, and *Deer*—that were still incomplete on the stocks. These and the *Coquette* formed the backbone of the Confederate government's fleet of blockade-runners. In 1864 he also contracted, as previously noted, with the Lairds to build two more erstwhile blockade-runners, *Enterprise* and *Adventure*. Bulloch would further contract that year with the William Denny and Brothers shipyard of Dumbarton, Scotland, for the construction of two more purported blockade-runners, *Ajax* and *Hercules*. None of these vessels actually served the South as the war ended before they could be delivered. *Ajax*, however, under the command of John Low, got as far as the West Indies before the conclusion of the war prevented her from running the blockade.

The Lairds also built the blockade-runners *Wren, Lark, Mary, Robert Todd, Isabel,* and *Penguin* for private owners. The first two were the property of John Laird Jr. *Mary* and *Robert Todd* were owned by Arthur B. Forwood, a Liverpool ship owner, and *Isabel* and *Penguin* were built to Charles K. Prioleau's order for Fraser, Trenholm, and Company. In addition, as a gift for the Confederate government, Prioleau also contracted the construction of the small but exceptionally sturdy *Alexandra* at the Miller shipyard, which had built the *Florida*. It is not known if she was intended to be a blockade-runner, cruiser, or both since the ship was never delivered.

Over time Bulloch became more and more concerned about the possibility that the British authorities might step in to end this collaboration among several British shipbuilders and the Confederate agents. So he went to France and contracted the construction of four commerce-destroying cruisers and two ironclads. The ironclads were named *Sphinx* and *Cheops* to make it appear that they were being built for the khedive of Egypt.

In addition, other naval purchasing agents were arriving in Great Britain and setting up shop. Among them was George Sinclair, whom Bulloch assisted in getting the keel laid for another cruiser based upon the design of the *Alabama*. The proposed cruiser was built using wooden planking on an iron frame, and certain vital parts of the ship were armored. Toward the end of 1862 Matthew Fontaine Maury arrived to begin his quasi-exile in Europe. Maury soon arranged to purchase the iron-hulled merchant ship *Japan* and the former Royal Navy dispatch vessel *Victor*, which became the Confederate cruisers *Georgia II* and *Rappahannock*, respectively. Neither ship, however, was particular successful.

While contracting for the construction of the cruisers and ironclads in France, Bulloch became involved with the firm of Bravary and Company of Paris. The firm was noted for a willingness to undertake risky and questionable contracts without asking too many questions. As a preventive measure, Bulloch had documents prepared transferring ownership of the Laird Rams to the French firm. The ships were named *El Tousson* and *El Monassir*. Again the cover story was that they were to be sold to the khedive of Egypt. Bulloch took care that the documents did not show any links to the Confederate government if the issue ever came to the attention of a British or French court.

Suddenly Bulloch experienced severe financial difficulties. The primary reason was that the Confederate States of America had utterly failed to establish its foreign credit abroad, particularly in Europe. The situation became so desperate that he was forced to sell the ironclad being built in Scotland to raise the money needed to complete *El Tousson* and *El Monassir.*

IRONICALLY THE Confederate government had a chance in 1860 and 1861 to firmly establish its foreign credit in Europe, but in a move of monumental foolishness permitted this vital opportunity to be lost. Historian Barbara W. Tuchman in *The March of Folly* defined misgovernment by folly as "being the pursuit of policy contrary to the self-interest of the constituency or state involved." She maintained that to qualify as folly (1) the policy adopted must have been perceived as counterproductive in its own time, (2) a feasible alternative course of action must have been available, and (3) the flawed policy should persist beyond any one political lifetime. The Confederacy paid such a full, complete, and immediate price for its folly that perhaps the third criterion can be overlooked.

At the time the secession crisis began, it seems elemental that the government of the Confederate States of America should have been seeking to export as much cotton as quickly as possible before the Union navy could assemble the ships required to make Lincoln's blockade effective. The Confederacy had a window of opportunity in which it could have easily and firmly established its foreign credit for years to come.

Raimondo Luraghi argues forcefully in *A History of the Confederate Navy* that such a course of action was glaringly obvious. If there were no immediate cotton exports there would be no money; no money meant no ships; no ships meant no cotton exports. He believes the unequivocal policy the Confederacy should have followed would have been to send to Europe, the West Indies, or any other neutral markets the greatest possible amount of cotton before warfare closed oceanic routes to Southern trade. Another action he suggests was that the Confederate government should have seized at least part of the cotton crop or nationalized foreign trade.

Any such suggestion, however, foundered on the South's traditional insistence upon free trade and then by the decision of the Confederate Congress to place a duty of $2.50 per ton on cotton exports. Although not a heavy tax burden, the measure coincided with repeated attempts by well-meaning groups to establish a cotton embargo. These efforts stemmed from the belief that such an embargo would threaten Britain's and France's textile industries and pressure would be brought to bear on those governments to officially recognize the Confederacy and possibly intervene in order to secure supplies of raw cotton for their mills. The theorists failed to recognize that years of bumper crops would delay such pressures or that alternative sources of supply might be found. They were—in Egypt and India, countries that were under the de facto if not direct control of the British Empire.

Although the Confederate government never officially declared such an embargo, its opposition was so badly handled that a de facto embargo was established in the face of an alternative proposed by Charles K. Prioleau and George A. Trenholm.

During 1860 Britain was still liquidating the English East India Company, which had ruled India since the late eighteenth century. In the aftermath of the 1857 Sepoy Rebellion, Britain was establishing direct rule. On the auction block as part of the liquidation were ten steamships, or East Indiamen. Some were wooden hulled and some were iron hulled, but in keeping with the East Indiaman tradition, they had all been built to serve as either merchant ships or as men-of-war.

Trenholm and Prioleau placed an option for the purchase of these ships on behalf of the Confederate government. The cost of the ships, ready for sea, was two million pounds, roughly equivalent to forty thousand bales of cotton. Before the blockade was established, these ships could have moved between the South and Cuba or the Caribbean, dropping off Southern cotton for reshipment directly to Europe and returning with military supplies.

When the Union blockade finally became effective, the ships could have been resold thus recouping the original investment. Or as David Hollet (in *The Alabama Affair*), Jack Greene, and Alessandro Massignani point out, the ships could have been converted into warships. If such a force could have been quickly armed and manned and utilized as a coordinated naval squadron, the possibilities would have been staggering. These ships could have provided an adequate naval force to oppose and even check the early Federal amphibious operations.

The Confederate government rejected the proposal, however. The trade embargo thus adopted by default proved itself to be an utter failure. This single example also highlights the failure of the Confederate leadership to take quick and decisive action at the beginning of the conflict, thus squandering the only real hope for the establishment of an independent Confederate States of America.

WHILE BULLOCH was making the arrangements to sell the Scottish ironclad to secure the funds to finish the Laird Rams, a major crisis struck. In April 1863 the British government—either to appease the Union government or to determine how far the Foreign Enlistment Act could be stretched—took legal action to seize the *Alexandra*. In keeping with Bulloch's dicta that no British- or French-built ship should appear overtly warlike, the *Alexandra* had no discernible military characteristics except for her unusual sturdiness. The British decision to challenge the *Alexandra* was a political one, since there was no question but that she was being built for the Confederacy. Prioleau had openly admitted from the beginning that the ship was to be a gift to the Confederate government. The sudden action by the British government was apparently sparked by a long statement made on April 6, 1863, at the Liverpool Customs House by Clarence Yonge, Bulloch's former clerk.

Yonge had been dismissed from the *Alabama*'s crew for drunkenness and theft during a stopover at Jamaica. There Yonge married a mulatto woman. He was found by Union agents and secretly sent to Adams, Moran, and Dudley in Liverpool, where he thereupon divulged everything he knew about Bulloch's enterprises. He testified about correspondence he had handled for Bulloch and disclosed how the procurement agent had managed the construction of the cruisers *Florida* and *Alabama*. Yonge also testified about James H. North's activities in Scotland. In addition, he stated that he had seen the plans for the Laird Rams and had gone to the shipyard, where he had noted that *El Tousson* and *El Monassir* matched exactly the plans he had seen.

Bulloch immediately hired the best attorney he could find in Britain to fight the government action. The case, however, did not go to trial until June 22, 1863, and until it was settled all naval projects currently under construction in Britain were either slowed down or otherwise suspended.

The barrister won the case on July 20, 1863, and it appeared that Bulloch had achieved a major legal triumph for the Confederate government. This victory, however, was only a paper achievement, because the British government was persuaded that the Foreign Enlistment Act would not prevent Britain's entangling itself in the American Civil War. The British government therefore refused to release the *Alexandra*.

Bulloch saw the writing on the wall and desperately attempted to save the Laird Rams by continuing the legal fiction that the ships were to be sold through Bravary and Company to Egypt. The British government contacted the khedive of Egypt. When he disavowed the sale, the British government acted on September 17, 1863, and ordered the seizure of both ships. They were eventually incorporated into the Royal Navy as HMS *Wyvern* and *Scorpion*. At the same time the British government also seized George Sinclair's cruiser, and the French government ordered the confiscation of the four cruisers and two ironclads being built for the Confederacy. Eventually one of the ironclads was released to Bulloch, and she went to sea as the CSS *Stonewall* just as the war was ending and far too late for her to be of any practical use to the Confederate navy.

Although Bulloch had suffered a disaster of the first magnitude, he was not yet done. The procurement agent had first seen the steamer *Sea King* at about the same time that the Laird Rams had been seized by the British government. He discovered that the ship was new and intended for the India trade. She was about to make her maiden voyage to Bombay and was expected to return in eight or nine months. Bullock also learned that she had the same type of propeller-lifting device as the *Alabama*.

When the commerce raider *Alabama* was engaged and destroyed by the Union cruiser *Kearsarge* in June 1864, Bulloch immediately began looking for a replacement. He found it when he heard that the *Sea King* had returned and that she was for sale. Through intermediaries unaffiliated with the Confederate government, the Confederate navy, or Bulloch himself, he arranged to purchase the ship. He also chartered the merchant ship *Laurel*, which he loaded with ordnance, munitions, and other naval stores. The two ships rendezvoused at the island of Madeira. They then sailed in company to the deserted island of Las Desertas, where the *Laurel*'s cargo was transferred to the *Sea King*.

Lt. James Iredell Waddell revealed his appointment to command the ship, now known as the CSS *Shenandoah*. He enlisted a crew of twenty-three from the crews of the *Laurel* and the former *Sea King*, including several former crew members of the *Alabama*. For a short time Waddell considered abandoning the effort, but he decided to seek recruits while the ship was at sea. Thus was born the last of the Confederate commerce-destroying cruisers.

11

Raiders on the High Seas

I N SOME WAYS THE commerce-destroying portion of Stephen R. Mallory's naval strategy succeeded beyond his wildest dreams. The Confederate cruisers took at least 245 prizes, most of which were destroyed outright. The Northern merchant marine, which had once covered the world's oceans, by the end of the war was in an irreversible decline, and by the beginning of the twentieth century had practically disappeared.

This damage was done by just ten ships. Mallory and his captains demonstrated how a campaign against an enemy's maritime commerce should be conducted. Their example was followed by Germany during World Wars I and II against Britain and by the U.S. Navy against Japan in World War II.

One measure of the commerce-destroying campaign's effectiveness can be seen in a real way by the massive increases in insurance rates during the war. This in turn induced many Northern ship owners to have their vessels reregistered under foreign flags, a practice that continues to the present (mostly to avoid U.S. government regulations). At the beginning of the war in 1861 the United States had registered 2.5 million tons of shipping engaged in foreign trade. At the end of the war that figure had fallen to 1.5 million tons and continued to decline until it was momentarily arrested by World War I.

In addition, Mallory had targeted the New England whaling industry for destruction, hoping to punish the region that had been home to the most rabid abolitionists in the North. Strategically, he hoped that so much damage to Northern mercantile interests would evoke demands for peace.

Furthermore, the exploits of the Confederate navy had done much to raise and maintain Southern morale following the March 1862 victory at Hampton Roads, the triumph of the *Arkansas* at Vicksburg, the sinking of the Union gunboat *Hatteras* by the Confederate commerce-destroying cruiser *Alabama,* and the raid by the CSS *Archer,* one of the commerce raider *Florida*'s clones, into the harbor of Portland, Maine, where Lt. C. W. Read captured the revenue cutter USS *Caleb Cushing.* The cutter, however, was destroyed, and Read and his raiders were captured through the quick reaction of the local military and naval officials.

Joining the Confederate navy in commerce raiding were the privateers who succeeded in capturing another 103 merchant ships. The actual losses were much lower, because most of the prizes were eventually recaptured when their prize crews attempted to return to their home ports through the blockade. Mallory finally gained control of the privateers when they were absorbed into the volunteer navy. By that time, however, privateering had mostly died out as decisions by various European governments and the Union blockade had eliminated the profitability of privateering.

Thus the story of Mallory's commerce-destroying cruisers contains some of the most colorful exploits in the short history of the Confederate navy. The various ships and their accomplishments include:

Sumter

THE FIRST of the Confederate navy commerce raiders left New Orleans and put to sea on June 30, 1861, under Cmdr. Raphael Semmes. She barely escaped having her career abruptly terminated.

On the day the *Sumter* put to sea, the Union vessels *Powhatan* and *Brooklyn* were covering the two main outlets of the Mississippi River into the Gulf of Mexico. The *Sumter*'s guns were no match for either warship. For several days Semmes watched for any sign that the blockaders might relax. On June 30 the way seemed clear.

Brooklyn had left her station to chase a distant vessel, so Semmes decided to make for the open sea. On the *Brooklyn,* however, a sharp-eyed lookout noticed the telltale trail of smoke from *Sumter*'s funnel. *Brooklyn*'s captain assumed that the emerging vessel was a blockade-runner and changed course to begin his pursuit. Meanwhile, *Sumter* lost valuable time when she had to squeeze past a stranded vessel on the bar. At that point, *Brooklyn* was only seven miles away and doing eleven and a half knots; *Sumter*'s speed was nine knots.

The gap between the two vessels rapidly closed, soon down to four miles. Then *Sumter*'s boilers started foaming when they were suddenly contaminated with saltwater, which caused the steam pressure to increase from eighteen to twenty-five pounds—a dangerous level. To lighten the ship so as to reduce the strain on her engines and to increase her speed, Semmes dumped fifteen hundred tons of drinking water. He knew that he could replace the water at any number of deserted or neutral islands in either the Gulf or the Caribbean.

Sumter had one advantage in her race to the open waters of the Gulf: her sail rigging featured larger-than-normal fore and aft sails, which meant she could sail close to the wind and still take advantage of her steam engine. As her speed increased, she began to pull away. *Brooklyn* depended solely on her engines. A sudden rain squall hid the two opponents for a moment, and when it lifted *Brooklyn* was still too close for comfort.

Sumter's chief engineer reported that the boilers had stopped foaming, removing the danger that they might explode under the strain. In addition, there was a fresh breeze of which Semmes took immediate advantage. *Brooklyn,* however, was forced to take in sail. *Sumter* could still utilize her full sail rig and was soon drawing away again. After a chase that had lasted three and a half hours, *Brooklyn* gave up the hunt and returned to her blockading station.

Semmes decided to begin operations off South America and proceeded to the waters off Brazil. His first prize was the *Golden Rocket.* After removing her crew, coal, provisions, sailing gear, and chronometer, the ship was set afire. This became standard operating procedure for all of the Confederate commerce raiders. Occasionally a vessel would be spared and bonded. This meant that the captured vessel's captain, acting as agent for the owners, signed an agreement or bond agreeing to pay a ransom to the Confederate government at the end of the war for sparing the vessel. Prisoners who had been accumulated from previous captured and destroyed ships would be loaded aboard, and the ship would be allowed to go on her way. The prizes were destroyed because no neutral ports would accept them, and it was nearly impossible to get them through the blockade into Confederate ports. In addition, drawing on the *Sumter*'s crew to man the prizes would have created a serious drain on her manpower. Semmes did not care for destroying such fine vessels. He was a naval officer, and he yearned to fight the Union directly.

Sumter was nearly caught by the Federal cruiser *Iroquois* while the Confederate raider was coaling at the French port of St. Pierre on the West Indian island of Martinique. The Union vessel waited nine days for the *Sumter* to come out, but the Confederate ship escaped during the night and made straight for Spain, arriving at Cadiz on January 4, 1862. Semmes put into the port to make repairs. Forced by U.S. diplomatic maneuvering to move on to British-held Gibraltar, the ship was blockaded there by several Union warships. Another blow fell when an inspection revealed that her engines had been so badly strained by her cruise as to be almost useless.

Semmes therefore decommissioned the ship and headed for Britain and consultations with James D. Bulloch on the first leg of his journey back to the Confederacy. He would eventually take a long detour, and it would be another two and a half years before he could continue his trip home. *Sumter* was sold at auction to Fraser, Trenholm, and Company, which not only represented the Confederate government's financial interests in Europe but was also heavily involved in the business of blockade-running. Renamed *Gibraltar,* she was turned into a blockade-runner.

During her cruise *Sumter* had taken a total of eighteen prizes and destroyed seven of them. Although the results seem rather light, this cruise initiated an increase in insurance rates that eventually forced the sale of many American merchant ships to foreign buyers and the reregistering of others under foreign flags.

Nashville/Rattlesnake

THE CSS *Nashville* made one cruise as part of the Confederate navy under the command of Lt. R. B. Pegram. The primary purpose of the voyage, which began when she ran the blockade on October 21, 1861, was to show the Confederate flag in European waters. A secondary purpose was to serve as a decoy for two commissioners—John Slidell and James M. Mason—who were on their way to Europe to seek recognition of the Confederate government by Britain and France. Her cruise also had the side effect of forcing the British to grant Confederate ships belligerent rights when the ship put in at Southampton in Britain.

The *Nashville* returned to Beaufort, North Carolina, at the end of February 1862, having captured two Union merchant ships, destroying both.

Decommissioned and sold, she became the blockade-runner *Thomas L. Wragg* and made several trips in and out of Savannah during the summer of 1862. Assisting her in her career as a blockade-runner was the fact that she resembled the USS *Keystone State,* a former merchant ship that had been purchased by the Union navy, converted into a gunboat, and used to blockade a number of Southern ports, including Charleston and Savannah. The owners of *Thomas L. Wragg,* however, realized that as the blockade tightened she was no longer suitable to continue serving as a blockade-runner. They decided to convert her into a privateer as part of the new volunteer navy. Her name was once again changed, this time to CSS *Rattlesnake,* and she was armed with four old cannon. A crew of 130 was recruited to provide prize crews for her prospective captures and thus increase the time she could stay at sea.

Painted gray to reduce her visibility, she was waiting in the Ogeechee River above Fort McAllister, the back door to Savannah, for an opportunity to slip through the blockade. On February 23, 1863, despite foggy conditions, the blockaders moved in to attack Fort McAllister, close the access to Savannah, and destroy the

Rattlesnake. While the rest of the Union flotilla engaged Fort McAllister, the ironclad *Montauk*, under the command of Cmdr. John L. Worden (the first captain of the USS *Monitor*) concentrated on the *Rattlesnake*, which had run aground while trying to move out of range of the Union warships. The *Montauk* closed to a distance of fifteen hundred yards and opened fire. The range closed to twelve hundred yards, despite the fire directed at the Federal ship by Fort McAllister's gunners. Only the upper works of the *Rattlesnake* were visible, but *Montauk*'s gunners had the range and used seven-second fuses to inflict massive damage on the privateer. Even when a fog descended again, the Federal gunners kept the range.

Soon the *Rattlesnake* was ablaze from stem to stern and finally exploded with a roar when the fires reached her magazine. The rest of the Union flotilla, however, was unable to force Fort McAllister to surrender. They retreated because of the falling tide, and the back door to Savannah remained open. The only real damage to the Union vessels occurred when *Montauk* struck a stationary torpedo. Mud sealed the hole in her hull when she was purposely grounded. The hole was patched, and later the ironclad returned to base for permanent repairs.

Alabama

THE SUCCESS of his cruise aboard the *Sumter* earned Raphael Semmes promotion to captain. He was given command of the British-built cruiser *Alabama*, which had been contracted by James D. Bulloch and built in the Laird shipyard in Birkenhead as Hull No. 290 before being temporarily christened the *Enrica*.

By August 24, 1862, *Alabama* was ready to begin a commerce-destroying cruise that was to last for the next twenty-two months. During her single cruise she captured sixty-four U.S. vessels valued at $6 million, most of which she destroyed. This total also included a Union gunboat. The *Alabama* began her career by penetrating the New England whaling fleet off the Azores and capturing a number of vessels. From there she moved on to the Newfoundland Banks, capturing and destroying more ships.

The Confederate raider then weathered a severe storm and headed for Martinique, where Semmes intended to replenish her dwindling coal supplies. Upon arrival on November 18, 1863, she met the *Agrippina,* whose charter Bulloch had extended once he returned to Liverpool so she could serve as *Alabama*'s supply ship. Once she joined *Agrippina,* a new rendezvous was set because of the arrival of the Federal cruiser *San Jacinto.* Upon spotting the *Alabama,* the Union ship remained in position, hovering just off the harbor entrance and waiting for *Alabama* to emerge. During a dark night, the *Alabama* slipped past her.

Semmes had learned from newspapers aboard a captured vessel that a Union expedition was due to sail for the Gulf of Mexico. He surmised that the force would be making for the city of Galveston and decided to try to intercept the convoy of transports and disrupt the expedition. Actually, the expedition was conveying reinforcements and a new commander to the Union forces garrisoned in New Orleans. Arriving off Galveston on January 11, 1863, he found the port covered by five blockaders. No transports were in sight.

One of the blockading ships, the gunboat *Hatteras,* a converted merchant ship, was dispatched to investigate the intruder. After leading the Federal vessel away from her consorts, Semmes turned on the Union gunboat at about 6:35 P.M. as night fell. He fired five-second-fused shells in a broadside at a point-blank range of just forty yards. The impact created rents and holes in the hull of the *Hatteras* that were at least five or six feet wide. In seventeen minutes it was all over. *Hatteras* surrendered in a sinking condition, and Semmes rescued 141 survivors.

Overcrowding caused by his many prisoners forced Semmes to head for Jamaica to set them ashore on neutral soil. During this visit his paymaster, Clarence Yonge, was accused of drunkenness and theft. Unfortunately, Semmes chose to have him put ashore rather than kept aboard in irons. This decision resulted in Yonge's eventual betrayal of Bulloch's activities in Britain and the collapse of Bulloch's efforts to obtain warships for the Confederate navy in Britain and France.

From Jamaica, *Alabama* slowly made her way to Bahia, Brazil, where she arrived in May after capturing and destroying another twenty Union merchant vessels. Using one of the captured ships, Semmes decided to clone the *Alabama.* Armed and commissioned as the cruiser CSS *Tuscaloosa,* she was used at first as a scout and then dispatched to cruise independently. She failed to make any captures before she was seized by British authorities in January 1864.

Alabama had a narrow escape from the Federal cruiser *Vanderbilt* off the Cape of Good Hope. *Vanderbilt* was a former passenger ship that had been converted into a steam ram for use against the ironclad *Virginia.* After *Virginia* was scuttled, she was refitted as a cruiser and dispatched on a yearlong cruise to chase down the *Alabama.* Later Semmes learned that the Northern cruiser *Wyoming* was patrolling the Sunda Straits. Seeking to repeat his success against the *Hatteras,* Semmes attempted to intercept the *Wyoming* but could not find her. From there *Alabama* headed for the China Sea, destroying more Yankee merchant shipping. At the British port and naval base of Singapore he found twenty-two laid-up Union merchantmen, which demonstrated to Semmes the effectiveness of his cruise.

The *Alabama* then headed back to the Cape of Good Hope, taking her last two captures. At Cape Town, Semmes took on coal and surveyed his ship. The examination found that the commerce raider was in dire need of repairs that could only be obtained in a European port. He made the fateful decision of laying in a course for Cherbourg. On June 11, 1864, the *Alabama* anchored at the French port, and Semmes asked the authorities for permission to land prisoners and repair his ship.

As soon as the U.S. minister in Paris, William L. Dayton, received word that the *Alabama* was at Cherbourg, he sent an urgent telegraph to the Dutch port of Flushing. Anchored there was the cruiser *Kearsarge* under the command of Capt. John A. Winslow.

Winslow was in the right place at the right time due to his pursuit of the Confederate cruiser *Rappahannock.* After that Confederate ship had made her way to Calais, Winslow and his ship had been dispatched to keep an eye on her. Because France favored the Confederacy, Winslow decided to base his ship at the nearby and much friendlier port of Flushing. Upon receiving Dayton's message, Winslow hurriedly weighed anchor and proceeded to Cherbourg, arriving on June 14. Shortly after the arrival of the Union vessel, the French authorities informed Semmes that he could remain in the port only as long as it took to complete the necessary preparations to safely take his ship back to sea.

Semmes had three options: fight, run, or decommission and abandon his ship as he had done with the *Sumter*. He chose to fight. Even if he could avoid *Kearsarge,* his ship had nowhere to go. Her bottom was foul, her ammunition was running low, and her gunpowder was showing signs of decay. During the last target practice, one-third of the shells were found to be defective. In examining his opponent Semmes could discern no particular advantage the *Kearsarge* had over the *Alabama*. Some of the Federal's guns were of larger caliber, but the weight of metal of her broadsides only amounted to seventy pounds more than his own.

What Semmes did not know was that Winslow had adopted the common expedient of draping anchor chains around his ship's hull to provide some makeshift armor protection. Semmes could not see this because Winslow thought the chains looked untidy and had covered them with thin planking.

After Semmes delivered an official challenge to Winslow, he spent the next few days with the executive officer, Lt. John McIntosh Kell, and drilled his crew in boarding tactics. He intended to disable and capture the Union cruiser, possibly even exchanging her for his own worn-out ship and continue his commerce-destroying career. Semmes well knew that his vessel could not withstand a sustained action. Nonetheless, on the morning of June 21, he took the *Alabama* out to meet the *Kearsarge*.

Kearsarge took position and waited about nine miles off the coast—far enough out to sea so that there would be no risk of violating French neutrality. The Federal vessel was faster than the *Alabama* and thus controlled the conditions of the coming battle. The Confederate ship fired the first shots, but they fell short. In fact, Semmes's gunners consistently fired short throughout the action. Many of the shells that did hit the *Kearsarge* failed to explode, including one that embedded itself in *Kearsarge*'s stern post. Thus Semmes lost his best chance to win the battle.

The two ships circled each other, firing constantly, barely a half- to three-quarters of a mile apart. All of the advantages of speed, accurate firepower, mobility, and even armor protection lay with the Union cruiser. After being hulled a number of times, the *Alabama* began to take on water faster than her pumps could eliminate it. When the rising water put out her engine fires, Semmes knew that the end had come.

To save his men's lives he ordered *Alabama*'s flag to be lowered, but Winslow feared a trick and continued firing. When the Confederate's guns ceased firing, Winslow ordered his gunners to cease fire. *Kearsarge* was not able to participate in the rescue of the *Alabama*'s crew because all of her boats had been smashed by Confederate shells during the battle. A number of spectator craft, including the British yacht *Deerhound*, were more than willing to provide assistance. Semmes and forty-one of his officers and men were rescued by the *Deerhound*, which refused to turn them over to Winslow. The British yacht took them to England where they were landed at Southampton. Other survivors were picked up by two French vessels, and some of them were turned over to Winslow and the *Kearsarge* but others were landed at Cherbourg.

Altogether Semmes had lost twenty-six men killed in battle or by drowning and another twenty-one men were wounded. *Kearsarge* had lost only one man killed and three wounded. Although *Alabama* had fired 370 shells at the *Kearsarge*, the damage to the Federal vessel was slight.

Semmes eventually made it through the blockade to the Confederacy and was given command of the James River Squadron, which was tasked with protecting the river approaches to the Confederate capital at Richmond. He was also awarded the rank of rear admiral, becoming the Confederate navy's second admiral.

Florida

THE DARK and stormy night that Lt. John N. Maffitt and his commerce-destroying cruiser *Florida* had been waiting for at Mobile finally arrived on January 17, 1863. As the rain eased at around 2 A.M. the *Florida* slipped out to sea in a thick mist and easily got past two Union blockading warships. Telltale sparks from her twin funnels revealed her presence to a third blockader. *Florida* set all sails, and Maffitt called for full steam ahead.

As she fled the scene, the Confederate raider was making fourteen and a half knots at one point. At 5 A.M. the only blockading ship that could have caught her, USS *R. R. Cuyler,* was spotted just three miles off. Maffitt immediately ordered all sails to be taken in and shut down her engines. High waves on the rough seas hid the *Florida*'s low-lying hull. Once she was clear of the blockaders, she continued on her way.

During *Florida*'s first cruise, which ended in August 1863, she captured twenty-four vessels. Using one of her prizes, she cloned herself, dispatching the CSS *Clarence* under the command of Lt. C. W. Read. The tender's crew and armament were moved successively to other prizes that became the CSS *Tacony* and the CSS *Archer* respectively. By the time the voyage ended with Read's failed raid on Portland, Maine, he had captured and destroyed a total of twenty-one ships.

Florida's first cruise ended when she put into the French port of Brest for repairs that took about six months. During this time Maffitt, because of ill health, turned command of the ship over to Lt. Charles M. Morris. Her second cruise lasted from March to September 1864, during which she added another thirteen captures. One of them was the steamship *Electric Spark,* the only steam-powered ship to be captured by any of the Confederate raiders or privateers during the war. Morris then headed *Florida* for the Brazilian coast.

The Union cruiser *Wachusett,* under the command of Cmdr. Napoleon Collins since January 1864, had been hunting for Confederate raiders off the coast of Brazil. The Federal ship was moving north from the Brazilian capital of Rio de Janeiro because the *Florida* was rumored to be in the area. *Wachusett* anchored at the port of Bahia, seeking more news of the *Florida*. Then the *Florida*—to Collins's happy surprise—came to him when a lookout reported at 7:15 P.M. on October 4 that a strange sail was entering the harbor. Collins dispatched a small boat to identify the stranger. He could scarcely believe his luck when the boat reported that the strange vessel was the *Florida*. Collins immediately got up steam, had his anchor chain heaved short, and called his crew to general quarters.

For her part the *Florida* had no intention of causing trouble. Morris told the port authorities he was there to procure provisions and make minor repairs. Since Brazil was a neutral nation, he expected to be accorded the customary belligerent's rights, which the port officials quickly granted.

Collins, however, was not about to lose the prey he had been seeking for the last six months. In consultations with the U.S. consul, Thomas F. Wilson, he decided to ram and sink the *Florida* and let the diplomats sort things out later.

Late on the night of October 7, Collins made his move. A sudden noise gave the *Florida*'s crew enough of a warning that *Wachusett* struck only a glancing blow, but the force of the collision knocked down the ship's mizzenmast, her main boom, and carried away a portion of her bulwarks. After a short scuffle, the surprised Confederates surrendered and *Wachusett* towed her prize out of the harbor, under ineffectual fire from the irate Brazilians.

Florida was taken to Hampton Roads and anchored. On November 19 while the Union, Confederate, and Brazilian governments argued over her, she was rammed again—this time by the army transport *Alliance* in what was both a highly convenient and highly suspicious accident. The Confederate cruiser took on water and sank, due to the "failure" of her pumps—nine days later.

Secretary of State William Seward responded to the Brazilians' diplomatic protest over the incident on December 26 by insisting that no Confederate ship was entitled to belligerent's rights. He later admitted that Collins and the American consul had exceeded their authority and promised that Collins would be court-martialed and that Wilson would be dismissed. Seward said the sinking of the *Florida* had been due to an unforeseen accident over which the United States had no responsibility.

Napoleon Collins, in one of the shortest court-martials on record, on April 7, 1865, pleaded guilty and was ordered dismissed from the service. As he was preparing to appeal the verdict, Secretary of the Navy Gideon Welles set it aside and restored Collins to active duty.

Although the sinking of the *Florida* was suspect, it probably brought a considerable sigh of relief to any number of officials in Washington, D.C., and Rio de Janeiro.

Georgiana

AMONG THE blockade-runners and warships built for the Confederacy by Laird and Sons was the *Georgiana,* although there is no documentation to that effect. The cover story given to British officials by the Lairds was that the ship was being built for the Chinese naval service. The Lairds also built two other vessels for the "Chinese navy," *Tiensin* and *Kwang Tung.* The *Kwang Tung* eventually became the blockade-runner *Mary.*

Georgiana left Liverpool on January 22, 1863, bound for Nassau and with the intention of running the blockade into Charleston, where she was to have been armed and outfitted as a cruiser. After being detained for some time at Nassau, the ship proceeded to Charleston but was intercepted by blockaders. Her commander decided to run the ship aground at Long Island Beach on the South Carolina coast to avoid capture. Strenuous efforts were made by the blockaders to obtain her cargo, which consisted partly of military stores and was known to be quite valuable. The Confederates, in an effort to keep the ship from falling into Union hands, drove off Federal landing parties by bringing up several field artillery batteries. Unfortunately, in attempting to keep her from falling into Federal hands, the *Georgiana* was destroyed by the Confederate gunners.

Aside from the loss of her cargo, the destruction of the *Georgiana* was a severe blow to the Confederate navy. *Georgiana* had been stronger and faster than any of the other Confederate raiders, including *Alabama.* As such she had tremendous potential as a commerce-destroying cruiser.

Georgia

Japan, A screw-propeller, brig-rigged, iron-hulled merchant ship, was purchased on the Clyde at Dumbarton, Scotland, by Matthew Fontaine Maury for the Confederate navy in March 1863. The vessel soon departed Greenock, Scotland, with a crew of fifty under the pretense that she was on a trading voyage to Singapore. Once out of British territorial waters, the ship rendezvoused with the steamer *Alar* near the French port of

Ushant. She took on two 8-inch rifles and two 24-pounder and one 32-pounder smoothbores.

On April 9, 1863, she was officially commissioned as the CSS *Georgia*. Cmdr. William Maury, a cousin of her purchaser, commanded the new cruiser.

On her single raiding cruise the *Georgia* went first to Brazil and then to the Cape of Good Hope. During the course of her travels she took nine prizes, burning five of them. *Georgia*, however, proved to be a poor sailor. As she cruised in the South Atlantic, her hull was badly fouled by marine growth, greatly reducing her speed. She put into Cherbourg on the night of October 28–29, 1863, for repairs and to clean her hull, remaining there for several months.

In February 1864 the ship was judged to be unfit for further service. It was decided to use her armaments and supply another ship purchased by Maury, the former British dispatch vessel *Victor*, and she was sent to a position off the coast of Morocco to await her replacement. The former Royal Navy vessel never arrived. *Georgia* waited for several weeks, during which her crew had a brief skirmish with hostile Arabs.

From there *Georgia* returned to France then slipped past two Union warships on patrol off the coast to arrive at Liverpool in May. Upon landing, she was decommissioned and sold as a blockade-runner. On her first voyage in that role, she was captured by the USS *Niagara*, sent to Boston, and condemned as a prize.

Rappahannock

ORIGINALLY BUILT for the Royal Navy as the HMS *Victor* in 1857, this ship was put up for sale in 1863 and purchased that November by Matthew Fontaine Maury. He intended to use her as a replacement for the CSS *Georgia*, which had proven to be an unacceptable raider.

The cover story was that the former *Victor* was to be used in the China trade. British authorities, however, suspected her true purpose and ordered the ship to be detained. Quick action enabled her to escape from the Sheerness Dockyard at the mouth of the Thames River estuary.

So hastily was the ship put to sea that a number of surprised dockyard workers were still aboard. While passing down the River Thames, the ship's engine burned out a bearing, confirming the wisdom of the Royal Navy in its decision to sell the ship. The engines could not be restarted, and she drifted into the channel in the general direction of France. In this condition the vessel was hurriedly commissioned as the CSS *Rappahannock* and drifted until she entered French territorial waters near Calais. At this point she was anchored, and the captain contacted French authorities for permission to enter the port as a ship-of-war in distress and in need of repair. Despite the imprudence and audacity of her request, *Rappahannock* was allowed to enter the port.

From his headquarters in Paris, Confederate Com. Samuel Barron detailed one of his staff, Lt. C. M. Fauntleroy, to command the newly commissioned cruiser. He oversaw repairs to his ship's engines, attempted to recruit additional crew, and continued preparations to take her to sea. These actions were eventually stopped when the French government stationed a gunboat across her bows. Her only use to the South was in requiring one or two Union ships to remain off Calais to keep an eye on her. As such the *Rappahannock* was laid up at Calais and used by the Confederates as a stores and accommodation ship. At the end of the war she was turned over to the U.S. government.

Chickamauga

IN THE fall of 1864 the blockade-runner *Edith*—home-ported at Wilmington and owned jointly by the Confederate government and a group of investors—was purchased outright by the Confederate navy. She was armed with a 9-inch Dahlgren smoothbore, one 32-pounder, and a 12-pounder. When the conversion was completed she was commissioned as the commerce raider CSS *Chickamauga* under the command of Lt. John Wilkinson.

Chickamauga was more substantially built that most blockade-runners, but Wilkinson thought her unfit to serve as a cruiser because of her limited coal supply. She was also schooner rigged, which was unusual for a blockade-runner, and she had relatively short masts. The vessel was primarily a steamship, and her limited sails were used mostly to steady her as she could only make a speed of around three knots under sail alone. Under less-than-favorable winds she could not even make steerage under sail.

Wilkinson took his cruiser out to sea on October 29, 1864. He successfully threw off the blockaders at the mouth of the Cape Fear River, distracting them by firing signal rockets that provided them with false information about her course and speed.

In preparing for the cruise a large amount of coal was stored in every conceivable space. Her crew even slept on piled sacks of coal. She also carried six pilots, each qualified for a different Southern port.

The *Chickamauga* steamed north to Long Island Sound, capturing seven Union merchantmen along the way. From there she moved on to Bermuda for repairs and coal, arriving on November 7, 1864. Several deserters jumped ship and landed in the midst of an epidemic of yellow fever.

On November 15 the *Chickamauga* left St. George's Island for the return voyage to Wilmington. No additional Union merchant ships were encountered. By November 18 she was off the mouth of the Cape Fear River in a heavy fog. As the fog lifted, two blockading vessels bore down on the Confederate cruiser. The *Chickamauga* made a dash for safety and after a short exchange of fire with the blockaders, she managed to reach safety under the guns of Fort Fisher.

In December *Chickamauga* helped fight off an amphibious attack aimed at capturing Fort Fisher. Some of her crew helped serve the guns in the fort, and the ship herself was used to bring in ammunition. The cruiser also supported the fort during a second attack, on January 15. When the fort and later the city of Wilmington surrendered, the cruiser was moved up the Cape Fear River, where she was scuttled by her crew.

Tallahassee/Olustee

THE BLOCKADE-RUNNER *Atlanta* was built on the River Thames in England for the Chatham and Dover Railroad as a high-speed ferry on the English channel. She was capable of making the twenty-mile Calais-Dover crossing in seventy-seven minutes.

Upon completion it was realized that her speed would make her an ideal blockade-runner, and she was purchased and diverted for that purpose.

Based out of Wilmington, like the *Chickamauga,* she was purchased by the Confederate government during the early summer of 1864 and armed with one 7-inch rifle, two 24-pounders, and two 32-pounders. The vessel was commissioned as the cruiser *Tallahassee.* Under Cmdr. J. T. Wood she was taken through the blockade in early August, making a successful nineteen-day cruise. The *Tallahassee* moved up the Atlantic coast to Halifax, Nova Scotia. Lack of fuel, however, ended the cruise, and she returned to Wilmington after capturing and/or destroying thirty-three Union merchantmen.

On her return she was renamed *Olustee* and made a second raiding cruise. During this voyage she captured six ships before being forced to return again to Wilmington because of a lack of fuel. As the *Olustee* tried to enter the harbor at Wilmington, the vessel was attacked by several Union gunboats but managed to evade capture.

The cruiser was then disarmed, reconverted back into a blockade-runner, and renamed *Chamelion.* Command was given to John Wilkinson, formerly the captain of the *Chickamauga.* Although she was able to reach Bermuda, where she loaded badly needed supplies for the Confederate army, she was unable to slip back into Wilmington through the blockade. After she was turned back from two other Southern ports, Wilkinson reluctantly steamed to Liverpool, where he turned her over to James D. Bulloch on April 9, 1865, the same day that Lee surrendered the Army of Northern Virginia at Appomattox Court House. Soon after that the ship was seized by the British government and turned over to the United States.

Shenandoah

UNDER THE command of Lt. James Iredell Waddel, the *Shenandoah* made her first capture on October 30, 1864, after leaving the vicinity of the island of Madeira, where she was armed and commissioned. She made her way south, capturing several more ships, and in mid-December rounded the Cape of Good Hope on her way to Australia, arriving there on January 25, 1865. The ship was extremely shorthanded as only twenty seamen had signed on when she was commissioned. Waddell was forced to recruit additional men from among the crews of his various prizes. It was a surprisingly easy task, as it turned out.

Shenandoah remained in Australia until February 18 while her propeller was being repaired. Meanwhile, several of her crew deserted. Waddell, however, was able to recruit more than enough men from among the Australians to make up the difference. He then moved on through several severe storms until he reached Ascension Island, Ponape, where he captured four New England whalers. His mission was the destruction of the whaling fleet.

The Confederate cruiser reached the Bering Sea on June 16, 1865. Within six days of his arrival, he had captured twenty-four whalers, burning all but four, which he used to release his prisoners.

After this success Waddell turned south. Although informed by one of his captured captains that the war was over, Waddell was not convinced. Captured newspapers told of the Confederate government's relocation to Danville, North Carolina, and Jefferson Davis's proclamation that the war would continue. Convinced that the Confederacy survived, Waddell continued his depredations and captured another nineteen ships. All but four were burned, and his prisoners were released to the remaining ships.

Waddell's ultimate target was now the city of San Francisco, which was protected by the *Passaic*-class monitor *Camanche*. He intended to capture the ironclad by surprise and demand a ransom from the city.

On August 2, 1865, as he neared his target, he hailed the British bark *Baracouta* and was told and finally believed that the war was over.

He decided that *Shenandoah* should return to Britain. For more than two months she avoided all contact with other ships and finally anchored in Britain's Mersey River on November 6, 1865, where she was surrendered to the British government. This last Confederate cruiser was turned over to the United States, which sold her to the sultan of Zanzibar as his private yacht. The vessel later sank in a storm off the island of Socotra while on a trip to Bombay. All told, she had taken at least forty-seven ships, most of which were destroyed, and she was the first and only Confederate warship to circumnavigate the globe.

Confederate Privateers

DURING THE course of the war, the Confederate government issued a total of fifty-seven letters of marque and reprisal to individuals or syndicates that fitted out privateers. The first letters of marque was issued May 10, 1861, to the *Triton,* a thirty-ton schooner based out of Brunswick, Georgia. The majority of the letters of marque were issued for vessels based in New Orleans and Charleston. By the end of 1862 only a handful remained. Ironically, the most successful of the privateers were those who operated along the Mississippi River, but they never amounted to more than an expensive nuisance.

Ships used in privateering ranged in size from the *Triton* to the 1,644-ton steamer *Phoenix.* Most of the vessels tended to be sailing ships, but there were also a few steamers. The most interesting craft was a three-man submarine, the *Pioneer,* home based at New Orleans. Her owners hoped she would claim the bounty offered by the Confederate government for sinking a Union warship.

Operationally, the privateers were concentrated in the Gulf of Mexico and the Caribbean. Because neutral harbors were closed to them, most privateers conducted short forays into waters close to their home ports then followed their prizes back to those home ports.

WHILE THE Confederate navy's commerce-destroying efforts were, on the one hand, the most successful part of Mallory's strategic plans for the navy, on the other hand, they were totally ineffective in achieving his strategic objectives. The secretary had hoped that the rampages by his cruisers would force Welles to detach ships from the blockade to chase them down and cause New England maritime interests to turn against the war. Welles did detach some ships from the blockade to hunt down the cruisers, going so far as to create a squadron in the West Indies specifically tasked with running down and destroying Confederate cruisers and privateers.

Welles, however, never lost sight of the fact that the blockade must be maintained if the Union was going to win the war. Therefore—despite the pressures put upon him and his department by politicians, newspapers, and the maritime mercantile interests—the blockade was paramount over all other considerations.

Although the New England maritime interests strenuously voiced their concerns, the depredations exacted by Mallory's cruisers were simply insufficient to hurt the rest of the country, which was in the midst of a major economic boom due to the war. This simultaneous industrial economic expansion in the Northeast and prosperity in agricultural exports, mostly wheat, from the Midwest largely offset the losses suffered by the maritime mercantile interests. Thus the Confederate commerce-destroying effort was really irrelevant.

The problem with commerce destroying is that this strategic policy is most effective against nations that depend on their overseas trade for raw materials with which to manufacture their products and to transport their products to the markets where they are sold. In such scenarios, the most important imports are generally foodstuffs and most exports are manufactured goods. The two nations most vulnerable to this kind of warfare were Great Britain and Japan, island nations dependent upon their maritime mercantile commerce for their survival. Their vulnerability to this kind of warfare was demonstrated by Germany's campaign of unrestricted submarine warfare against Britain in the Atlantic during World Wars I and II and the U.S. Navy's similar campaign against Japan during World War II. Britain was able to economically survive the experience because it was able to develop adequate countermeasures and tactics. The Japanese could not.

Continental nations, such as the United States, are not nearly as vulnerable because they are generally able to feed their population and absorb such losses to their maritime mercantile commerce, even to the extent of allowing it to be carried primarily by the merchant ships of other nations.

12

Carolina and Combined Operations

THE THIRD YEAR OF the war, 1864, was an election year. Lincoln was running for a second term, and in both the North and South the election was seen as a referendum on the war. If Lincoln won, he would have the political support to force the war to a successful conclusion for the Union. If he lost, it seemed likely that the people of the North no longer supported the war. In such a situation, many in the South were convinced that the North would be open to a negotiated peace that included independence for the Confederacy.

Thus in the spring of 1864 the effort to break the blockade became a political issue as well as a strategic war aim. While cruisers and blockade-runners played cat and mouse with the Union navy on the sea, the South renewed the struggle to destroy the Federal bases established on the Carolina coast in 1861 and 1862.

An attack in February against the Union base at New Bern failed. The operation was an army affair commanded by Maj. Gen. George E. Pickett, the commander of the Department of Cape Fear and North Carolina. Two months later, on April 15, 1864, P. G. T. Beauregard replaced Pickett. The initiative came from Richmond, likely (although there is no direct evidence) from Secretary of the Navy Mallory. Beauregard was a better strategist than field commander, and he perennially submitted war plans to Richmond. Some of these proposals were grandiose and impractical, but others were eminently workable. The problem for Beauregard's superiors lay in determining the one from the other.

The plan for the operation against the Federal bases in North Carolina centered around the four ironclads under construction in the Tar Heel State: *Raleigh* and *North Carolina,* which were to protect the port of Wilmington, and *Albemarle* and *Neuse,* which were assigned to the North Carolina sounds.

Raleigh AND *North Carolina* were built in Wilmington in 1862 according to plans provided by John L. Porter, one of the architects of the *Virginia. Raleigh* was constructed at the J. L. Cassidy and Sons shipyard, and *North Carolina* took shape at Berry and Brothers. Construction was hampered by limited resources and a lack of materials. Both factors contributed to considerable delays in their completion. These delays were only made worse when the shipwrights went on strike because the Department of the Navy had inadequate funds to pay them. Other delays occurred in late 1862 and again in 1863, when three serious outbreaks of yellow fever forced workers to flee the city. Finally, when they were on the verge of completion, one of the shipyards suffered a severe fire, which occasioned even more delay.

The two ships entered service in late 1863. At about the same time, a third Wilmington ironclad, named *Wilmington,* was laid down but never completed, enduring much the same history of delays as the two other vessels. *North Carolina*'s engines had been taken from an old tugboat. They were unreliable, so the ship was used mostly as a floating battery to protect the blockade-runners' anchorage at Smithville on the New Inlet of the Cape Fear River.

To contest Federal control of the North Carolina sounds established by the operations at Hatteras Inlet in 1861 and Roanoke Island in 1862, the Confederates established a number of inland navy yards. A total of eighteen warships were under construction. Again those efforts were hampered by limited resources, poor transportation, and a shortage of skilled workers.

Among the contracts were three given to Gilbert Elliott and William Martin for the construction of two ironclads and a wooden gunboat. Only one vessel was completed, however: the

CSS *Albemarle*. Construction did not begin until January 1863, when John L. Porter was appointed to superintend the work. When he arrived he found the shipyard to be a former cornfield at Edwards Ferry on the Roanoke River. After a year Porter was replaced by Cmdr. James W. Cooke, who brought extra men and equipment to the project.

When the ship was completed, *Albemarle*'s modified hull allowed her to float in only six feet of water. This was done by giving her a flat bottom and a flared side in place of the knuckle—a design that quickly became associated with Confederate ironclads specifically built for shallow-water operations. In addition, she also had a sixty-foot-long octagonal shield that was covered with two layers of two-inch iron plating. Her prow, strengthened for ramming, was also plated with two-inch-thick iron plates and was tapered to a point. The ship's battery was made of two 7-inch Brooke rifles mounted on pivots within her casement. They were designed to fire fore and aft and on both broadsides.

Neuse was an *Albemarle*-type ironclad laid down at Whitehall by Elliot Smith and Company in 1863. She had the same hull design as the *Albemarle* and was also intended to operate in shallow coastal and riverine waters. While under construction the *Neuse* was shelled and damaged by a Federal raiding force in December 1863. After her hull was repaired, she was handed over to the Confederate navy and towed to Kingston, North Carolina, to be completed. *Neuse* was commissioned around the same time as the *Albemarle*, in April 1864. Like *Albemarle* she was also fitted with two 7-inch Brooke rifles.

Gideon Welles had begun receiving reports about the *Albemarle* and *Neuse* as early as the spring of 1863. All that was known, though, was that ironclad rams were being built somewhere up the Roanoke and Neuse Rivers. Lt. Cmdr. Charles W. Flusher, commander of the wooden gunboat *Miami,* was assigned to investigate. Flusher did not have much luck with his sources and received only conflicting reports from spies and scouts.

Confederate Com. William F. Lynch was then in command of the squadron defending Wilmington. He had been something of a lightning rod across the Confederacy, overseeing many Southern naval disasters. In early 1862 he had succeeded Samuel Barron as commander of naval forces on the North Carolina coast, and these forces were later destroyed at the battle of Elizabeth City. Later that same year Lynch had succeeded George N. Hollins in command of naval forces on the Mississippi. There he had failed to provide the leadership that might have prevented the unnecessary destruction of the gunboats that had escaped the disasters of the battle of Memphis and Island No. 10. This had forced the *Arkansas* to go it alone when she saved Vicksburg from two Union fleets. Then Lynch had failed to prevent the *Arkansas* from being sent off on what amounted to a suicide mission when she should have been retained for the continued defense of Vicksburg. Now he was back in North Carolina to supervise ironclad construction projects, particularly the *Raleigh* and *North Carolina*. As the senior naval officer in the state, he also had command authority over the *Albemarle* and *Neuse* as well as other Confederate warships operating in the sounds.

THE EVENTS that began with the *Albemarle*'s sortie on April 17, 1864, and ended about nineteen days later on May 5 and 6, represented a single coordinated operation aimed at destroying the infrastructure of the blockade represented by the Union supply bases. For this operation Beauregard was given a division of troops drawn from Robert E. Lee's Army of Northern Virginia under the command of Brig. Gen. Robert F. Hoke.

On April 10 Charles W. Flusher received word from three separate sources that the *Albemarle* was about to come out, accompanied by Confederate troops—Hoke's command. Flusher prepared to meet the Southern ship with the gunboats *Miami, Southfield, Whitehead,* and *Ceres* and sank a number of blocking ships to impede the approaches to the Federal base at Plymouth. The town had been seized by Union troops as a subsidiary to the Hatteras Inlet and Roanoke Island operations in 1861–62. It had since been used as a base and coaling depot for the Federals' shallow-draft unarmored coastal and riverine gunboats, which were the mainstay of the blockade along the North Carolina coast.

Albemarle entered the area on April 17 after she successfully maneuvered through the Roanoke River obstructions without so much as a scrape on her keel. Opposing her were the only two

Union gunboats on the scene, *Miami* and *Southfield,* which Flusher had lashed together; they blocked the approach to Plymouth along the Roanoke River. In a fierce action the *Albemarle* attacked the two gunboats. Flusher tried to ram the Confederate ironclad, but *Albemarle* struck first. The Confederate rammed the *Miami* then struck the *Southfield* slantwise. Her bow hit *Southfield*'s side and penetrated her forward room and into her fire room.

The two Union ships opened fire, but their guns were largely ineffective. Solid shot fired at close range bounded off the ironclad's sides. Seeking a vulnerable spot in the Confederate's armor, Flusher himself directed the gunners of a forward-mounted 9-inch Dahlgren. Under his direction the gun fired three shells. The third shell shattered on *Albemarle*'s armor, and pieces of it flew back into the Federal gun crew. Flusher was killed when a fragment of his own shell ripped into his chest.

Meanwhile, *Southfield* was sinking and threatening to take the other two vessels down with her. The crew of the *Miami* frantically cut loose whatever lashings had not been broken by the force of the blow from *Albemarle*'s ram. The Confederate ship's ram was also entangled in the lashings. Water poured through the ironclad's forward gun ports until the ship broke free and bobbed back to the surface of the river like a cork. With *Southfield* sunk and Flusher dead, *Miami* and the other two small gunboats at Plymouth fled.

Albemarle's skipper, James W. Cooke, did not bother to pursue the Federals. The next day the Confederate ironclad appeared off Plymouth to support Hoke's attack on the Union base. *Albemarle*'s two heavy guns bombarded the town all that day and all that night. Gen. Matt Whitaker Ransom's brigade of Hoke's division was directed against the forts on the eastern and southern faces of the town. The brigade engulfed the Federal forces defending Conaby Creek and assaulted Fort Comfort on the eastern side. The Southerners routed the Union garrison and pushed into the town itself, where street-to-street and house-to-house fighting ensued. On April 20 the Confederate troops resumed their attack with naval fire support provided by *Albemarle*'s guns. By this time Ransom's brigade had silenced the Federals' heavy artillery that had held the *Albemarle* at bay and prevented her from providing close support. In addition, most of the defenses except for Fort Williams had been knocked out. Here the fire support provided by *Albemarle*'s two rifled guns kept the defenders away from the ramparts. At 10 A.M. the fort and the Union base at Plymouth surrendered.

Hoke's troops took almost three thousand prisoners and captured twenty-eight heavy guns, five thousand rifles, seven hundred barrels of flour, a large amount of other supplies and ammunition, and three hundred tons of coal badly needed by the Confederate navy. Southern strategists believed the Plymouth naval base itself would be the ideal launching point for an offensive to clear the Union forces from the sounds.

On April 26, 1864, Hoke began marching toward his next target—Washington, North Carolina. The Federal garrison evacuated this coastal town on April 27, since the loss of naval power in this coastal zone made it impossible for Union forces to hold the town. With only one ironclad, used with imagination and daring, the Confederates had won a dazzling victory and had taken a huge step toward liberating the entire coastal area. Hoke's next target was the naval base at New Bern.

Plans originally required the ironclads *Albemarle* and *Neuse* and the small gunboats *Cotton Plant* and *Bombshell* to support Hoke's attack on New Bern. The *Neuse*, under the command of Lt. Benjamin P. Loyall, weighed anchor on April 22 and began to descend the Neuse River. Unfortunately the water had fallen too low even for her light draft, and she ran aground on a sandbank. Her crew tried to refloat her, but the water level had fallen seven feet in just four days. *Neuse* remained stuck on the sandbank until the water level rose again—in the fall.

Albemarle, Cotton Plant, and *Bombshell*'s part of the operation called for them to leave the Roanoke River for the sea, cross the sounds, which were infested with Union gunboats, and proceed up the estuary of the Neuse River, which was full of obstructions. James W. Cooke felt he had a good chance of success since there were no Union ironclads on the sounds, and the Federal gunboats could not stand against his ironclad.

There were no Union ironclads on the sounds because their drafts were too deep for the sounds' shallow waters, and sufficient shallow-draft ironclads were simply not available. To address the situation, Gustavus V. Fox, the U.S. assistant secretary of the navy, concentrated a force of powerful wooden gunboats here— namely, *Mettabesett, Sassacus, Wyalusing, Miami, Whitehead, Commodore Hull,* and *Ceres*—all under the command of Capt. Melancton Smith.

When the approach of *Albemarle* and her consorts was reported to Smith, he ordered his ships forward. His four largest were in a line ahead, shielding his three smaller gunboats from the guns of the Confederate ships. The battle opened at 5 P.M. on May 5, 1864, when *Albemarle* fired on the Union ships at a range of eight hundred yards.

Albemarle's second shell struck *Mettabesett,* Smith's flagship, destroying some of her rigging and wounding several of her crew. *Sassacus,* second in the main Union line, opened fire with a full broadside upon *Albemarle,* doing her absolutely no damage at all. Next Cooke tried to ram *Mettabesett,* but the Union ship had enough speed to avoid what might have been a fatal blow.

Sassacus had opened the distance between herself and *Albemarle* in an attempt to capture the *Bombshell.* Now she suddenly turned to starboard and steamed at full speed toward *Albemarle* and rammed her. The blow made *Albemarle* heel over considerably and threw most of her crew, including Cooke, to the deck. *Sassacus,* however, had not been designed as a ram, and the blow only did minor damage to the *Albemarle* while inflicting major damage on the Federal gunboat. Cooke quickly rallied his crew and fired his guns point-blank into the *Sassacus.* One of the shells burst her boiler. The explosion of the boiler knocked *Sassacus* out of the fight for good.

The Union ships managed to cut off the *Bombshell* from support from the *Albemarle,* and she was captured by Smith's smaller gunboats. Cooke was able to cover *Cotton Plant* and prevent her from suffering a similar fate. The battle continued, and *Albemarle* targeted the Union ships with well-aimed shot and shell until the *Wyalusing* was forced to withdraw in a sinking condition. By 7:30 P.M. the battle was over. *Sassacus* and *Wyalusing* were severely damaged with five dead and twenty-five wounded. Smith had had enough and withdrew his battered flotilla.

The battle prevented the *Albemarle* from continuing her cruise. Her funnel was almost destroyed, causing her steam pressure to fall to near zero, which carried the risk of her becoming immobilized while under enemy fire. Cooke used the expedients of throwing oil and greasy materials on the fires to cause the boiler pressure to raise enough to move his ship. In addition, one of *Albemarle*'s guns was disabled when its muzzle had been shot away, which reduced the ironclad's firepower to a single gun. Cooke was forced to return to Plymouth for repairs.

The next day the combined operation kicked off. Intended as a diversion to keep reinforcements from being dispatched to Smith's Union flotilla on the afternoon of May 6, the ironclad *Raleigh,* backed by the gunboats *Yadkin* and *Equator,* steamed from Wilmington down the Cape Fear River to the sea. Their objectives were the blockading ships. Following behind were a number of blockade-runners intending to exploit the confusion of the attack to break out into the Atlantic. This was a highly risky enterprise since the river was also falling and the *Raleigh* was not a shallow-draft ironclad like the *Albemarle* and the *Neuse*. Steps were taken to lighten the *Raleigh* so she could cross the bar safety. The effort was successful, and the three Confederate warships began looking for prey. *Raleigh,* however, became separated from her consorts as night fell.

Sometime around 8 P.M., in the gathering dusk, *Raleigh* suddenly appeared directly in the path of the Union ships *Britannia* and *Nansemond*. The startled crew of the *Britannia* managed to open fire first then saw that the shells had no effect and immediately fled the scene. The night protected both Federal vessels from *Raleigh,* although *Nansemond* did exchange fire with the Confederate ironclad around 11:45 P.M. When dawn broke only four blockaders were visible, the rest having fled. As soon as her crew could see her enemies, the *Raleigh* resumed the battle. The USS *Howquah* was hit by the ironclad's gunners in her funnel and immediately withdrew. *Nansemond, Mount Vernon,* and *Kansas* also reversed course and departed for the high seas. The Union ships were faster than the *Raleigh*. Because the combat had taken place at relatively long range, the Confederate was unable to engage and dispatch any of her opponents.

By 8 A.M. the *Raleigh* commanded the sea around her but also lost contact with her two escorts. Lynch decided to reverse course and return to Wilmington. *Raleigh* managed to pass safely over the bar but ran aground as she approached the Smithville blockade-runner anchorage, about three miles up the Cape Fear River's New Inlet. Since she had broken her back in the grounding, all efforts to refloat her failed. Eventually she was judged a wreck, and her guns and armor were salvaged. The loss of the *Raleigh* was ascribed to a weakness in her hull that represented either a design flaw or a failure in her construction.

The Union navy, however, was ignorant of her loss for some time. Fear of the *Raleigh* caused the blockaders to keep their distance. The Federals were still studying ways to eliminate the *Raleigh* at least two weeks later, unaware that the Southerners had already lost the ship.

Meanwhile, Hoke's troops had invested New Bern on May 4 and demanded the surrender of the town. They were obliged to abandon this attempt, however, when Ulysess S. Grant crossed the Rapidan River with the Army of the Potomac while Benjamin F. Butler was moving up the James River with the Army of the James. Their target was, of course, Richmond. Beauregard was therefore compelled to send Hoke's troops to meet this threat. Thus the successful operation in the North Carolina sounds had to be abandoned.

The departure of the troops stripped North Carolina of manpower, but as long as the *Albemarle* remained at Plymouth, no Union attempt to strengthen or extend their then existing North Carolina holdings could succeed. Thus *Albemarle* single-handedly served the purpose of a fleet and validated once again Mallory's coastal defense strategy. The Confederacy, however, would never again have a similar opportunity, because the days of the North Carolina ironclads were numbered.

The first to be lost was the *Raleigh's* sister ship, the immobile *North Carolina*, which served as a floating battery at the blockade-runner anchorage at Smithville. She proved to have even worse hull problems than engine problems, and she sank at her moorings on September 27, 1864, due to numerous leaks caused by marine worms, or teredos. The lack of seasoned materials during the vessel's construction meant that her wooden hull was not protected from the worms by the usual copper sheathing.

Within a month *Albemarle* too would be gone. Ever since the ship had fought Smith's flotilla to a standstill, the Federals had pondered her destruction. William B. Cushing submitted two plans to Rear Adm. Samuel P. Lee, commander of the North Atlantic Blockading Squadron. The first called for an assault unit of one hundred men to advance through the swamps on inflatable rafts and swarm the ironclad. The second took a page from the Confederates' book and suggested that torpedo launches might eliminate the feared *Albemarle*. Lee submitted both schemes to the assistant secretary of the navy. Fox was impressed and authorized the torpedo launch operation.

Cushing went to New York City to obtain two thirty-foot-long steam-powered picket boats. Each was fitted with a 12-pounder howitzer in the bow and a starboard side-mounted fourteen-foot-long torpedo boom. During the attack the boom would be lowered to contact the target, and the torpedo would be detonated. While en route to North Carolina, one of the boats was lost.

In North Carolina, Cushing's original sponsor, Lee, had been replaced by Rear Adm. David D. Porter. The change was made in part due to the poor showing of Lee's squadron against the *Albemarle* and *Raleigh*. In addition, it appeared that the Union was in danger of losing control of the North Carolina sounds. Since Cushing's project had the approval of Fox, Porter allowed him to proceed.

Due to the poor living conditions aboard the *Albemarle*, caused by the constant trickling of water along her inside walls, most of her crew spent their off-duty time ashore and slept in a nearby shed. Cushing knew that there would be only a few guards aboard the Confederate ship at night. He waited for a dark night that would allow the best opportunity to approach the anchored ironclad.

On October 27, 1864, Cushing and seven volunteers slipped into the Roanoke River. The steam-powered launch also towed a cutter with a thirteen-man boarding party, which was intended to take care of the picket protecting the *Albemarle*. At 3 A.M. the launch was within thirty feet of the lookouts, but the raiding party was not spotted. Cushing considered the possibility of boarding and commandeering the ironclad. As he turned in to land his men, one of the guards shouted a warning.

Cushing cut the cutter loose and steered his launch toward the ironclad. The ship's guards opened fire with small arms. Cushing's coat was shredded by a charge of buckshot, and the sole of one of his shoes was carried away. Also protecting the ironclad was a tangle of floating logs. Cushing had foreseen they would be slimy from long immersion in the dank water. While his men fired the launch's howitzer at the ironclad, Cushing guided the launch over the logs, lowered the boom, and detonated the torpedo. Instantly the launch was swamped. Some of the men thought their craft had been hit by a shell. In actuality the water had been thrown into the open boat by the force of the torpedo explosion. The charge opened a gigantic hole in *Albemarle*'s side, and the iron-clad sank immediately to the bottom of the Roanoke River.

Most of Cushing's raiders surrendered. Cushing himself and another man swam away. The other sailor drowned, but Cushing got to the bank of the river and followed it to the sea. He came across a rowboat the following evening and set out in it to find the fleet. After ten hours of rowing, he was rescued by the gunboat *Valley City* and taken to the squadron's flagship, *Malvern* (the former blockade-runner *Ella and Annie*), and made his report to Porter. With the *Albemarle* eliminated, Union troops and their naval supports easily retook Plymouth.

Porter now turned his eye toward taking Wilmington. He wanted to eliminate this major blockade-running port in the same way his foster brother—David G. Farragut—had taken New Orleans and Mobile. In addition, Federal planners were interested in using the port to support Maj. Gen. William Tecumseh Sherman, who had completed his March to the Sea and begun to march through the Carolinas. Benjamin F. Butler, due to his experience and knowledge of amphibious operations, was assigned to command the sixty-five hundred troops allocated for the effort. The attacking force was assembled at Hampton Roads and arrived off Fort Fisher—the port's protecting fortification—by December 20, 1864.

The loss of both *Raleigh* and *North Carolina* had left the vitally important port without any ironclads to reinforce land fortifications like Fort Fisher. The ironclad *Wilmington* was still under construction. She was intended to be a fast, light-draft double-casemate ironclad with twin engines and an eight-foot-diameter screw propeller. Four boilers were to supply the steam, and she had a single funnel between two fixed and rounded casemates. Each of the casemates was to be fitted with a large-caliber pivot-mounted rifle that could fire through any of three gun ports.

As with *Raleigh* and *North Carolina*, construction of the *Wilmington* was behind schedule. As the Porter-Butler expedition neared the city, she was still not completed. The lack of ironclad naval support unfortunately unhinged Mallory's heretofore successful coastal defense strategy.

The key to the land-based defenses of the city of Wilmington was Fort Fisher. The fortification was constructed on a large sand spit that formed a peninsula lying on a roughly north-south axis. The Cape Fear River was to the west, and the Atlantic was to the east. Fisher's powerful batteries were protected by mounds of sand, and her garrison was protected by a number of bombproof shelters dug into the sand.

Butler and Porter devised a clever stratagem aimed at minimizing the loss of life. On December 23 the supply ship *Louisiana* was towed to within 450 yards of the fort. Her hull was loaded with 350 tons of gunpowder. The Federals planned to blow her up, believing that the concussion from the massive explosion would sweep across the fort and disable both the structure and defenders. The chief engineer of the army declared the idea preposterous, but Butler and Porter proceeded. At 1:40 A.M. on December 24 the powder ship was detonated. The result was a colossal failure. A Confederate prisoner questioned after the fall of the city about the effect of the blast said it "woke up everybody in the fort."

Porter began a bombardment of the fort at midday on December 24 and continued for five and a half hours. His rate of fire reached 115 rounds per minute. During the bombardment the troop transports arrived, and Butler began moving his men ashore. They landed at the north end of the fort and edged their way toward the Confederate position. As they approached the fort, Butler was shocked to discover that aside from minor damage the fort was virtually untouched; the sand had swallowed the Federal shot and muffled the effect. As soon as the naval fire lifted, Col. William Lamb, the commandant of the fort, was able to man his guns and ramparts.

Not seeing how he could avoid a hopeless bloodbath, Butler withdrew without attempting an attack—to the immense disgust of Admiral Porter.

A second attack was made in mid-January 1865. This time the army commander was Maj. Gen. Alfred Terry, and he was given twelve thousand men and a siege train to do the job. The fleet returned to Fort Fisher on January 12, 1865, with a second bombardment beginning the next day. Porter had learned from his mistakes: there was no *Louisiana* bomb this time, and he moved his ships much closer to the fort.

Porter was able to do this because there was little or no interference from the Confederate navy. Without ironclads, the gunboats and the cruiser *Chickamauga* tasked with helping to defend Wilmington were easily brushed aside by the Union fleet. If *Raleigh*, *Wilmington*, or even *North Carolina* had been available, they could have prevented Porter's Union ships from effectively closing the range with Fort Walker, which was the decisive factor in the battle.

Porter's ships concentrated their fire at the north face of the fort, dismounting guns and blowing wide gaps in the palisades defending the fort. Terry efficiently moved his troops ashore with adequate provisions and ammunition. In addition, Porter also landed sixteen hundred sailors and four hundred marines to assault the sea face. The attack by Porter's landing force was brave but uncoordinated. They were repulsed with heavy losses although their attack caused the Southerners to divert troops to the sea face, weakening the north front, where Terry's troops broke through. The fort surrendered at 10 P.M. after seven hours of combat.

Terry and his troops moved onto the city, which surrendered on February 22, 1865. With the fall of the city, the last incomplete ironclad, *Wilmington*, was destroyed while still on the stocks.

The fall of Wilmington helped to demonstrate how important ironclads were to Mallory's coastal defense strategy. If the *Raleigh*,

North Carolina, or *Wilmington* had been available, it is possible that they could have kept Porter's fleet from firing so effectively. If Fort Fisher had not fallen, the city could have held out longer than it did, possibly until after the surrender of Joseph Johnston's army on April 26, 1865. Of the South's six primary coastal ports—Richmond, Wilmington, Charleston, Savannah, Mobile, and New Orleans—only two were taken by direct military assault. New Orleans fell before the ironclads under construction there were either operational or fully completed. Wilmington fell after her protecting ironclads had been eliminated. Although the city of Mobile did not fall to the Union army until the closing months of the war, it had been effectively neutralized when the August 1864 battle of Mobile Bay gave Farragut effective control of the city's sole harbor entrance.

The approaching end of the war was signaled by the destruction of the last of the North Carolina ironclads, the unlucky *Neuse.* In the fall of 1864 the water level of the Neuse River finally raised enough to release *Neuse* from her sandbank. She was used thereafter to protect the river as well as the countryside around her from enemy raids. By this time Sherman and his army had entered North Carolina, and Union columns had spread throughout the state. The ship was cornered. Confederate authorities, surrounded by Sherman's troops, begged for help from the ironclad to cover their retreat. *Neuse* used her guns to scatter some Union cavalry, but finally she was scuttled on March 13, 1865, to prevent her capture.

13

Farragut's Fatal Final Strike

REAR ADM. DAVID G. FARRAGUT returned to the war's center stage during the late summer of 1864. After the *Arkansas* forced him to withdraw his seagoing warships from the vicinity of Vicksburg, it was clear that the navy would need more than token army support to take the Mississippi River fortress city. Even Secretary of the Navy Gideon Welles had to admit that only a large army—with naval support on the Mississippi River—would be sufficient to take the city and finally close the "Father of Waters" to the Confederates.

It would take over a year and the combined talents of Maj. Gen. Ulysses S. Grant and Rear Adm. David D. Porter, Farragut's foster brother, before the river fortress would fall and the Anaconda Plan would be fulfilled.

Farragut, with more than a sigh of relief, had meanwhile returned to the Gulf of Mexico and immediately fixed his attention on the city of Mobile and Mobile Bay. It was Farragut and not the Navy Department who determined to tie off another major Confederate economic artery at Mobile. It was Farragut who realized that the best way to blockade or close a port was to take the port. While he did not have the physical means to take the city of Mobile, which would have required an occupying army, he did have the means of seizing control of Mobile Bay.

203

With the fall of New Orleans on April 29, 1862, Mobile had been left as the only port of consequence controlled by the Confederates along the Gulf of Mexico. Tampa, Galveston, and Matamoros (safely in neutral Mexico opposite the city of Brownsville across the Rio Grande) remained open to the Confederacy practically to the end of the war, but they lacked the rail and water connections to supply the interior of the South and specifically the Army of Northern Virginia and the Army of Tennessee.

After the fall of Vicksburg, Ulysses S. Grant, William Tecumseh Sherman, and Farragut attempted to answer the question that had been left unanswered ever since the aged General Scott had first formulated the Anaconda Plan. The fall of Vicksburg and the closing of the Mississippi River did not in itself end the Confederacy. Scott had viewed the fight as a limited war being fought by limited means, and he assumed that once the Mississippi had fallen under Union control, the Confederate government would realize it would be impossible to win independence by force and the individual states would negotiate readmission into the Union.

That did not happen because the Civil War had changed from being a limited war for limited aims into a total war for total aims: either the South would win its independence or the North would conquer the South. Farragut believed that one answer to the question of "Then what?"—after achieving the goals of Scott's plan—was the city of Mobile and Mobile Bay.

Grant agreed that Mobile Bay might well prove to be the soft underbelly of the Confederacy. In late 1863 he told Maj. Gen. Henry W. Halleck, the general in chief, that an expedition against Mobile could detach Mississippi, Alabama, and most of the state of Georgia from the Confederacy. As soon as Grant was made general in chief on March 9, 1864, he wanted to seize Mobile so as to threaten Joseph E. Johnston and the Army of Tennessee from the rear while Sherman pressed them from the front.

These tentative plans came to naught when the troops Grant needed for the offensive were diverted to the disastrous Red River campaign under Maj. Gen. Nathaniel Banks, another political general who failed in the field. Banks's mission had been to invade Texas for the sake of cotton and to frighten the French emperor Napoleon III out of Mexico. The Banks expedition foundered at the battle of Sabine Crossroads in Louisiana on April 8, 1864, and forced Grant to choose other strategic projects.

Although the army, as represented by Grant, had dropped its plans for Mobile, Farragut made sure that the navy did not. He continued to study Mobile, Mobile Bay, and their defenses.

Mobile is situated at the head of Mobile Bay, about thirty miles from the bay's entrance and the waters of the Gulf of Mexico. Before the war began the city had been one of the South's primary ports for the shipment of cotton to Europe. Its population of thirty thousand people included a number of foreign nationals, and its French and Spanish heritage made it a cosmopolitan community. As a port, however, Mobile left a lot to be desired.

The harbor was well protected, but the passage leading to the open waters of the Gulf was difficult, as the Confederate raider cruiser *Florida* had already discovered. Although the entrance to the bay was three miles wide, a number of natural obstacles greatly reduced the channel. To port was Dauphin Island and its major defensive work, Fort Gaines. To starboard was Mobile Point, which was defended by Fort Morgan. A third work, Fort Powell, was just outside the bay. Most of the three-mile span of the mouth of the bay was extremely shallow. In fact there was only one navigable channel, which was on the starboard side as it was approached, running very close to Mobile Point. Thus any ship entering the channel was well within the range of the guns of Fort Morgan.

Water depth farther up the bay remained fairly shallow, and eventually this sole navigable channel reached Dog River Bar. This east-west obstruction had a depth of water of ten feet or less, depending upon the tide. Before the war most of Mobile's commerce had been handled by lighters that loaded and unloaded at the city's wharves and ferried cargo back and forth to ships riding at anchor much closer to the waters of the Gulf.

The city itself had been built upon the banks of the Mobile River, which provided easy access to the rich agricultural areas of the interior of Alabama and Mississippi. Thirty miles above the city the Tombigbee and Alabama Rivers joined to form the Mobile River. Through this river system steamboats and other river craft brought huge quantities of cotton to the city for shipment abroad and also took imported munitions and other goods back to the interior. Aside from waterborne transportation there was also the Mobile and Ohio Railroad, one of the longest in the South, which had its southern terminus at Mobile. This railroad ran all the way north to Columbus, Kentucky.

For the city of Mobile the Civil War began when Forts Gaines and Morgan were surrendered to the state when Alabama seceded in January 1861. The blockade came to Mobile on May 26, 1861, when then Lt. David D. Porter dropped anchor at the entrance to the harbor aboard the USS *Powhatan*. The Confederate navy made its appearance at Mobile Bay when a coastwise packet was converted into the gunboat CSS *Florida*, which skirmished off and on with the blockaders until she was captured in March 1862. The city's greatest defense, however, was Union indifference.

Although both Grant and Farragut both wanted the city, its seizure was not a high priority for either Lincoln or Secretary of the Navy Welles. Mobile did not become a serious target for the Union navy until the Mississippi River had been cleared of Confederate strongholds by the surrender of the fortress cities of Vicksburg and Port Hudson in the summer of 1863. Even then it took the dogged persistence of Farragut over a period of months before an attack upon the port was authorized.

Mobile's comparative importance to the Confederacy, on the other hand, can best be inferred by the appointment of the senior-most-ranking officer in the navy, Adm. Franklin Buchanan, to take command of the naval forces defending the city. There was, however, no unified command in either a formal or informal sense. In the formal sense Buchanan commanded the naval forces and Maj. Gen. Dabney H. Maury commanded the forts and troops protecting the city and Mobile Bay. Informally, Buchanan and Maury did not achieve the level of cooperation that Beauregard established with Duncan N. Ingraham and John Randolph Tucker. Finally, the command responsibilities of neither Buchanan nor Maury were clearly defined.

Not only was Buchanan the highest-ranking Confederate naval officer, he was also one of the most highly respected naval officers in the South. A native of Maryland, Buchanan had been the first commandant of the U.S. Naval Academy. Maryland was part of the Upper South and a slave state. At the beginning of the war Buchanan had been so certain that Maryland would secede that he had tendered his resignation as soon as Fort Sumter fell. When Maryland did not secede, Buchanan attempted to withdraw his resignation. Welles, however, was thoroughly disgusted with resigning officers and refused to reinstate Buchanan.

As the senior ranking officer in the Confederate navy, Buchanan had commanded the *Virginia* at Hampton Roads during the first day of the battle there and had overseen the destruction of the *Congress* and the *Cumberland,* even though his brother was serving as a navy paymaster aboard the *Congress.* After he was wounded in the leg at Hampton Roads, Buchanan had been promoted to admiral, becoming one of only two in the Confederate navy. He spent much of the rest of 1862 recovering from his wound.

Buchanan was still not completely recovered when in August 1862 he was ordered by Mallory to take command at Mobile Bay. His predecessor, Flag Off. Victor Randolph, had been in charge there since the previous February. Randolph, unfortunately, was an example of why Mallory crusaded against seniority in the navy. Randolph was a native of Alabama and had joined the U.S. Navy during the War of 1812. Almost fifty years later he gained prominence within the Confederacy when on January 12, 1861, he led a small force to demand the surrender of the Pensacola Navy Yard. Randolph was one of the most senior naval officers to join the Confederate navy, and he expected to receive a command commensurate with his seniority in the old navy. He and Mallory, however, soon quarreled, and it was suspected that Randolph had been sent to Mobile more because it was as far away from Richmond as Mallory could send him rather than because of Randolph's native-son relationship to Alabama.

His home state roots made little difference, because Randolph failed to make friends and influence people there either. He also failed to take the initiative to attack the blockading warships at Mobile Bay, most of which were sailing ships, as George N. Hollins had done at New Orleans, as Duncan N. Ingraham later did at Charleston, and as Josiah Tattnall attempted at Savannah. Randolph developed only a tiny force consisting of three gunboats and an ironclad. Instead of doing anything, he apparently sat there, watched the blockade, and sent irritating letters to Mallory insisting that he be reinforced with ironclads, which did not then exist. Eventually, Mallory had had enough. He removed Randolph from command and ordered him court-martialed.

Upon taking charge at Mobile, Buchanan found the existing gunboat flotilla (what few of them were gunboats) "to be in a state of efficiency, highly creditable to their officers and the service." Randolph apparently had maintained a workable force even if he did little or nothing with it. The Mobile Bay Squadron was comprised of the ironclad *Baltic* and the gunboats *Gaines, Selma,* and *Morgan.*

Baltic had been a wooden side-wheel steamer originally built in 1860 as a tow boat for the Southern Steamship Company. She was purchased by Alabama for conversion into an ironclad. When the conversion was completed, she was eventually turned over to the Confederate navy for service at Mobile when the Alabama State Navy was disbanded. Her armament consisted of one 42-pounder, two 32-pounders, and two 12-pounder howitzers, all of which were smoothbores.

In February 1863 the *Baltic* was reported as unfit for further service and thus was unable to take part in the defense of the bay against Farragut. Her armor was removed and earmarked for the CSS *Nashville II,* an ironclad then under construction. Prior to that, however, she became the first minelayer in American naval history and was used to lay 180 stationary torpedoes, or naval mines, at the entrance to the bay but leaving a gap for blockade-runners to slip through.

Gaines had been hastily built at Mobile during 1861–62. Her hull consisted of unseasoned timber, and although not considered an ironclad, she was partly plated with two inches of armor. She was a side-wheeler with a top speed of ten knots. In 1863 her armament had included six 8-inch smoothbores in broadside with two 6-inch rifled cannon mounted on pivots. When Farragut forced his way into Mobile Bay, the gunboat's armament had been reduced to six guns, one 8-inch pivot-mounted rifle, and five 32-pounders.

The gunboat *Selma* had originally been built for coastal trading in Mobile in 1856 under the name *Florida.* Shortly after Fort

Sumter surrendered, the ship had been taken into the Confederate navy. She was cut down and strengthened with extra framing, and three-eighths-inch iron plating was added to her upper deck where it was angled to provide some protection to her boilers and machinery. Like *Gaines, Selma* was a side-wheeler. As a warship she had a top speed of nine knots. Her armament included two 9-inch Dahlgren smoothbores, one 8-inch and one 6-inch smoothbore; all four guns were mounted on pivots.

Morgan was another side-wheel steamer. She had been purchased by the Confederate navy in 1861 and had been converted into a warship with a top speed of ten knots. Her armament included a 7-inch Brooke rifle, a 6-inch rifle, and four 32-pounder smoothbores.

The first thing Buchanan did was to expand the shipbuilding program. In short order, four ironclads were under construction: *Nashville II, Tennessee II, Huntsville,* and *Tuscaloosa II.* Buchanan found many problems along the way. Although there were plenty of raw materials, there was a lack of skilled workmen. In addition, engines, which were generally inadequate, had to be salvaged from other steamers. Finally, cannon were difficult to find and transport.

Moreover, the Submarine Battery Service was also busy at Mobile, and several submarines were built there. One of these was the *H. L. Hunley,* which was moved to Charleston, where it attacked and sank a Union warship and then was lost at sea.

On February 7, 1863, the *Huntsville* and *Tuscaloosa* were launched at Selma, Alabama. Neither was as yet finished, but it was decided to move them to Mobile where they would be completed. A few days later the *Tennessee* was also launched and towed by the *Baltic* to join the other two in Mobile for their final fitting out and commissioning. Buchanan pushed, prodded, demanded, threatened, and finally in the spring of 1863, the *Huntsville* and *Tuscaloosa* were completed, commissioned, and steamed into Mobile Bay for their engine trials.

The two ironclads were identical to each other. Each was armed with one 6.4-inch rifle and three 32-pounder smoothbores. The *Tuscaloosa*'s engine trials were held in early April and *Huntsville*'s about two weeks later. The results were disappointing. The two ships could hardly make three knots, which made them little more than barely mobile floating batteries. By the summer of 1863, the two were deemed operational, but due to their low speed, a decision was made not to use them in the bay. They were retained for the river defense of Mobile. Buchanan did everything he could to keep their weaknesses from being discovered by Farragut. He succeeded rather well—perhaps too well. The mere existence of the ironclads was the argument Farragut used to obtain permission for his attack.

After the disappointing performance of the *Huntsville* and *Tuscaloosa*, Buchanan pinned his hopes on the *Tennessee*, which was nearly completed, and the *Nashville*.

The larger of the two, *Nashville*, was laid down at Montgomery and then moved to Mobile after being launched. Since Buchanan had enough materials on hand to complete only one ironclad at a time, he decided to concentrate on the much more nearly complete *Tennessee*. By the time attention could be paid to *Nashville*, it was too late. The ship was never fully armored, and her sides were left unprotected. She was one of three paddle-wheel ironclads built or converted for the Confederacy. Eventually she was armed with three 7-inch Brooke rifles and one 24-pounder smoothbore howitzer. Like the *Huntsville* and *Tuscaloosa*, she eventually became part of Mobile's river defenses.

On the other hand, *Tennessee* was probably the single most powerful ironclad ever built and completed for the Confederate navy. By any standard she was a large and mighty warship. She had a rather broad beam in comparison with her length, but she was well armed and well protected. The armament included two 7-inch Brooke rifles and four 6.4-inch rifles. Heavy iron shutters were fixed over her gun ports, which were closed whenever the gun was run back inside the casemate. Her armor was five inches thick on her sides and six inches over her forward end. There was also two inches of armor on her decks.

Her shortcomings, however, were serious indeed. First, the automatic shutters over the gun ports were susceptible to jamming if struck directly by enemy fire. A more serious design flaw had been the placement of her tiller ropes in open channels on the deck, and the chains connecting the steering mechanism in the pilothouse ran back to the rudder along the top of her afterdeck.

Finally, her engines, which had been salvaged from the river steamer *Alonzo Child,* were inadequate, and additional problems were caused by their complicated gearing. She had a top speed of four knots.

Still the *Tennessee* was a formidable warship, and at the very least she frightened most of Farragut's officers, although Farragut himself was not overly impressed by rumors of her great strength. He was impressed enough by the fact that Buchanan had five ironclads, four of them completed, to set against the Union fleet of wooden warships. Farragut did not then know that *Baltic* had been decommissioned, nor did he know of the weaknesses of the *Huntsville* and *Tuscaloosa.* Farragut wanted ironclads of his own, and he wanted them badly.

Buchanan had another problem: finding crews for his warships. A product of the old navy, Buchanan was a tough, demanding martinet, not the sort of man to make an ideal recruiting officer. In the end, the army sent him 150 artillerymen to crew his guns. It was not an ideal solution, but like most of the makeshift solutions to the massive problems faced by the Confederate navy, it would have to do.

According to Jack Greene and Alessandro Massignani, when the *Tennessee* had been completed in May 1864, Buchanan considered using her immediately, as he had the *Virginia,* to take the war to the Union. He planned to have her loaded with coal and ammunition and to attack the wooden blockading vessels before they were aware of her presence. There were delays, however, in preparing for sea—including her being grounded for a time—and by May 21 the blockaders were aware of her presence. After that the number of Union wooden blockaders was increased from nine to thirteen to as many as eighteen ships. In addition, on July 20, 1864, a Union ironclad—the *Manhattan*—arrived.

THE *Tennessee* never sortied against the blockaders. If it had, the question remains whether or not the Confederate ironclad could have penetrated the blockade at Mobile and attacked a target of importance, such as Pensacola. Some historians believe Buchanan had a chance for such an attack as the guns of Fort Pickens, which blocked access to Pensacola and its navy yard, were few and old.

Yet they also believe that the blockaders he would have contended with in May and June could have overwhelmed the *Tennessee* if they had been resolutely led. If Farragut had been on the scene, that would certainly have been the case. The attempt might have been worth the effort rather than to wait for the Federals to mass several ironclads for their own attack on Mobile Bay—which of course is what happened.

Greene and Massignani also point out that if the Confederates had exploited the opportunity to obtain the East Indiamen in 1860 and 1861, assigned a greater portion of their war effort to building ironclads quickly and early, and had been much more aggressive with the ironclads they did have, it is possible that they might have secured control of the waters off some of their main ports. This possibility and its repercussions have not been fully appreciated by many, if not most, historians of the war.

If the South had maintained open ports—even if there were only one or two and even if only for a short time—this achievement could have encouraged foreign intervention on the side of the Confederacy. In addition, it offered the possibility of a naval victory for the South. Such a victory could very well have adversely affected Northern morale and threatened the Union's ability to win the war.

FARRAGUT WELL knew what kind of man his opponent was. In the old navy they had been friends with a shared background, as both of them were from the Upper South. Farragut had been born in East Tennessee and had spent what little boyhood he had in New Orleans before going to sea with his foster father. In addition, Farragut had been married in Norfolk and considered Virginia to be his home, as much as he had a home. He could not, however, abandon the flag he had served for over half a century. When Farragut had chosen to go north and Buchanan had chosen to go south, their friendship to all intents and purposes ended—particularly after the two had quarreled publicly over their separate decisions. So as commanders on opposite sides, the two officers had a very good idea of what the other would do in the approaching battle.

Like Buchanan after the battle of Hampton Roads, Farragut had been feted, toasted, and celebrated after the fall of New

Orleans as the Union's greatest living naval hero. He spent New Year's Day 1864 in New York City, where his family had relocated from Norfolk at the start of the war and where his flagship, *Hartford,* was being refitted. On January 6, 1864, he boarded the flagship to head back to the Gulf.

Although he had been away from the Gulf, he was apprised of developments through reports by his officers. He had already decided to let the Confederates keep their hold on the Texas Gulf Coast as the surrender of Vicksburg had effectively isolated Texas from the rest of the Confederacy. The West Gulf Blockading Squadron, however, remained an important command because Mobile was the last useful Gulf port remaining to the Confederacy, and the blockade there had to be maintained.

Farragut had been born, bred, and trained as a deep-water sailor. He remained, in his heart, a deep-water sailor even though his fame and victories had been achieved in shallow coastal waters. As a deep-water sailor he had an instinctive dislike for ironclads. He considered them to be—compared to his wooden ships—ugly, clumsy, and lacking in firepower. Still, Farragut realized that he had been lucky to attack New Orleans before the Confederates had completed or commissioned the two powerful ironclads *Louisiana* and *Mississippi.* He may not have liked ironclads, but he was forced to respect them, especially after his experience with the *Arkansas,* and to admit his fleet needed ironclads if he was going have a chance of successfully forcing his way past Buchanan's ironclads. This would be especially true if Buchanan's flagship, the mighty *Tennessee,* was anywhere as formidable as she was purported to be. At the same time, Farragut had no way of knowing that *Huntsville* and *Tuscaloosa* were little more than slow-moving floating batteries.

When Farragut returned to the Gulf, he wrote to his foster brother David D. Porter, then commanding the Union fleet on the Mississippi, on January 17, 1864, that he planned to force his way into Mobile Bay. He asked Porter if he could spare at least two ironclads to spearhead the attack. He also wrote Secretary of the Navy Gideon Welles requesting that two additional ironclads be transferred to his squadron from the Atlantic, where an ironclad fleet under John A. Dahlgren was attempting to address Welles's constant obsession, with Charleston.

Porter flatly refused to part with any of his ships. Welles too was unwilling to divert any ironclads from Charleston.

Farragut knew that his ships could bombard the Confederate fortifications and get around them with ease, but they were powerless to capture, occupy, and hold them. Until the forts guarding the entrance to Mobile Bay had been reduced, he would be unable to close the bay to blockade-runners. For those particular chores he needed army troops, and like the ironclads he requested, they were not available.

From early 1864 through the spring, Farragut shuttled between Pensacola and New Orleans with frequent visits to Mobile. He wrote constantly to Welles asking and demanding ironclads, troops, and coal, although neither the War nor Navy Department sent them to him.

Finally, toward the end of May, rumors began circulating that the *Tennessee* and *Nashville* were nearing completion and that, when they were ready, Buchanan was going to launch his own offensive. That news captured Washington's attention as well as Porter's.

In June the *Canonicus*-class monitors *Tecumseh* and *Manhattan* were transferred from Dahlgren's South Atlantic Blockading Squadron to Farragut's West Gulf Blockading Squadron, which by this time was mainly concentrated at the entrance to Mobile Bay awaiting an opportunity to strike. *Tecumseh* actually did not join Farragut's fleet until the evening before the battle. These were single-turret ironclads that mounted two 15-inch Dahlgren smoothbores. In addition, Porter ordered two ironclads, the *Milwaukee*-class heavy monitors *Chickasaw* and *Winnebago* to the Gulf. These were twin-turreted monitors that mounted four 11-inch Dahlgren smoothbores. They were considered to be among the finest ships of their type to be built during the Civil War. Finally, the army decided to cooperate as best it could.

Maj. Gen. William Tecumseh Sherman, who had succeeded Grant as western theater commander, saw the advantages a diversionary attack upon Mobile would give his own offensive in Georgia, namely, the conquest of Atlanta and the March to the Sea, which terminated at Savannah.

At a conference with Farragut aboard *Hartford,* Maj. Gen. Edward Canby and Maj. Gen. Gordon Granger informed the admiral that they did not have enough troops to take Mobile, but they did have sufficient men to take out Forts Gaines and Morgan as long as they moved against first one and then the other. Farragut recommended that the soldiers start with Fort Gaines, and the generals agreed.

Granger arrived with his troops on August 1 as agreed. The *Tecumseh*, however, was late in arriving, and Farragut was loath to launch the attack without her. When she finally arrived on the evening of August 4, Farragut decided to begin the assault the next day.

Farragut was probably the most experienced officer in the Union navy when it came to attacking land-based fortifications. He decided that a night attack, like the one at New Orleans, was inappropriate for Mobile Bay. Failure of command control and communications in the dark would simply invite catastrophe. Nor would he use a single-file attack column as he had at New Orleans, because a lone hit in a vulnerable place could stop a ship dead in the water. This would be disastrous in the narrow ship channel at Mobile Bay. He decided that his wooden ships would steam in pairs, lashed together, with the smaller ship on the side away from the enemy fortifications. If one ship in a pair was damaged, the other could pull both to safety.

Studying his charts and reconnaissance reports (some of the reconnaissance he had done himself), Farragut realized he would have to pass close—very close—to Fort Morgan on his starboard side. He did not want to be that close to the fort, but he had little choice because of the mines that had been laid by the *Baltic*. These further constricted an already narrow channel and forced his ships to steam well within the range of the Confederate guns.

Just ahead of the fort, Buchanan had anchored his squadron—*Tennessee, Gaines, Morgan,* and *Selma*—on a roughly northwest-southeast axis. Buchanan knew that the only way to prevent Farragut from closing off the entrance to the bay was to closely support the forts, especially Fort Morgan, with his ships. If he could keep Farragut's fleet outside the bay, he could prevent the landing of a force sufficient to invest and eventually capture Fort Morgan. As long as Fort Morgan remained under the Confederate flag and Farragut was unable to penetrate the entrance to the Mobile Bay, Mobile would remain an open port.

As Farragut's ships approached, they would provide a perfect target for Buchanan's ships, which by their deployment were in a position to rake Farragut's ships as they approached lashed together, two by two. Later this tactical position would be known as "crossing the T." It permitted Buchanan's ships to fire their full broadsides while Farragut's ships would be limited to responding only with their own bow guns. Buchanan also knew that as Farragut's fleet came parallel to Fort Morgan, Farragut would be required to alter his course to the northwest. While this would allow the Union ships to bring more of their guns to bear against Buchanan's squadron, it would also uncover the sterns of Farragut's ships to raking fire from the guns of Fort Morgan. A lot depended upon Fort Morgan.

Morgan was a pentagonal-shaped fortification constructed in 1818 as part of the coastal defense program following the War of 1812. By 1864 it was obsolete and unable to withstand the new powerful naval rifled guns. The fort, however, actually served to protect a water battery whose seven heavy guns, including an 8-inch rifle, were responsible for protecting the channel that led into Mobile Bay. Fort Gaines, situated on Dauphin Island, mounted twenty-six guns and helped to protect the main channel and the shallow secondary channel to the west of the island. Fort Powell was an earthwork built on an island in the channel and had another half-dozen heavy guns.

While Farragut had faced forts before, he had never had to consider maneuvering a fleet through a field of stationary torpedoes. In addition, he had been in combat only once against a truly powerful ironclad—the *Arkansas*—and he had lost. This reverse at Vicksburg had taught Farragut to respect ironclads—especially the Confederate variety.

After a final conference with his officers, Farragut agreed to one change in his battle plan. Originally, his flagship, *Hartford,* was to lead the attack. His captains, as they had at New Orleans, maintained he would have trouble controlling the fleet if he led the attack. They argued that *Brooklyn* should lead, particularly since she had been fitted with a special bow device designed to sweep stationary torpedoes. Thus in the same way that the *Baltic* had become the first minelayer, the *Brooklyn* was now the first minesweeper.

At 5:30 A.M. on August 5, 1864, the fleet got under way. The ironclads *Tecumseh, Manhattan, Chickasaw,* and *Winnebago* were positioned in their own line-ahead formation slightly forward and to starboard of the main fleet. Arranged parallel and to port of the ironclads were Farragut's seven pairs of wooden ships: *Brooklyn* and *Octorara, Hartford* and *Metacomet, Richmond* and *Port Royal, Lackawanna* and *Seminole, Monongahela* and *Kennebec, Ossipee* and *Itasca,* and *Oneida* and *Galena.* (*Galena* was the same ship as the second of the ironclads that was approved by the Ironclad Board. After the battle of Drewry's Bluff, the *Galena*'s armor was removed and the ship was recommissioned as a conventional wooden gunboat.)

The battle began when *Tecumseh* opened fire on Fort Morgan at 6:47 A.M. Within minutes the fort returned fire, and the battle quickly became a general action. As Farragut's fleet ranged in with their bow guns, Buchanan's little flotilla emerged from behind the fort, enfiladed Farragut's double line of ships, and opened fire.

There was very little wind to disperse the immense clouds of gun smoke generated by the intense fire, and it hung over the ships. The gun smoke made it difficult for Farragut to see what was going on. If he was going to control his fleet, he had to see what the situation was rather than relying on lookouts. Farragut elected to join the lookouts in the rigging. He took a position where he could see over the smoke and at the same time call orders out to the captain of the *Metacomet* and still communicate with his own flag captain, helmsman, and pilot. As the smoke grew heavier, Farragut climbed higher until he was braced against the futtock shrouds; he wrapped one of his arms around the shrouds and clutched his binoculars in his other hand.

The admiral's precarious position worried his flag captain, Percival Drayton, who feared that even a miss might dislodge the admiral from his precarious perch. Drayton, to Farragut's annoyance, ordered a seaman aloft to lash the admiral to the rigging for his own safety.

Once secured to his perch, Farragut saw that his fleet was facing great danger. First, the *Brooklyn* was backing down, her bow swinging toward Fort Morgan. This situation carried the seeds of disaster. If the other ships slowed, they would not be able to make steerage or hold their positions, and they would collide with each other. That kind of chaos could be quickly exploited by the Confederates. As he watched *Brooklyn* falter, Farragut saw the ironclad *Tecumseh,* just ahead and to *Brooklyn's* starboard side, suddenly change course. The original plan had called for *Tecumseh* to pass inboard of the minefield marker buoy. Her change of course, however, caused her to move farther into the channel, leaving the buoy to starboard and entering the field of stationary torpedoes.

On her new course, *Tecumseh* would cut directly across Farragut's battle line. The ironclad's captain, Cmdr. Tunis Augustus MacDonough Craven, had decided to alter the battle plan. Craven feared that should the four Union ironclads continue as planned, they could run aground and possibly allow the *Tennessee* to escape. Yet within minutes of changing course, the *Tecumseh* lurched from side to side, stopped dead in the water, and started sinking bow first. The general consensus was that she had struck a torpedo. Her stern came up, lifting her still turning propeller out of the water, and within minutes she was gone.

The *Brooklyn's* frantic efforts to avoid a collision with the *Tecumseh* as well as the ironclad's fate had instigated the original problem Farragut now perceived. *Brooklyn's* lookouts had sighted the buoy marking the minefield, and the ship's minesweeping device was entangled in some of the lines that connected the electrical detonators of the torpedoes with their frantic operators concealed on the shore. As he watched *Tecumseh* sink, Farragut instantly realized what had happened, but he immediately decided that he had no recourse but to steam ahead.

Farragut ordered Drayton to cut *Hartford* loose from *Metacomet* and to steam around *Brooklyn* and her consort to take the lead, even though this meant that she had to steam through the minefield. As *Hartford* passed *Brooklyn,* Farragut yelled to her captain, "What's the trouble?"

"Torpedoes!" he replied.

"Damn the torpedoes, full steam ahead!" Farragut is alleged to have roared to the pilot of the *Hartford.*

Hartford forged past *Brooklyn* and took the lead—the position Farragut had wanted her to take in the first place. Many of the *Hartford*'s crew believed that they were about to share the fate of the *Tecumseh*. Possibly most of the torpedoes—except for the one that had apparently sunk *Tecumseh*—were faulty, or perhaps they had been damaged by their long-term immersion in saltwater, which may have corroded their electrical contacts. Whatever the reason, the *Hartford*'s crew heard a succession of dull thuds along the ship's hull, but there was no explosion.

By 8 A.M. Farragut's force was inside the bay. Aside from the lost *Tecumseh*, one other ship had been badly damaged in passing Fort Morgan. The cruiser *Oneida* had occupied the most exposed position in the rear of the line, and she was limping along with *Galena*'s help.

Heavy gunfire from the Union ships had sent Morgan's gunners scurrying for cover. Now it was time to confront Buchanan and his ships.

The Confederate admiral and his four ships had not been idle as Farragut's fleet passed the fort. The gunboats *Morgan, Gaines,* and *Selma* had stayed ahead of the double column by about one thousand yards as Farragut's fleet approached, firing on the oblique. *Tennessee,* far too cumbersome for such a maneuver, made straight for the *Hartford* in an attempt to ram and sink the opposing flagship.

Without too much trouble *Hartford* slid past the ram and poured a broadside onto the *Tennessee*. Buchanan steamed past the rest of the Union line, pouring shot and shell into the ships and attempting to ram each one as it passed but failing each time. Although neither side was able to inflict any serious damage, both sides were heavily pounded.

As Buchanan moved down Farragut's line, the Union ships steamed on. The Federal admiral ordered the smaller gunboats to cast themselves loose from their bigger and slower consorts and to run down the three Confederate gunboats. *Metacomet* had lost no time awaiting orders after she had been cast loose from *Hartford*. Her target was the *Selma,* and within an hour the Confederate ship was her prize. The other Union gunboats were not quite so quick, and *Morgan* and *Gaines* were able to find shelter under the guns of Fort Morgan.

Tennessee, battered but not beaten, came rounding up the bay after going down the length of the Union line. It was thought that she too would take shelter under the guns of Fort Morgan, but taking shelter was never Buchanan's intention. As the situation became clear to his own officers, one asked, "Are you going into that fleet, Admiral?"

"I am, sir!" Buchanan growled back.

Tennessee's single-handed attack on Farragut's fleet could be seen as an act of rash desperation. Buchanan, however, could have succeeded in disabling or even sinking some of Farragut's ships. In addition, he would have the opportunity to engage the three remaining Union ironclads. It is conceivable that Buchanan could have succeeded in fighting through the Union fleet, returned to Mobile, and carried on a further defense of the city.

As *Tennessee* approached, Farragut ordered all of his ships—including ironclads—to attack and, if possible, ram the Confederate ironclad. What followed has been described as one of the closest and most heavily fought naval actions of the entire war.

One after another, *Monongahela, Lackawanna,* and *Hartford* rammed the *Tennessee*. They only succeeded in shaking her from funnel to keel while doing very little real damage. The actual damage was done when she was surrounded by the Union ironclads and showered with hits from their massive 11- and 15-inch Dahlgren smoothbores. Each time one of the rounds from the three Federal ironclads hit the Confederate ship, there was a violent noise and concussion. The experience was like being trapped inside a giant bell while it was being rung.

The impact of those massive shells and projectiles broke the backing of the *Tennessee*'s armor and let metal and wood splinters loose inside the *Tennessee*'s casemated hull, filling the air like so much shrapnel. Among the wounded was Buchanan, who was hit by a splinter in the same leg that had been wounded at Hampton Roads. Repeated hits also bent *Tennessee*'s armor beyond repair and jammed shut many of her gun ports. If that were not enough, the chains running from the pilothouse to the rudder were shot away and relieving tackle had to be rigged.

By this time *Tennessee*'s situation was desperate. She was unable to return the Union fire, her steering was crippled, and a great many of her crew were either dead or wounded. Finally, Buchanan's flag captain, Capt. James B. Johnston, ordered her flag to be hauled down and raised a white flag of surrender in its place. When the firing ceased, Johnston came aboard the *Hartford* and presented both his sword and that of the wounded Buchanan to Farragut.

Morgan and *Gaines* were all that was left of Buchanan's flotilla. *Morgan* succeeded in making a run for the city and its defenses. *Gaines* was not so lucky. She was too badly damaged to make a dash for safety, and her captain ordered her scuttled. After the battle Farragut immediately captured a Confederate submarine, leading to speculation that the *Tecumseh* was sunk by a submarine rather than a moored torpedo. In addition, at least one submarine was apparently used to ferry supplies to the forts protecting the bay.

While the battle was under way, other Union naval vessels bombarded Fort Powell on the approaches to Mobile Bay, forcing its abandonment and self-destruction when its magazines were detonated by the retreating garrison around noon on August 5. Granger's troops quickly took Fort Gaines, which was now isolated on its island, and then turned their attention to Fort Morgan, which managed to hold out until August 23 when it too surrendered.

There would be no immediate attempt to take the city of Mobile. By winning control of Mobile Bay, Farragut's fleet had effectively closed the port to all Confederate traffic. Thus there was no reason to target the city itself, and it could be safely left to wither on the vine.

The city would not fall until it was invested by a Union army under Maj. Gen. Edward Canby, supported by a powerful naval squadron under Rear Adm. Henry K. Thatcher. Although the Confederate naval forces helping to defend the city enjoyed several successes, the city was evacuated on April 10, 1865, and surrendered to Union forces on April 12. Com. Ebenezer Ferrand, commanding the Confederate squadron at Mobile, scuttled the *Huntsville* and *Tuscaloosa* and moved up the Tombigbee River with *Nashville* and the squadron's remaining ships. There they remained defiant until Ferrand was finally convinced that the war was over, and he surrendered the squadron on May 10.

It took a little time for the effect of Farragut's victory to begin to sink in. A month later Atlanta fell. In October came the triple victories of Winchester, Fisher's Hill, and Cedar Creek in the Shenandoah Valley. Finally, the people of the North began to realize that victory, so long out of reach, was approaching. The realization began to seep in among the Northerners at home and the Union forces in the field that they would win the war. On November 8, 1864, Lincoln was elected to a second term, and any hope the Confederacy had of obtaining independence through a peace of exhaustion vanished. Thus it was a naval victory that helped to guarantee that the Union would ultimately win the Civil War.

AFTERWORD

On Choosing the Wrong Model

This book is not intended as a history of the Confederate navy. Nor has it been intended as a history of the naval side of the American Civil War. The purpose, rather, has been to examine the naval strategies used by both sides during the war. There have been many works that have covered, or have attempted to cover, the military strategy of the war, but very little has been written about the naval strategy of the war.

In fact, there have been rather few naval theorists. The first of these was an American—Alfred Thayer Mahan—who first became influential when he was appointed president of the U.S. Naval War College in 1886. During his tenure he delivered a number of lectures that highlighted the importance of seapower, a term Mahan coined. These lectures later became the basis of a book—*The Influence of Sea Power upon History, 1660–1783*—which in turn became the bible for those who accepted Mahan's theories on the importance of seapower.

Unfortunately for the history of the world, one of Mahan's earliest and most fervent admirers was Kaiser Wilhelm II, emperor of Germany. The kaiser proved the adage that a little knowledge can be a dangerous thing.

The German emperor made the mistake of not realizing that in using the history of the British navy as the model upon which he based his theories of naval strategy, Mahan had focused his sights upon a very narrow target. True, the Royal Navy was the foundation and cornerstone upon which the British Empire rested, but what the kaiser did not realize was that what might have been true

223

for the British did not therefore also have to be true for other nations. The British model is unique because of a happy accident of geography. Britain, an island, is ideally positioned to be able to dominate the European seacoast from Scandinavia to Gibraltar.

In addition, as an island, Britain had no need of immense armies to defend itself from invasion. By dominating the coast of Europe with its navy, Britain protected itself from invasion almost as an unintended byproduct.

In fact only two other countries of the world have been so favored by geography (and/or history) as to be able to reproduce Britain's seapower: Japan and the United States. Japan has been so favored because it is also an island, positioned to dominate the main seacoast of Asia in exactly the same way that Britain dominated the seacoast of Europe. The United States is an entirely different proposition, however.

Of course, the first and most importance difference is that the United States is not an island, but it is favored like Britain and Japan through a historical situation rather than a geographical one. The United States so dominates the continents of North and South America, that is, the Western Hemisphere, that it has no possible challenger close to home. True, there is Canada to the north, which at first was a British possession and then the first of Britain's self-governing dominions. Yet by the nineteenth century, British power was so spread out and diluted over the rest of the world that, in the Western Hemisphere, it could not compare with the latent—and mostly unused—power concentrated within the United States. In fact, the only way that America could find such a challenge was to fight itself, which is exactly what happened during the Civil War.

It was during the Civil War that the Confederate navy demonstrated how an inferior naval force can hold off a vastly superior naval force. It would have been far better for Kaiser Wilhelm if he had decided to use a Confederate model for his navy rather than a British one. In fact, it would have been far better in 1914 if the governments of Europe had looked closely at the American Civil War rather than trying to repeat the Franco-Prussian War—a failure that unleashed the holocaust of two world wars, the repercussions of which are still reverberating after the conclusion of the twentieth century.

By choosing to emulate his British cousins, Kaiser Wilhelm set in motion the forces that guaranteed the coming of a generalized world war that would destroy the German Empire and totally disrupt the world order as it had existed up to 1914. The reason why was that he had chosen a provocation that Britain simply could not ignore. The result was a naval arms race to end all naval arms races, which in the end benefited no one.

The real reason that the growth of the Imperial German Navy so alarmed the British Royal Navy, the British government, and the British people, was that by the end of the nineteenth century Germany had become the foremost military power in Europe. The kaiser's decision to build a navy powerful enough to challenge British naval supremacy made an invasion of the British Isles possible. Britain in turn abandoned its policy of "splendid isolation" and the idea that it held and maintained the balance of power in Europe that had prevented a general European war for almost one hundred years.

Britain with its worldwide empire and commerce was the richest nation in Europe and was probably, at the end of the nineteenth century, running neck and neck with the United States as the richest power on the planet. Ever since the fall of Napoleon at the battle of Waterloo it had refused to join sides in any European conflict, with the exception of the Crimean War, while using its influence and its navy to keep any conflict from turning into a general European war. Germany's direct challenge to British naval supremacy therefore forced Britain to seek allies to counter the vastly superior German military. Therefore, instead of standing aloof, Britain found itself joined with France and Russia in the entente cordiale in an attempt to contain Germany. This alliance made World War I inevitable.

If the kaiser had chosen to implement a coastal defense policy similar to the policy adopted by Confederate Secretary of the Navy Stephen R. Mallory, he would not have posed a direct challenge to British naval supremacy, while at the same time protecting his own coasts from seaborne invasion. Thus the German emperor could have avoided World War I and everything that came after it.

Perhaps this is unfair to treat the kaiser so, because he never had a chance to learn the true story of the Confederate navy. The main reason for this lack of information was that at the end of the war the Confederate naval archives were destroyed, first at Richmond and then at Charlottesville, North Carolina. The kaiser could never learn about the alternative represented by the successes of the Confederate navy.

This lack of information about the Confederate navy's successes has continued until relatively recently. Mallory quite accurately assessed his own career as Confederate secretary of the navy after the war when he said: "I am satisfied that, with the means at our control and in view of the overwhelming force of the enemy at the outset of the struggle, our little navy accomplished more than could have been looked or hoped for . . . and, yet, not 10 men in 10,000 of the country, know or appreciate these facts."

Mallory's words are borne out because most Americans since the end of the war have considered the Confederate navy to have been an abject failure. It has always been well known that a major facet of Mallory's naval strategy was aimed at the breaking of the blockade through the use of ironclads. Naval construction was hindered by many factors that included the lack of an adequate industrial base, the lack of an adequate transportation system for raw materials, labor problems caused mostly by a lack of patriotism and shortsightedness among labor leaders and their rank and file, and the destruction or transfer of what existing facilities there were in the South. In addition, many of the ironclads that were placed under construction were destroyed before they could be completed, mostly to prevent their capture by the Union forces.

On the whole, however, it must be said that Mallory's revised naval strategy worked. Although ironclads were not the ultimate weapon he originally envisioned, they were of great importance. Their value as the ultimate protectors of the vital Southern blockade-running ports was incalculable. Although the Union was not the proper target for a commerce-destroying campaign, the operations of Mallory's commerce raiders set the pattern for the proper conduct of such a campaign. Mallory also sparked the creation of submarine warfare and the evolution of naval mine warfare.

His campaign against the entrenched principle of seniority became a weakness, however. Mallory's obsession caused him to denigrate and ultimately dispense with or waste the services of men like George N. Hollins and Josiah Tattnall. It did not help that events proved them right and Mallory wrong: Hollins in contending that Farragut's fleet was more of a menace to New Orleans than any Union Anaconda thrust down the Mississippi, and Tattnall in his cautious attacks on the blockaders at Savannah. Mallory's fixation particularly led him astray when he rejected the cautious Tattnall in favor of the rash William H. Webb, which resulted in the spectacular loss of the *Atlanta.*

Mallory, however, got along famously with that old sea dog Franklin Buchanan. Although some historians believe Buchanan could be just as rash as Webb, such as when he exposed himself to Union small-arms fire aboard the *Virginia* at the battle of Hampton Roads and when he plunged the *Tennessee* into the middle of Farragut's fleet at the battle of Mobile Bay. Others view his actions at Mobile to have been due less to rashness and more to a brave attempt to snatch something positive out of what appeared to be an impossible situation.

Gideon Welles, on the other hand, never developed a naval strategy to match that of Mallory's. Instead, he followed the national strategy as laid down by Lincoln and formulated by Scott. His contributions to the Union's naval war effort lay in the team approach he developed with himself as coach, Fox as quarterback, and Farragut, Porter, and others as his running backs. Welles's stumbling upon the principle of unified command—which the Confederate army and navy could never quite bring themselves to adopt, even with Beauregard's ability to obtain the cooperation of the local naval commanders within his department—was highly important to the success of the Union's combined army-navy Mississippi River campaigns at Forts Henry and Donelson, Island No. 10, Memphis, and finally Vicksburg.

Welles was not distracted by personal crusades, other than winning the war. His only concern with his officer corps was if they were doing the job. If they were, he kept them. If not, he sacked them. Samuel Du Pont deserved better. His successor, John A. Dahlgren, proved equally unable to crack the defenses at Charleston. Samuel P. Lee, on the other hand, was a victim of circumstances, having been caught flatfooted by the Confederate combined army-navy offensive between April 17 and May 6,

1864, aimed against the North Carolina bases that supported the blockade. Welles showed much more patience with Farragut during the Vicksburg fiasco than Mallory would have shown either Hollins or Tattnall.

Finally, Welles kept his eye on events. Although he followed the national strategy, he was not a prisoner of it. He was constantly looking for opportunities, he recognized them when they occurred, and he pounced on them with gusto when he found them. The ultimate example was his decision to drop the Anaconda Plan and to send Farragut to New Orleans, where the audacity of the thrust gained for the North the most elusive elements of strategic surprise.

Although their methods of operation were diametrically opposed, the two secretaries served their respective governments superbly.

Recently through the efforts of an Italian naval historian, Raimondo Luraghi, it has finally been possible to tell the full story of the Confederate navy. It took twenty years of research in various European archives to relocate much of the information that was lost when the Confederate navy's archives were destroyed. His *A History of the Confederate Navy* reveals that the Confederacy's naval strategy was much more successful than historians have realized up to this time. This in turn has made it possible for historians and others to understand at last how Mallory and his navy were able to keep the massively superior Union navy at bay for so long.

Luraghi demonstrates that much of the history written about Civil War naval operations was wrong because of a lack of basic information. He observes that one of the basic myths about the Civil War was that the only strategic objective of the Confederate navy was to break the blockade, thus because it failed in this mission, the Confederate navy must have been an abject failure. Luraghi notes that Mallory began the war nurturing the illusion that his Confederate navy could break the blockade and even seize local command of the sea through the use of the steam-powered ironclad, which he considered the ultimate naval weapon of the mid-nineteenth century.

Luraghi argues that the first year of the war showed Mallory that he had been in error and that the blockade was not the true, immediate, and most deadly danger facing the Confederacy from the sea. Instead, the real danger was the North's amphibious operations. Once Mallory grasped the true danger facing the South from the sea, he changed the primary objective of his navy from breaking the blockade (although as an objective it was never abandoned) to making the South safe from the threat of Union seaborne invasion.

Once this change had been implemented, the Confederate navy's success was remarkable, according to Luraghi. The Southern navy protected the rear of the Confederate armies, who were fighting on several fronts, from invasion from the sea and retained control of the vital port cities through which the blockade-runners brought crucial supplies for the armies. In the end, the collapse of the armies behind Mallory's coastal defense system brought everything crashing down.

In addition, the creation and implementation of strategy during the Civil War, both military and naval, says something about the nature of the experts. Abraham Lincoln, Edwin M. Stanton, and Gideon Welles were not experts in either field. Lincoln and Stanton were attorneys, and Welles was a journalist. Jefferson Davis—a graduate of West Point, a combat veteran of the Mexican War, and a former secretary of war—considered himself to be a military expert. Stephen R. Mallory was a recognized civilian naval expert. Because he believed himself to be an expert, Davis ran the military side of the Confederate war effort, and because Mallory was a recognized expert, Davis allowed him to run the naval side of the war effort.

The problem with experts is that they tend to focus only on their area of expertise. Yes, experts are needed, but what is also needed is someone who can look at the total range of operations and direct the efforts of the experts. In the Confederate government no one filled this need. Because Lincoln, Stanton, and Welles were not experts, they pieced together a comprehensive view of the various operations and left it to their experts—men like Gustavus Vasa Fox and Ulysses S. Grant—to address the details. Ultimately, this is another reason why the North won and the South lost the war. The Confederacy never had a unified national strategy, but the North did—from the beginning—once Lincoln accepted the basic tenets of the Anaconda Plan.

When James Iredell Waddell was convinced that the war was over and that the Confederacy had lost, he disarmed his cruiser—the *Shenandoah*—and returned to Great Britain, ultimately to relinquish his ship to the British authorities. In effect he wrote the end to the story of the Confederate navy. It was a military service that had begun from nothing. It strove valiantly against an enemy that, on paper, could only be described as overwhelming. It also managed to survive for a short time the total collapse of the government and the society that had created it. Its ships were the last of the Confederate armed forces to cease fighting, and they became the last vestige of the Confederate States of America.

As a military organization the officers and men of the Confederate navy could look back with pride upon their involvement in the war with the realization that their service never formally surrendered to the restored Union. Like Napoleon's Old Guard at Waterloo, it had died in the field instead.

SELECTED BIBLIOGRAPHY

Books

Anderson, Bern. *By Sea and by River: The Naval History of the Civil War.* New York: Alfred A. Knopf, 1962.

Campbell, R. Thomas. *Gray Thunder.* Chippensburg, Pa.: Burd Street Press, 1996.

Catton, Bruce. *The Civil War.* New York: American Heritage Publishing Co., The Fairfax Press, and Crown Publishers, 1960, 1980.

Coombe, Jack D. *Gunfire Around the Gulf: The Last Major Naval Campaigns of the Civil War.* New York: Bantam Books, 1999.

———. *Thunder Along the Mississippi: The River Battles That Split the Confederacy.* New York: Sarpedon Publishers, 1989.

Coski, John M. *Capital Navy: The Men, Ships and Operations of the James River Squadron.* Campbell, Calif.: Savas Publishing Co., 1996.

Davis, William C. *Rebels and Yankees: The Commanders of the Civil War.* New York: Salamander Books, 1990.

Donald, David, ed. *Why the North Won the Civil War.* New York and London: Collier Books, Macmillan Publishing Co., Collier Macmillan Publishers, 1960, 1962.

Dowdey, Clifford. *The History of the Confederacy 1832–1865.* New York: Marlboro Books, 1955.

Dufour, Charles L. *The Night the War Was Lost.* Garden City, N.Y.: Doubleday & Co., 1960.

Fowler, William F., Jr. *Under Two Flags: The American Navy in the Civil War.* New York and London: Avon Books, 1990.

Gibbon, Tony. *Warships and Naval Battles of the Civil War.* New York: Gallery Books, 1989.

Greene, Jack, and Massignani, Alessandro. *Ironclads at War.* Conshohocken, Pa.: Combined Publishing, 1998.

231

Hagan, Kenneth J. *This People's Navy: The Making of American Seapower.* New York: Macmillan, 1991.

Harwell, Richard B., ed. *The Civil War Reader.* New York: Konecky & Konecky, 1957, 1958.

Hoehling, A. A. *Damn the Torpedoes! Naval Incidents of the Civil War.* New York: Gramercy Books, 1989.

Hollett, David. *The Alabama Affair: The British Shipyards Conspiracy in the American Civil War.* Cheshire, England: Sigma Leisure, 1993.

Jones, Archer. *Civil War Command & Strategy.* New York: The Free Press, 1992.

Leckie, Robert. *None Died in Vain: The Saga of the American Civil War.* New York: Harper Collins Publishers, 1990.

Luraghi, Raimondo. *A History of the Confederate Navy.* Annapolis, Md.: Navy Institute Press, 1996.

MacMillan Reference USA. *Macmillan Information Now Encyclopedia: The Confederacy.* New York: Simon and Shuster Macmillan, 1993, 1998.

Mahan, Alfred Thayer. *The Influence of Sea Power Upon History 1660–1805.* Englewood Cliffs, N.J.: Prentice Hall, Inc. Greenwich, Conn.: Bison Books, 1980.

Massie, Robert K. *Dreadnought: Britain, Germany, and the Coming of the Great War.* New York: Random House, 1991.

McPherson, James M. *Abraham Lincoln and the Second American Revolution.* New York: Oxford University Press, 1990.

———. *Battle Cry of Freedom: The Civil War Era.* New York: Ballentine Books, 1998.

Mokin, Arthur. *Ironclad: The Monitor and the Merrimack.* Novata, Calif.: Presidio Press, 1991.

Potter, E. B. *The Naval Academy Illustrated History of the United States Navy.* New York: Galahad Books, 1971.

Rye, Scott. *Men and Ships of the Civil War.* Stanford, Conn.: Longmeadow Press, 1995.

Sears, Stephen W. *To the Gates of Richmond: The Peninsula Campaign.* New York: Ticknor & Fields, 1992.

Tuchman, Barbara W. *The March of Folly.* New York: Alfred A. Knopf, 1984.

Williams, T. Harry. *Lincoln and His Generals.* New York: Vintage Books, 1952.

Woodworth, Steven E., ed. *Leadership and Command in the American Civil War.* Campbell, Calif.: Savas Woodbury Publishers, 1995.

Periodicals

Basoco, Richard M. "The Cruise of 'Savez' Read." *Civil War Times Illustrated* 2, no. 8 (December 1963).

Bearss, Edwin C., and Grabau, Warren E. "How Porter's Flotilla Ran the Gauntlet Past Vicksburg." *Civil War Times Illustrated* 1, no. 8 (December 1962).

Canfield, Eugene B. "Porter's Mortar Schooners." *Civil War Times Illustrated* 6, no. 6 (October 1967).

DelGallo, Dino. "Mr. Mallory and the Terrapin." *Civil War Magazine,* no. 55 (February 1996).

Halsey, Ashley. "The Plan to Capture the *Monitor.*" *Civil War Times Illustrated* 5, no. 3 (June 1966).

———. "What Its Captain Thought of the Monitor *Passaic.*" *Civil War Times Illustrated* 4, no. 1 (April 1965).

Harding, Ursula, and James F. Harding. "The Guns of the *Keokuk.*" *Civil War Times Illustrated* 1, no. 7 (November 1962).

Huffstot, Robert S. "The *Carondelet* and Other Pook Turtles." *Civil War Times Illustrated* 6, no. 5 (August 1967).

———. "Story of the CSS *Arkansas.*" *Civil War Times Illustrated* 7, no. 4 (July 1968).

Jones, V. C. "How the South Created a Navy." *Civil War Times Illustrated* 8, no. 4 (July 1969).

———. "Mr. Lincoln's Blockade." *Civil War Times Illustrated* 10, no. 8 (December 1971).

———. "Preparation Paid Off for Farragut at Mobile Bay." *Civil War Times Illustrated* 3, no. 2 (May 1964).

———. "The Mighty Ram *Albemarle.*" *Civil War Times Illustrated* 1, no. 3 (June 1962).

Julian, Allen P. "Fort Pulaski." *Civil War Times Illustrated* 9, no. 2 (May 1970).

Kimball, W. J. "Ransom's North Carolina Brigade." *Civil War Times Illustrated* 1, no. 2 (May 1962).

Luvaas, Jay. "Burnside's Roanoke Island Campaign." *Civil War Times Illustrated* 7, no. 8 (December 1968).

———. "The Fall of Fort Fisher." *Civil War Times Illustrated* 3, no. 5 (August 1964).

McClary, Ben H., and Eller, Ernest M. "Matthew Fontaine Maury: 'The Pathfinder of the Seas.'" *Civil War Times Illustrated* 2, no. 3 (June 1963).

Melton, Maurice. "First and Last Cruise of the CSS *Atlanta*." *Civil War Times Illustrated* 10, no. 7 (November 1971).

Merli, Frank J., and Green, Thomas W. "Could the Laird Rams Have Lifted the Blockade?" *Civil War Times Illustrated* 2, no. 1 (April 1963).

Miller, William J. "Farragut at New Orleans: A Conversation with Chester Hearn." *Civil War Magazine*, no. 55 (February 1996).

Mosser, Jeffry S. "Fort McAllister's Trial by Fire." *America's Civil War* (March 1998).

Musicant, Ivan. "The Fires of Norfolk." *American Heritage: Civil War Chronicles*, 1999.

Myers, Cynthia. "The Cotton Road Between Houston and Matamoros Was a Vital Lifeline for the Blockade-Choked Confederacy." *America's Civil War* (March 1998).

Nash, Howard P., Jr. "The CSS *Alabama:* Roving Terror of the Seas." *Civil War Times Illustrated* 2, no. 5 (August 1963).

———. "The Ignominious Stone Fleet." *Civil War Times Illustrated* 3, no. 3 (June 1964).

———. "The Story of Island No. 10." *Civil War Times Illustrated* 5, no. 8 (December 1966).

O'Flaherty, Daniel. "The Blockade That Failed." *American Heritage: Civil War Chronicles*, 1993.

Orth, Michael. "The CSS *Stonewall*." *Civil War Times Illustrated* 5, no. 1 (April 1966).

Patterson, Gerald A. "George E. Pickett—A Personality Profile." *Civil War Times Illustrated* 5, no. 2 (May 1966).

Pickney, Roger. "Yankees on King Cotton's Coast." *Civil War Times Illustrated* 37, no. 1 (March 1998).

Ragan, Mark K. "New Light on Submarine Warfare." *North & South: The Magazine of Civil War Conflict* 2, no. 3 (March 1999).

Ripley, Warren. "Fort Sumter." *Civil War Times Illustrated* 9, no. 1 (April 1970).

Schuster, Carol O. "Confederate Corsairs: Commerce Raiders of the Confederate Navy." *Command: Military History, Strategy & Analysis*, no. 46 (December 1997).

Taylor, John M. "Shark Hunt." *Civil War Times Illustrated* 38, no. 6 (December 1999).

INDEX

235